Ian Buruma

A JAPANESE MIRROR

Heroes and Villains in
Japanese Culture

V

VINTAGE

FOR SUMIE

Published by Vintage 1995

2 4 6 8 10 9 7 5 3

Copyright © Ian Buruma 1984

This book is sold subject to the condition that it shall not
by way of trade or otherwise, be lent, resold, hired out,
or otherwise circulated without the publisher's prior
consent in any form of binding or cover other than that
in which it is published and without a similar condition
including this condition being imposed on the subse-
quent purchaser

First published in Great Britain by
Jonathan Cape Ltd, 1984

Vintage
Random House, 20 Vauxhall Bridge Road, London SW1V 2SA

Random House Australia (Pty) Limited
20 Alfred Street, Milsons Point, Sydney
New South Wales 2061, Australia

Random House New Zealand Limited
18 Poland Road, Glenfield,
Auckland 10, New Zealand

Random House South Africa (Pty) Limited
PO Box 337, Bergvlei, South Africa

Random House UK Limited Reg. No. 954009

A CIP catalogue record for this book
is available from the British Library

ISBN 0 09 938921 5

Papers used by Random House UK Ltd are natural, recy-
clable products made from wood grown in sustainable
forests. The manufacturing processes conform to
the environmental regulations of the country of origin

Printed and bound in Great Britain by
The Guernsey Press Co. Ltd., Guernsey, Channel Islands

Contents

Illustrations

Plates

Figures

Preface

An elderly aunt once asked me on a Sunday afternoon what I was reading. A Japanese novel, I replied. How extraordinary, she thought, 'but the feelings of those people must be quite different from ours, how can it mean anything to you?' Many people, like my aunt, still find it hard to believe that the Japanese are not simply exotic, transistor-making birds, but people who feel the same way about many things as we do. They assume that because their writing is back to front, their feelings must be too.

Perhaps because on the surface things seem so utterly different and so violently paradoxical, Japan provokes a sudden urge in many foreigners to express their culture shock in writing; to explain to the incredulous folk back home just what they saw behind the looking-glass. This often results in the half-informed Japan-seen-through-blue-eyes kind of comment that appears to delight the Japanese. They appreciate the attention and it confirms that cosily insular idea that foreigners could not possibly understand them.

It is hard to avoid the clichés about Japan, because both Japanese and foreigners seem to feel most comfortable with them. This book is an attempt to draw a picture of the Japanese as they imagine themselves to be, and as they would like themselves to be. This will naturally include many of the cultural clichés that have been built up through the ages. But primarily it is a book about the imagination. Sometimes the imagination belongs to individual artists who would never pretend to speak for anybody but themselves. I have included them, nevertheless, because they represent something wider than themselves, something that tells us about the culture that nurtured them.

More often, however, I shall try to show the products of a more popular, more collective imagination: films, comics, plays and books catering to the taste of the maximum amount of people, and thus often the lowest common denominator. This is not always the best art, though it is certainly not to be despised, but it is often revealing of the people at whom it is aimed. Because of this, I have devoted more space to the raunchy, violent and often morbid side of Japanese culture than to the more delicate and refined forms with which we are more familiar in the West.

It is not always easy to separate fantasy from reality. People's aspirations are in a sense part of reality. Certainly even the pulpiest of pop culture has some connection with the real world. It is, if not a mirror image, at least a reflection of it. Few Americans are really like John Wayne, but many would like to be, which is significant. Heroes do not just drop from Heaven. They are to a large extent home-grown.

The examples of heroes, villains and ordinary people I have chosen for this book represent what I think are typical aspects of Japanese culture. They play the starring roles in the myths and legends – old and new – that hold the national identity together. What must be borne in mind, however, is that what is typical is not necessarily uniquely Japanese. It is the expression of fantasies that often differs from one nation to another rather than the fantasies themselves.

Most heroes and heroines, even those who seem to reflect only their own age (in both senses of the word), have illustrious predecessors just like them. There is something universal too in many heroes – certain characters pop up in almost every culture – but there are also types who keep on bouncing back in an endless cycle of reincarnation throughout the history of one culture.

So I shall start at the very beginning, with the first Japanese gods. After all, the emperors and the principal clans were once thought to have been directly descended from them. It is striking, moreover, how human the Japanese gods, as described in legendary chronicles, seem. So human, in fact, that many traits of the Japanese people, imagined or real, can be traced back to them.

The first half of the book is about women and the second about men. The women are divided roughly into the two roles they traditionally play in so many societies: the mother and the prostitute. Both are extremely important in Japan. Though their roles are socially perhaps more strictly divided than anywhere else, they have certain things in common. Both, of course, are shaped by the fantasies of men.

Sandwiched in between the males and females is a chapter about the third sex, that is, men acting the roles of women and vice versa. It is in this twilight world of transvestism, still a vital element in the Japanese theatre, that cultural sex roles are most clearly defined.

Much space in the men's section is devoted to the traditional world of Japanese gangsters, the *yakuza*. This is because this fantasy world constitutes an almost perfect microcosm of Japanese society.

There is no point in studying another culture if this does not teach us anything about our own. It has been said that Japan is the ideal place from which to observe the rest of the world. One can see why, for perched out there on the extreme edge of Asia it often seems as if one is looking at the world from the outside.

Despite the extraordinary development of communications technology, mass tourism and other factors that are supposed to have created a global village, Japan is in many respects the loneliest, most isolated member of the modern world. If we in the West, in our blissful ignorance, often find the Japanese odd, so do most Asians.

The reason is partly geographical, of course. But like the North Sea in the case of Britain, the water separating Japan from the Asian continent is psychological as well as physical: Japanese do not really feel part of Asia. But then they do not really feel part of anything. They prefer to think that they are unique, a sentiment that has no doubt been strengthened by almost three centuries of virtual isolation from the rest of the world during the Edo period.

Japan, at times, really does feel like the other side of Alice's looking-glass. Whether or not this is just an illusion is less important than the fact that it is so universally believed both by foreigners and Japanese themselves. Thus living in Japan as a *Gaijin* (literally 'outside person') means being a constantly scrutinized odd man out. As a result one cannot help but scrutinize oneself. This can easily lead to a common fallacy that whatever is true of the Japanese could not possibly be so for foreigners and vice versa. The two are so mutually exclusive in many Japanese – and foreign – minds that there are even scientists who think they can prove it.[1] The most bizarre – but by no means only – example is the much praised Dr Tsunoda who claims that the Japanese actually have different and entirely unique brains.

I do not subscribe to the myth of Japanese uniqueness. On the contrary, because of her long periods of isolation, Japan has retained much that in the course of our own history has been lost, hidden or unrecognizably changed. Although Japan today on the surface seems more advanced and modern than, say, decaying Britain, underneath she is in many ways closer to the European Middle Ages, before Christianity obliterated the last vestiges of paganism.

The Japanese gods seem more human than the Christian Holy Trinity because they share our human weaknesses and further-more accept them. This acceptance is one of the outstanding and most pleasant features of Japanese society and it is, I believe, the most important lesson for a Westerner to learn. This has nothing to do with mysticism or superior wisdom. Neither is it simply a matter of passive Buddhist resignation, which can be a mixed blessing. It is certainly not a question of being better or worse; but just of accepting humanity for what it is, unburdened by the moral prejudices than can and so often do limit human life in the West.

Thus, while the heroes and heroines in this book tell us something about the culture that created them, if we look at them honestly, they tell us far more about ourselves.

In researching this book I have been greatly helped by many people, but special thanks are due to Tsuda Michio and my wife, Tani Sumie, without whom I would not even have begun to study Japan. For introductions, encouragement and much of their time, I am in debt to Kujo Eiko of the Tenjo Sajiki theatre group and her brother, Tanaka Hideaki.

Many errors and infelicities were ironed out at various stages of the manuscript by Henry H. Smith, Hanca Leppink, David van het Reve, Philippe Pons and Ann Buruma.

I would also like to thank Shimizu Akira and the staff of the Film Library Council in Tokyo, as well as Shibata Kazuko of the Furansu Eigasha for their generous assistance in providing screenings and stills. Help was also given by many members of the publicity departments of Toho, Nikkatsu and Toei, to whom I am grateful. Still photographs were also kindly provided by the Takarazuka Theatre, Shochikku and the Kabukiza.

My thanks are also due to the following: Ronald Bell for Plates 1, 2 and 3; June Magazine for Plate 24; and Phaidon Press for Plate 10 and the back jacket, 'A *saké* party', both reproduced from J. Hillier, *Utamaro: Colour Prints and Paintings*, 1961. For the use of drawings from comic-books I am grateful to Futaba-sha Publishers, pp. 106 and 108–9 (artist: Kamimura Kazuo); Jump Comics, published by Shueisha, p. 144 (artist: Motomiya Hiroshi); June Magazine (No. 2, 1982), pp. 126–7; Margaret Comics, published by Shueisha, p. 120 (artist: Ikeda Riyoko); Hobunsha, p. 138 (artist: Baron Yoshimoto); and Shueisha Publishers, p. 146 (artist: Shoji Toshio).

The verse on p. 86 is from *Major Plays of Chikamatsu*, translated by Donald Keene, 1961, reproduced by courtesy of Columbia University Press. The quotations on p. 78 and passim from Ivan Morris, *The World of the Shining Prince*, © Ivan Morris 1964, appear by permission of Oxford University Press.

Finally a very special thank you to Donald Richie and Karel van Wolferen, whose steady encouragement, suggestions and ideas were not only invaluable, but essential to the completion of this project.

Japanese names throughout the book have been written in the Japanese order, that is, family names first. Where translations have not been attributed to other sources, they are my own.

1983 I.B.

The mirror, they say, 'reflects eternal purity'. It does not foster vanity nor reflect the 'interfering self'. It reflects the depth of the soul.

Ruth Benedict, *The Chrysanthemum and the Sword*

1

Mirror of the Gods

Man has always created gods in his own image. The Japanese are no exception. The oldest gods and myths are not necessarily unique to Japan. Some of them probably originated on the Asian continent, but they were soon adapted to a Japanese way of life and thinking.

In the beginning, however, there were no gods at all. There was, instead, something resembling an egg. Out of this egg came seven generations of gods, including a brother and sister called Izanagi and Izanami. It is with them that the Japanese myth really began.[1]

These two were groping around in the hot lava of Chaos with the 'Jewel-spear of Heaven' when some brine dropped off its tip, coagulating in the sea to make an island. On this island they erected a phallic pillar separating Heaven and Earth. Then they noticed that he had something she did not and decided to put two and two together. The art of kissing was learnt by watching a pair of amorous doves and the rest of the happy union was inspired by the movements of a wagtail.

Izanami gave birth to the Japanese islands as well as to a large number of deities, but the god of fire proved to be too much for her. During his painful birth, she badly burnt her genitals. And after one last exertion whereby she bore the gods of metal, clay and water from her vomit, faeces and urine, Izanami perished and disappeared into the nether regions.

She was followed into the underworld by her grief-stricken brother/husband. She begged him not to look at her in her horrible state, but he could not resist a peek, and seeing her putrifying body swarming with maggots, he exclaimed: 'What a hideous and polluted land I have come to unawares!'

Thus shamed, the furious Izanami sent the Ugly Females of the Underworld after him with the express order to kill him. He barely managed to escape from these furies and then he was able to stop his sister/wife from catching him only by blocking her way with a rock. Shaken by these events, he announced his divorce from her in the traditional Japanese manner: a word from the husband was enough to sever the relationship. In retaliation Izanami vowed that she would strangle a thousand people a day in his land. Whereupon he replied that he would set up fifteen hundred houses for childbirth in one day.

Back from the underworld, Izanagi took great pains to purify himself from the pollution of the dead. He had a thorough bath in the Tachibana river and once again deities were born: Amaterasu, the Sun Goddess, crawled out of his left eye, and her brother Susanoo, the Wind God, emerged from his nose. Amaterasu was allotted the Plain of High Heaven and Susanoo was put in charge of the seas. Far from happy to accept this duty, however, he howled and screamed, desperate to be with his mother in the underworld. But before his descent into the land of darkness, he decided to pay his sister a visit in Heaven.

Apart from having a mother-fixation, Susanoo was a rough-neck. After arriving in his sister's domain, he smashed the divisions in the rice-fields; he relieved himself in a most unseemly manner during sacred rites; but his worst prank of all was to fling a flayed colt into the hall where the Sun Goddess and her entourage were busy weaving sacred garments. This so distressed one of the weaving maidens that she accidentally pricked her genitals and died.[2]

Amaterasu was a patient goddess and she loved her brother dearly. At first she put up with his behaviour, making excuses for him and indulging him, hoping that would make him stop. But now he had gone too far. In a huff she retired into a dark cave near Ise (which is now a popular tourist spot). As a result the world was plunged into complete darkness.

The gods decided to hold a meeting. In their very Japanese attempt to reach consensus, 'the voices of the myriad deities were like swarming flies in the fifth moon . . .'[3] Several attempts were made to lure the goddess from her cave. She would not budge. Finally a tub was placed upside down in front of the cave and Ama no Uzume, the Dread Female of Heaven, climbed on top of it. In the style of an ancient shamaness, she went into a trance, and began to stamp her feet, slowly at first, but progressively faster, rolling her eyes and wildly waving her spear. She went into an erotic frenzy, which, cheered on by the other deities, reached its shuddering climax when she revealed her breasts and then 'pushed her skirt-string down to her private parts'.[4] With all eyes on her sacred genitals, the gods burst out laughing so loudly that the whole universe could hear them.

Amaterasu, who could not bear other people having fun without her, put her head out of the cave to see what was so funny. Immediately a mirror was pushed in front of her and the Dread Female of Heaven cried out that a new goddess had been found. Amaterasu completely lost her composure and frantically reached out to grasp her reflected image. This gave the Strong-handed Male a chance to grab hold of her and he pulled her out of her hiding place. The world was light again.

Culture of any kind is always influenced by many fads and fashions. Japanese culture has been worked on by history, both native and foreign, by Buddhism, Confucianism, and even at times by Christianity. But underneath the changing surface it has never quite let go of its oldest native roots which are connected to the Shinto cult. By this I do not mean the nationalistic State Shinto concocted by politicians in the late nineteenth century when they were pushing for a strong national identity, but the whole range of sensual nature worship, folk beliefs, ancient deities and rituals. It is the creed of a nation of born farmers, which Japan in many ways still is.

The word Shinto was first coined in the seventh century to distinguish it from Buddhism, called *Butsudo*. It means Way of the Gods, but it can hardly be called a religion, for there is almost no trace in it of abstract speculation, neither is there much awareness of, or even interest in, another world outside our own. Heaven in the minds of the ancient Japanese was a cosy sort of place full of industrious villagers tending rice-fields.[5] There is no evidence of a system of ethics or statecraft, such as we see in China. The earliest myths are, in fact, typically Japanese dramas revolving around human relationships, liberally spiced with sex.

Shinto has many rituals, but no dogma. A person is Shinto in the same way that he is born Japanese.[6] It is a collection of myths and ceremonies that give form to a way of life. It is a celebration, not a belief. There is no such thing as a Shintoist, for there is no Shintoism.

Women play a somewhat ambivalent, though significant part in Shinto. Virgins still serve in the holy shrines. And one of the most celebrated figures in Japanese life from ancient times to this day is the mother, hence perhaps the importance of the Sun Goddess, Amaterasu. In patriarchal societies the sun tends to be masculine. In Bengal, for instance, there is a yearly celebration of the marriage between the earth goddess and the sun god.[7] As in the Japanese creation myth, the sun rising from the sea is a symbol of the life force in India, but it is associated with Shiva, a male god. In Shinto, which bears traces of a matriarchal culture, it is the other way round: earth is ruled by a male, the spear-carrying Okuninushi. But the source of life is water and the sun rising from it, the symbol of Japan, is female. So too, is the symbolism of fire. In Japan Izanami gives birth to fire and dies as a result.[8] In Greece, which is a patriarchal society, the myth tells of a male hero, Prometheus, who steals fire from the gods and is severely punished for it.

Worship of nature obviously includes sex. Like most Japanese, the gods felt no guilt about sex as such. Once the wagtail showed the way Izanami and Izanagi could not stop. Sex is an essential, indeed central part of nature. There is no question of sin. The brother and sister gods were not the only ones in the Japanese pantheon to so enjoy themselves. The Master of the Land (Okuninushi) had numerous lovers in the world he pacified and the only time he ran into trouble was when he refused to go to bed with his lover's ugly sister. For this breach of good manners, the Japanese emperors – his descendants – were doomed to be mortal.

It is often said that one can get away with almost anything in Japan as long as one is not caught and thus socially shamed. In other words, hedonism is held in check by social taboos. This is putting it rather simply, but let us compare Izanagi and Izanami with Adam and Eve. The latter were thrown out of the Garden of Eden because Eve took a bite from the apple. They were made conscious of good and evil and only thus was it possible to sin.

Japan has no such myth. Izanagi and Izanami were not directly punished for anything they did. They were certainly not removed from any Garden of Eden. Their crisis came when Izanami was seen by her husband in a state of pollution. The disaster concerned her shame rather than anything she consciously did. Although the gods enjoyed sex with impunity, they were terrified of pollution, especially the pollution of death. Izanagi, seeing the putrid body of his sister, barely escaped death himself. One could perhaps say that pollution is the Japanese version of original sin. One must add that women in Shinto, as in many religions, are considered to be more polluted than men, because blood is a form of pollution. In some parts of Japan women used to be segregated in special huts during menstruation.[9]

The connection between sex and death is certainly not typically Japanese. Georges Bataille, among others, has written eloquently about this concept.[10] But although sex as such is not a sin in Japanese thought, there does seem to be a strong fear of the destructive forces sexual passion can unleash, especially in women. (Needless to say, this too is not uniquely Japanese, as one can see in the work of many Catholic artists.)

Jealousy in particular is one such force the Japanese fear. This explains their deeply ambivalent attitude to women. They worship them, especially as mothers, but also fear them as corrupters of purity. Izanami is the creator of life as well as the personification of death and pollution. Her jealousy further prompted her to vow to strangle a thousand people a day. She had no reason to be jealous of another woman, however, for, as far as we know, there was not one in Izanagi's life. But she hated losing her marital status. And social status, however hard it may be to be bullied by possessive mothers-in-law or neglected by unfaithful husbands, is something most Japanese women cannot do without. Any threat to take it away from them can unleash jealousy of the most violent kind and there is sufficient evidence that men live in morbid fear of it. It is still customary for brides to wear a white hood at their wedding. It looks like a loosely wrapped turban made out of a bed-sheet and it is called a *tsunakakushi*, a 'concealer of horns', the horns namely of jealousy.[11]

In 'The Tale of Genji', written at the beginning of the eleventh century, a Buddhist monk tries to dissuade a mother from letting her daughter have an affair with a married man. He argues that:

> Women are born with a heavy load of guilt. As a retribution of the evil passions in their nature they are condemned to flounder about in the darkness of the long night. If your daughter incurs the jealousy of this man's wife, she will be shackled with fetters from which she can never free herself in this life or the next.[12]

In *The Life of an Amorous Woman*, a seventeenth-century novel about a fallen lady, Ihara Saikaku describes how a group of upper-class women gather in a so-called 'jealousy meeting' (*rinki-ko*) to complain about their philandering husbands.[13] One after the other, the women, beside themselves with rage, come forward to vent their pent-up emotions by thrashing an effigy of a woman, symbol of all the wicked ladies who led their men astray. Typically it is always the other woman, and not the husband himself, who has to bear the brunt of jealousy.

The most fearsome jealous wives are vengeful spirits who are finishing a job they had left undone when they were still alive. Old plays and folk tales are full of ghosts and spirits of betrayed wives tormenting husbands and rivals, usually ending in cruel and violent death. These horror stories are still performed in theatres and cinemas, traditionally during the clammy summer months, when people are in need of something to chill them.

Like earthquakes and other natural calamities common in the Japanese isles, jealousy, pollution and death simply happen. They will always be with us. But they do not occur because of a sinful act. The concept of sin was, and still is, alien to Japanese thought. The Japanese gods (*kami*) are like most people, neither wholly good, nor completely bad. There is no Satan in Japan.

One could argue perhaps that Susanoo, the Sun Goddess's brother, is 'bad', but certainly not in any metaphysical or absolute sense. He is the Wind God: his badness just blows. His worst crime, serious enough in Japanese society, is his erratic, selfish and rudely destructive behaviour. He is an unruly adolescent indulging in what is called *mewaku kakeru* (to cause bother) – a verb, incidentally, often used by the Japanese to describe their behaviour in Asia during the war. Their violence too was like the wind; that it often blew like a hurricane wasn't their fault: it just happened.

Susanoo's punishment is a common one in traditional society: he is banished, compelled to be a drifter. This is an unpleasant fate, but it makes him a rather typical Japanese hero.[14] The violent man breaking the social rules is not always condemned in Japan – as a fantasy, that is. Social rules, rather than an abstract system of morals, control Japanese behaviour. But they are so pervasive that it takes a hero to break them. The only way for him to do so is to be outside society, for in the end, the community is always stronger than the individual.

So in their hero worship the Japanese often have it both ways: the security of a closed social system is preserved, but the heroic outsider lets people taste vicariously the forbidden fruit of extreme individualism. Also the impetuous violence of the unruly hero (*burai*) and his contempt for the rules of society are sometimes seen as forms of sincerity, of pure nature reasserting itself against man-made rules. Finally, the hero resembles nothing so much as an angry child ranting and raving against uncomprehending adults. Thus, far from being a model of evil, the screaming Wind-God is regarded with a certain affection. His badness is not evil, but simply a part of human nature which civilized people can learn to suppress, as indeed Susanoo himself manages to do after getting most respectably married to the Rice-Princess. With her he settles down to a life of the blandest domesticity.

Amaterasu's reaction to her fierce brother's abominations is quite compliant at first. She indulges his whims like a doting mother blind to her boy's faults: after all, he cannot help the way he is. When things finally go too far, it is she who retreats into the cave, not he. One could conclude, as many casual observers of the Japanese scene do, that men rule their women like spoiled despots. This is a superficial view, however, for at a very basic level (and Shinto is fairly basic) women have an awesome power over their men.

In myths the magic of the vagina is more potent than that of the phallus. There is a phallic god called Sarutahiko, blessed with a long, red nose. This walking penis, symbol of the force of life, is so powerful that demons flee at the sight of him. And yet it is said that when the Dread Female of Heaven pushed down her skirt-string even he lost his strength and wilted like a dead flower.[15]

The exhibition of the Dread Female's private parts, which so greatly amused the gods, probably had a magical significance. Early sculptures have been excavated showing female divinities exposing their genitals.[16] This image was later transposed to Kannon, the Buddhist Goddess of Mercy.[17] 'Going to see Kannon' is still a popular slang expression for visiting a striptease parlour. And only in Japan would an internationally known film-star insist on kissing his mother's genitals publicly at her funeral. This was widely reported in the press, with respect rather than shock or even much surprise.[18]

There are many legends about the magical qualities of the female organ. To mention just one: two women were chased by a group of demons. They tried to get away in a rowing boat, but still the demons kept up their pursuit. Then, just at the critical moment, a goddess appeared, advising the women to reveal their private parts. She proceeded to do so herself. The women, a little bashfully at first, followed her example and the demons gave up the chase, roaring with laughter.[19]

This laughter among gods, demons and men is not just a sign of good fun. It may be that too, but it is also a liberation from fear. Laughter in Japan, like anywhere else, is often a mechanism for breaking the tension, in the same way that people laugh at violence in the cinema. The female sex in all its impenetrable mystery is feared as much as it is worshipped. Or, more accurately, it is worshipped because it is feared. As in many cultures, there are legends about this fearsome side of female power: about clam-like vaginas that snip off male genitals like steel traps.

Buddhism helped to strengthen these fears. There is no room for women in Buddhist Nirvana. They have to be reborn as men first. According to a well-known sutra 'woman is an emissary from Hell; she will destroy the germ of the Buddha. Her appearance seems holy, but she has the heart of a demon.'[20]

The female body is a source of pollution. Murasaki Shikibu, the authoress of 'The Tale of Genji', certainly not a prudish work, described the naked body as 'unforgettably horrible'. None the less nudity in Japan is a strange and paradoxical thing, for people do take baths in public, in certain rural areas even mixed baths. Yet a large number of schoolboys and old ladies are hired as part-time workers at Japanese customs offices to delete with ink and razor any pubic hair that might be showing in imported publications. But striptease of the crudest kind is allowed to take place in Japan unimpeded. Morality is very much a matter of time and place and nothing is absolute.

The fascination in religious ceremonies, myths and the popular arts for the sexual organs (the grotesque stylization of male and female genitals in erotic woodblock prints, for example) is as much a celebration of life and fertility as a form of exorcism. It is as if one can ward off the dangers inherent in the mysteries of nature by laughter or stylization, by turning raw nature into man-made symbols. In various parts of Japan there are literally 'laughing festivals', where people laugh at local shrines to please the gods. Inside these shrines one often finds images of female and male sexual organs.

Though absolute Evil seems to be absent from Japanese thought, every form of pollution, including wounds, sores, blood, death and even simple uncleanliness is to be feared. The traditional antidote to the polluting forces of nature is purification. Izanagi's ablutions in the Tachibana river after his return from the Underworld are a typical example. Naturally, purification in one form or another exists in religious ceremonies everywhere, but in few cultures is it taken as seriously and is it as much a part of daily life as in Japan.

One finds evidence of it in the most disparate places: in the wrestling ring, for example, which sumo-wrestlers sprinkle with purifying salt before every bout. Little heaps of salt can also be seen in front of homes, on the doorsteps of bars, massage parlours or any other place where pleasure is bought and sold. The Japanese feeling for purity manifests itself in other, less obvious ways: the ubiquitous habit of wearing white gloves by people performing public functions, for instance. Politicians making speeches wear them, taxi drivers are never without them, policemen and even elevator operators in department stores wear them; everywhere one goes in Japan, one sees this ceremonial white on people's hands.

Bathing is a cult. Keeping clean is so universal a preoccupation that all one smells in packed commuter trains during rush hours

in Tokyo is a faint whiff of soap. Most Shinto festivals involve
ritual bathing. The first bathhouses, still a social institution in
cities, were part of Buddhist temples, dating from the seventh
century. But, like many religious habits in Japan – drinking *saké* is
another – bathing soon became a sensual experience enjoyed for
its own sake.

The Japanese have the same attitude to bathing as Frenchmen
reserve for eating: they do it with a mixture of connoisseurship
and physical abandon. A bath can be enjoyed alone, but it is more
often taken with many others, keeping up with the latest gossip
while scrubbing one's neighbour's back. Bathing has become a
major gimmick in holiday resorts built around hot springs. One
place features a gigantic heart-shaped bath with room for
hundreds of romping honeymoon couples; at another resort one
can bathe in a solid gold bath in the shape of a large chicken,
which costs 1,500 yen (five dollars) a minute to sit in; and there is
even a bath that moves up a mountain on tracks so that one can
enjoy the view while soaking in the tubs.

But pleasure has its reverse side in Japan. Purification rituals
in Shinto are an example of what has been called the stoic hedonism of the Japanese.[21] As in many cultures, though few are
as extreme, there is a strong belief in Japan that physical suffering and deprivation are purifying experiences. Standing on
smouldering bonfires or wading through icy rivers stark naked in
mid-winter – to name but two uncomfortable examples – and
sensual pleasure, even erotic ecstasy, go hand in hand in the
Japanese celebration of the gods.

These celebrations are called *matsuri*. They are like Latin
carnivals or fiestas, celebrations as well as outlets for popular
frustration; every Japanese city, town and village has a *matsuri*,
often more than one. These fiestas have been influenced by
Buddhism, but they are basically Shinto, and they are always
exuberant, sometimes escalating into real violence. Experiencing
a *matsuri* one has the impression of massive energy constantly
teetering on the edge of chaos, like a primitive tribal dance. In
some villages huge phalluses are carried through the streets like
battering rams, and are violently mated with swaying female
symbols held by sweating and heaving youths from a neighbouring shrine.

The novelist Mishima Yukio, who committed suicide in 1970,

called the *matsuri* 'a vulgar mating of humanity and eternity, which could be consummated only through some such pious immorality as this'.[22] What shocked and obviously titillated him as a boy was 'the expression of the most wanton and undisguised rapture in the world . . . '[23]

Pain and ecstasy, sex and death, worship and fear, purity and pollution are all vital elements in the Japanese festival. The Shinto gods are very Japanese in their tastes: they do not demand sacrifices – apart from some food – prayers or a dogma of faith; instead they demand to be entertained, like the Sun Goddess; they want to celebrate, to laugh. Above all, they want spectacle, masquerade, and the sexier the better. In a sense, they invite the people to break the very taboos they themselves symbolize.

It is this theatre for the gods that forms the basis of popular culture in Japan. This primitive, often obscene, frequently violent side of Japanese culture has persisted to this day, despite the frequent official disapproval of its raunchier manifestations and the superimposition of more austere and alien forms.

The first performer of this kind of spectacle was of course the Dread Female of Heaven. Her sacred striptease was the prototype of what was later known as *Kagura*, literally 'that which pleases the gods'. Though *Kagura* is still performed at shrines it has lost much of its popular appeal. But its spirit can still be seen in more modern dramatic forms. The contemporary striptease parlour is one example.

The 'Toji Deluxe' is a well known striptease parlour in Kyoto. It is a garish, neon-lit place in a dark, dreary street behind the station. The entrance is decorated with great garlands of plastic flowers, like colourful funeral wreaths. The customer is led through a purple-lit hall into an inner chamber where the entertainment takes place. It is a huge space bathed in a warm pink light. In the middle stands a large, slowly revolving stage.

High above the spectators is a second tier of revolving stages made of transparent plastic. The walls and ceilings are completely covered with mirrors, multiplying the ten or so girls into a kind of cubist harem painting.

The audience is welcomed by a male voice crackling through a loudspeaker and several women dressed in flimsy nightdresses toddle on to the ramps (some hastily handing their babies to colleagues backstage), carrying what look like picnic hampers, neatly covered with colourful cloths. These baskets are placed on the stage and the cloths carefully spread out. Then, with an exquisite sense of decorum, the girls unpack their accoutrements, vibrators, cucumbers and condoms and put them side by side, in a neat little row, as if preparing for a traditional tea-ceremony.

This done, the girls stand up and to the loud and scratchy tune of 'Strangers in the Night' they adopt a few perfunctory poses; not so much a dance as a series of tableaux vivants. Their faces remain impassive. Japanese dancers, classical and modern, often seem to wear a mask of complete detachment, as if their motions are automatic, the human will numbed into submission.

But then a slight smile shines through: not the plastic grin of American show-girls or the studied naughtiness of the French music-hall, but more like a maternal assurance that there is nothing whatsoever to fear.

Still smiling they invite members of the audience to join them on stage. Blushing and giggling, neatly dressed men on company outings are pushed on to the stage by their colleagues. Their ensuing attempts to have sex with the dancers are part of the entertainment. Not surprisingly in the circumstances, these attempts mostly fail, much to the merriment of the audience.

The show must go on, however, and with more blushing and giggling the young company employees are hastily pushed off the platform, whence they struggle awkwardly back to their seats with their trousers still dangling round their ankles. The best part, the real show, the thing that most men have paid to see, is still to come: the *Tokudashi* (special event), also known as the 'open', for reasons that will become clear.

The girls shuffle over to the edge of the stage, crouch and, leaning back as far as they can, slowly open their legs just a few inches from the flushed faces in the front row. The audience, suddenly very quiet now, leans forward to get a better view of this mesmerizing sight, this magical organ, revealed in all its mysterious glory.

The women, still with their maternal smiles, slowly move around, crablike, from person to person, softly encouraging the spectators to take a closer look. To aid the men in their explorations, they hand out magnifying glasses and small hand-torches, which pass from hand to hand. All the attention is focussed on that one spot of the female anatomy; instead of being the humiliated objects of masculine desire, the women seem in complete control, like matriarchal goddesses.

The tension of this remarkable ceremony is broken in the end by wild applause, and loud, liberating laughter. Several men produce handkerchiefs to wipe the sweat off their heated brows.

All this is a long way from the austere, controlled, exquisitely restrained, melancholy beauty most people in the West have come to associate with Japan. It is true that the contrast between the native, Shinto-inspired, popular culture and the more aristocratic, Buddhist-inspired aesthetic is so strong that one could almost speak of two separate cultures.[24]

This is partly a matter of class. Foreign influence is generally felt first by those with the time and money to indulge in exotic fashions. Indeed much in the aristocratic tradition was imported from more sophisticated societies (mainly China and Korea). Thus the first Buddhists in Japan were aristocrats at the court of Prince Shotoku in the beginning of the seventh century. And during the Heian period (794–1185) all the male literati wrote in Chinese – the women did not and consequently they were the pioneers in native Japanese literature.

Importing upper-class culture is not a typically Japanese phenomenon. French culture in Europe was eagerly lapped up in the nineteenth-century salons of the upper classes. But the impact of foreign importations, usually at a much higher stage of development, on an isolated island culture was enormous and in some ways traumatic. Moreover Buddhism and Confucianism with their strong emphasis on ethics and morality were useful tools to keep the masses under control. The seventh-century rulers of Japan deemed Buddhism 'excellent for protecting the state'.[25]

But the native tradition never disappeared. Unlike Europe, where Christianity was quite successful in squashing or at least replacing ancient forms of worship, primitive cults in Japan were never crushed by more sophisticated official creeds. Though the distinctions, especially at the most popular level, are somewhat blurred at the edges, Buddhist temples and Shinto shrines still exist side by side. Rites of both creeds are observed, though not always at the same time or place. This might be due to the Japanese lack of concern for ideology or dogma. Instead great importance is attached to externals, to the attitudes proper to assume on each occasion, because 'appearance' is more important than 'being'.[26]

Aristocratic culture, because of its Buddhist influence, emphasizes restraint and austere perfection to the point of morbidity: not surprisingly, the Japanese, high and low, use Buddhist rituals to bury their dead. In popular Shinto culture everything human and sensual is stressed and sometimes grotesquely exaggerated. Again not surprisingly, marriage is usually a Shinto ceremony, though nowadays many young couples, though not in any sense believers or even formal members, find it more chic to marry in Christian churches, which are most willing to oblige. In terms of traditional culture this means that the austerity of the No theatre, suffused with Zen Buddhism, co-exists with the violent extravagance of Kabuki.

Nevertheless, if one should ask a Japanese if he is a Buddhist or a Shintoist, he would not know what to say. Both, is the most likely answer. Or he might mumble something about the Japanese being non-religious. There are, however, hidden conflicts between the morality of the rulers and their officialdom, supported by Buddhism, Confucianism or even State Shinto, all depending on the period in history, and the Shinto way of life. Power in Japan has never rested so much on the letter of the law, as on a type of social totalitarianism. People were often made to behave according to imported codes, which they did not really share. Thus the tension between official and popular culture is always simmering under the surface. The harder the official pressure is, the more grotesque the manifestations of popular culture become. This was most apparent during the Edo period (1615–1867), the influence of which is still strongly felt today.

From the moment they came to power, the Tokugawa shoguns, who ruled during the entire Edo period, did all they could to suppress anything that could possibly pose a threat to their authority. The creed that served the authoritarian government best was Confucianism, especially the school of Chu Hsi, a twelfth-century Chinese philosopher, emphasizing loyalty and duty; originally to one's parents, but most conveniently expanded to include one's rulers, in effect the Tokugawa rulers themselves. It must be stressed that loyalty in Japan became something far more absolute than the original Chinese model.

Being terrified of disorder, the Tokugawa government tried with varying degrees of success to clamp down on the hedonistic, extravagant and erotic aspects of popular culture. This tug of war between officialdom and the common people is indeed still going on. Censorship and other other forms of control were based on the official morality, which was not an internalized religious morality, but included anything that supported the power of the state; the power of the state *was* the official morality.[27]

Homosexual prostitution, for example, was officially banned in 1648, although homosexuality was in no way thought to be sinful. Particularly amongst the samurai it was considered quite normal, desirable even. The reason for the crack-down was that upper-class warriors mixed with lower-class actors, hustlers and other members of the demi-monde. Worse still, they affected their habits. This was not acceptable, for Tokugawa power was based on rigid class divisions.

The subservient position of women in feudal society was also given the Confucian stamp of approval. The scholar Kaibara Ekiken (1630–1714) wrote that 'a woman must regard her husband as her lord and serve him with all the reverence and all the adoration of which she is capable. The chief duty of woman, her duty throughout life, is to obey.' This seems a far cry from the world of the Sun Goddess and Izanami, where shamanesses held sway and even, like Himiko in the third century A.D., became queens of the land; or the Heian court, where promiscuous ladies were the arbiters, if not of real power, at least of taste. The Tokugawa government did everything to stamp out the last vestiges of matriarchy for ever.

To a large degree it succeeded in its aims. It became difficult and even dangerous for people to behave as independent individuals: everybody was judged by his or her rank in the social hierarchy, a habit which has, unfortunately, stuck. The only escape from this oppressive system was, as usual, the spectacle, the matsuri, the cruel world of theatres and brothels.

Within the strict boundaries of licensed areas, permitted and controlled by the government, people could let themselves go. The gods were entertained by female impersonators, male prostitutes, woodblock artists and courtesans. Popular urban culture of the Edo period, especially during the relatively prosperous seventeenth century, was intimately connected to this narrow world of pleasure. Writers, musicians, actors and painters, all were to be found in the officially despised but commonly adored 'floating world'. The importance of this cannot be overestimated. One could say that little has fundamentally changed: violent entertainment and grotesque erotica are still important outlets in what continues to be an oppressive social system. Thus they have a social and political significance far beyond similar fare in the West.

Following the Meiji Restoration in 1868, when the Tokugawa regime came to an end, Japan entered the era of 'Civilization and Enlightenment' (*Bunmei Kaika*). She began to borrow from the West in the same wholesale way she had done eleven centuries before from China. This did not mean that the Tokugawa legacy of social oppression could be discarded as easily as the native kimono. Moreover, the influence from the then still highly puritanical West helped push the Sun Goddess even further into her cave.

Released from its self-imposed isolation, Japan became a little self-conscious. The Japanese 'were like an anxious housewife preparing to receive guests, hiding away in closets common articles of daily use and laying aside comfortable everyday clothes, hoping to impress the guests with the immaculate idealized life of her household, without so much as a speck of dust in view.'[28] It seems trains even had signs in them dissuading passengers from the old custom of tucking in the hems of their kimonos: 'DO NOT BARE THE THIGHS'.[29] One still sees similar signs in Western-style hotels, where foreigners might be shocked by the sight of Japanese men walking around in their pyjamas, or worse, their underwear, though both are common enough sights in places not normally frequented by overseas visitors.

But much has changed since the Japanese were first civilized and enlightened. Now that 'Western' culture has reached even the simplest Japanese home through television, advertising and organized foreign holidays, the surface of Japanese life has changed almost beyond recognition. All the same, enough remains under the concrete and glass façade of the Economic Miracle to amuse the gods. Despite all the changes Japan is a profoundly traditional country. Every new building has a shrine on the roof, dedicated to the fox Inari, guardian of rice-crops and export figures. In many ways the Japanese continue to be a nation of farmers not quite sure what to make of their new affluence.

The film director Imamura Shohei has called the modern surface of Japan an illusion. 'Reality', he says, 'is those little shrines, the superstition and the irrationality that pervade the Japanese consciousness under the veneer of the business suits and advanced technology.'[30]

In the last few decades the more primitive aspects of Japanese culture, things 'reeking of mud' (*dorokusai*), have enjoyed a kind of renaissance. The Japanese are now secure enough, it would appear, not to worry too much about specks of dust coming into view – though many would still prefer foreigners not to notice. Since the 1960s especially, Japanese scholars have been digging their muddy spades into the more scabrous corners of popular culture. Certain Kabuki plays, long considered too vulgar for a civilized and enlightened world, are being performed again, albeit somewhat toned down. And the *matsuri* are enjoying a televised boom.

This does not mean that the Japanese are living in an age of unbridled earthy hedonism, dancing in the streets all night. On the contrary, some controls are tighter than ever. It would be truer to say that what were once expressions of dangerous, subversive spontaneity have now entered the sphere of harmless folklore. But popular expression need not be traditional in form: it is the spirit that counts. And I think it will seem from the images in films, books, comics and plays which I shall discuss, how close the contemporary Japanese still are, despite the vicissitudes of history, to the original gods they created.

2

The Eternal Mother

Oh, that my dear mother
Were a jewel-piece
That I might place in my hair-knot
And always wear above me.

Manyoshu, eighth century

It is said that kamikaze pilots always screamed the same famous
last words before crashing their planes into American battleships: 'Long live the emperor!' ('Tenno Heika banzai!') Some of
them may indeed have done so. But most, according to less
reverent informants, simply shouted at the top of their terrified
voices: 'Mother!'

I visited an old kamikaze air base recently. The best-selling
souvenir in the dingy museum was a record album entitled 'The
Suicide Pilot's Mother':

You are the suicide pilot's mother
So please don't cry
Laugh as you send us off
We'll show you how to die
Mother, Oh Mother!

When Takakura Ken, the most popular macho star in gangster
films, is thrown into a maximum security jail in one of his many
movies, after stabbing a rival boss to death, all he worries about is

his mother. He hears – and so do we – his sister's voice on the soundtrack: 'Dear brother, do you know that mother calls out your name every single day?' At that point the hardened gangster hero and his fans in the auditorium break down and cry.

An ultra-rich businessman in his seventies, with shady political and criminal connections, has launched an expensive campaign to clean up his grubby public image. How? By buying television time for 'commercials' showing pictures of himself as a young man gallantly carrying his mother on his back.

Every night thousands of Japanese businessmen find refuge from the Economic Miracle in tiny bars, sometimes with names like 'Mother's Taste' or just 'Mother'. There, aided by whisky and water, they retreat into early childhood, seeking the ever-attentive ears of the ladies they call 'mama-san', who, with the practised patience of psychiatrists, listen to their problems: about how the wife keeps nagging and how the section-chief in the company is no good and how nobody appreciates their hard work. After some kind words of advice and plenty of soothing encouragement from the mama-san, Japan's economic warriors stagger home, holding each other up, jumping on and off each other's backs, and shrieking with the sheer joy of being eight years old again.

At home *kachan*, literally Mummy, but often used to refer to the wife, is waiting for her husband. After he stumbles in, she takes his shoes and socks off, feeds him if necessary, listens to some drunken abuse and puts him to bed.

. Little seems to have changed since Susanoo screamed for his mother instead of commanding the ocean as he was told. Or indeed since his sister Amaterasu patiently put up with his offensive behaviour. It is often hard to avoid feeling that in male–female relationships in Japan every woman is a mother and every man a son.

Kurt Singer, one of the wittiest foreign observers of the Japanese scene in the 1930s, said this about it:

Seeing the Japanese mother in the street, serenely sauntering and humming, with her child attached to her back, one feels that it is through her that the stream of Japanese life runs and refreshes itself. The over-busy and excessively self-conscious males appear, compared to her, a mere protuberance, unattractive and lacking authenticity; useful or noisome instruments, hardly initiated in the mystery of being.[1]

Being a Japanese child, especially a boy, and most of all an eldest son, is as close as one can get to being God. I am not just being flippant. According to an eminent American scholar:

> An analogy may be drawn between a child in a tantrum and a god in the Japanese pantheon who vents his anger by causing trouble for humans. Both the child and the god are expected to be placated and quietened down by some sort of pacifier. Indeed, the folk belief has it that a child is god's gift or a god himself to be looked after.[2]

Appeasement appears to be the Japanese mother's favourite tactic. Bad behaviour, even rank destructiveness of what Singer calls 'the divine tyrant' is often met with compliant smiles and instant forgiveness. Girls are indulged less, for they are trained to be mothers, thus to be giving rather than taking. Appeasement seems to be currently fashionable in the West too. What is remarkable in Japan, however, is for how long it goes on. Even when a child grows up to, say, six years old, feeding him sweets, even just before meals, is still a common way of appeasing temper tantrums.

The treatment of young children is in a way similar to that of drunks and foreigners. They are not held socially responsible for anything they do or say, for they know no shame. They must be pampered not punished. This wonderful state of grace is one good reason for foreigners to live in Japan and Japanese males to spend much of their non-working hours in a state of inebriation or even, if necessary, to fake it.

Much in the traditional way of child-rearing seems to foster passive dependence. The child is rarely left alone, day or night, for it usually sleeps with the mother. When it goes out the child is not pushed ahead in a pram, to face the world alone, but is tightly bound to the mother's back in a snug cocoon. When the mother bows, the child does too, so the social graces are acquired automatically while feeling the mother's heartbeat. Thus emotional security tends to depend almost entirely on the physical presence of the mother.

In the worst, but not in the least rare cases this leads to a clinging relationship stifling any individual independence. Children learn that a show of passive dependence is the best way to get favours as well as affection. There is a verb for this in Japanese: *amaeru*, translated in the dictionary as 'to presume upon another's love; to play the baby'. According to the psychiatrist Doi Takeo this is the main key to understanding the Japanese personality.[3] It goes on in adult life too: juniors do it to seniors in companies, or any other group, women do it to men, men do it to their mothers, and sometimes wives, the Japanese government does it to stronger powers, such as the United States. An education fostering this type of passive dependency obviously does not encourage much personal initiative or sense of responsibility.

An added complication is that the mother needs the child's dependence to satisfy her own emotional needs. The child's attempt to act contrary to the mother's desire (and thus act independently) tends to provoke anxiety in the mother, since she may feel that she is no longer needed.[4]

If anything, this phenomenon has grown worse in recent times. In this age of birth-control and nuclear families, wives, cooped up in small high-rise apartments with nothing but a television-set for company, easily become fixated on their children. They are often their only satisfaction, their only link to the outside world, in short, their only reason to live, particularly when their marriages are not based on romantic illusions.

No wonder then that the separation from the mother at a later stage of development should be so traumatic. The mother tries to hang on as long as she possibly can. The child retains a lifelong nostalgia (mixed, no doubt, with more or less suppressed aggression) for that early childhood paradise. The yearning for that particular Arcadia is a very important aspect of Japanese culture, for it can be as collective as it is personal.

The novelist Tanizaki Junichiro (1886–1965) is a good, though perhaps slightly eccentric example. He could never forget his mother, the beautiful Seki, 'whose breasts I sucked until I was six'.[5] This, incidentally, is not unusual in Japan, where weaning tends to take place rather late. In *Days of my Youth* (*Yosho Jidai*, 1957) he wrote about his mother that 'not only did she have a beautiful face, but the skin of her thighs was so lovely, so white and so delicate that I experienced a thrill every time I looked at her, when we took a bath together'.

Tanizaki's mother-worship was like a cult. Apparently he was close to his grandfather who, rather unusually for a Japanese, belonged to the Greek Orthodox church. Tanizaki remembered how his grandfather would pray to the Virgin Mary and how he himself, as a little boy, would 'gaze at Mary holding the infant Christ . . . and with a feeling of almost indescribable awe I would watch those merciful, soulful eyes, and I never wanted to leave her side'.[6]

One of Tanizaki's most elegiac mother stories is *The Bridge of Dreams* (*Yume no Ukibashi*), written in 1959. The hero Tadasu is haunted by his memories of two mothers: his real mother who died when he was five, and his stepmother. Often the two merge in his mind, and he cannot remember which was which. He does remember, though, that he slept with his first mother, 'a small, delicately built woman, with plump little dumpling-like feet . . .' (Tanizaki was a connoisseur of women's feet.) He would suck his mother's breasts and 'the milk flowed out nicely. The mingled scents of her hair and milk hovered there in her bosom, around my face. As dark as it was, I could still dimly see her white breasts.'[7]

Several years later, after his mother's death, he sleeps with his nurse, still remembering 'that sweet, dimly white dream world there in her warm bosom among the mingled scents of her hair and milk . . . Why had it disappeared? . . . was that what death meant?' One is reminded again of Susanoo's craving for his mother in the underworld. Is there a connection perhaps between mother-worship and the wish to die? Singer has remarked that 'the readiness of the Japanese to die, casting away their lives or dying by their own hands, may echo this desire of their divine ancestor.'[8]

He did write this at a time (the end of the Second World War) when many Japanese showed a greater readiness to leave this world than is usual today. But even allowing for that, I doubt whether the supposed Japanese death wish ought to be taken so literally. The longing described by Tanizaki is not for death so much as for that dimly white dreamworld, that supremely sensual state of unconsciousness. Many Zen-ish meditation techniques are geared to achieve exactly that: to dull, even deny the conscious mind, to sink into a state of ego-less sensuality like a warm, collective, Japanese bath.

When the hero is about fourteen, his stepmother has a child, who is swiftly removed for adoption in some remote country area. Thus the illusion that the second mother is identical to the first is preserved. He soon goes back to his old habits too: ' . . . I leaned down and buried my face in her bosom, greedily sucking the milk that came gushing out. "Mama," I murmured instinctively, in a spoiled, childish voice.'

The Garden of Eden-like state of early childhood does, however, come to an end. Around the age of six children are handed over to the care of schoolteachers and other outside agents of education. The chains of social conformity are progressively tightened from then on. The psychological importance of this cannot be overestimated. The spoilt little gods, living at the centre of their pampered universe, are required to become rigorous conformists. The shock is considerable, for, unlike most children in the West who, as an ideal at least, are taught that they are not the only ones in the world, the Japanese child is quite unprepared for this. Moreover, he will never really get used to the idea. Obsequious conformity and callous egotism can alternate in many a Japanese personality with disturbing and unpredictable ease.

Life is especially hard on boys, for they are to be achievers. It is through their future success that families prosper. Only through the son's achievements can the mother assert her power. This means that an obedient son must pass all the right exams to get into all the right schools to enter all the right companies, and yes, even to marry the right woman.

While these obedient sons spend most of their time hunched over their books memorizing facts, their mothers engage in the most appalling one-upmanship with other mothers, using the sons as pawns in a continuous game of social snakes and ladders. These so-called *kyoiku mamas* (education mamas), driving their sons in the pursuit of exams, surpass many a Hollywood stage mother in sheer pushiness. Although this can be exploited – 'If you don't bring me more chocolate, I won't work for my exam' – *kyoiku mamas* are not universally popular figures.

Already in 1894, when the phenomenon was not nearly as widespread, the novelist Higuchi Ichiyo wrote a vitriolic short story about just such a mother, 'whose aspirations rose higher than Mount Fuji, though her station in life kept her back amongst the foothills'. She engineers a 'good marriage' for her son, ruthlessly pushing the girl he actually loves out of the way, creating misery for everybody but herself.[9]

Like the Jewish mother, the Japanese mama is always suffering and sacrificing. This can be, and frequently is, turned against the child. Every failure could be felt as a betrayal of maternal sacrifice. No achievement could ever repay her devotion. Guilt is one of the most durable pillars of maternal power.[10] Suicide notes left by children who failed their exams are the most eloquent proof of this. Most are pathetic apologies to the mothers they could not live up to.

There is a special genre in the Japanese cinema dedicated to maternal suffering, the so-called *hahamono*, literally 'mother things'. In these ostensible celebrations of the sacrificing, always sacrificing mother, feelings of guilt and hidden aggression are exploited with a ruthlessness that could only spring from complete innocence, or utter cynicism; but, as the latter is notably absent in Japan, one can only assume the former to be the case.

A typical example of the genre and also one of the best made, is entitled 'A Japanese Tragedy' ('Nippon no Higeki', 1953), an apt title for more reasons than one. The star playing the mother is Mochizuki Yuko, a specialist in 'mother things' and thus, before her death a few years ago, affectionately known as *Nippon no haha*, mother of Japan. She exploited this image quite effectively in a political career, after retiring from the film world. The story is set just after the war, when Japan was destroyed and everybody had to scrounge for the next meal. Mochizuki Yuko is a poor war widow, making every possible sacrifice for her son and daughter. And how she suffers! She is thrown out of her husband's house by her brother-in-law and she slides lower and lower down the scales of poverty until finally she has to suffer nightly humiliations as a barmaid in a vulgar seaside resort. For the children she will do anything.

But are they grateful? Of course not. They despise her. The daughter runs off with a married schoolteacher and the son manages to get himself adopted by a wealthy doctor in Tokyo. In an excrutiatingly sad scene near the end of the film, he tells his mother not to come round any more, as he is no longer officially her son. The poor, sacrificing mother of Japan has no choice but to do what poor, sacrificing mothers always do in these cases: she jumps in front of the nearest oncoming train. There, that will show them. This is followed by a loud rustle of handkerchiefs in the auditorium: these entertainments used to be classified by the distributors on the posters as two or three handkerchief films, depending on the number of expected tears to be mopped away.

In another 'mother thing', simply entitled 'Mother' ('Haha'), from the same period, a poor sacrificing mother is discarded by her callous children after a lifetime of devoted duty. With no place to go and no one to turn to, she is compelled to eke out a living by doing menial work in factories and hospitals. In the end she is rescued by her one faithful son, a fisherman, who had not realized what had happened in his absence. He curses his brothers and sisters for what they did. But the ever-forgiving mother just smiles beatifically and says, 'Please don't say that, my dear. To me you're all equally sweet.'

This is what that 'sweet, dimly white dream world' of the mother's bosom is ultimately all about. Everyone is the same. All are equally sweet. Individual differences are wiped out, just as they are, ideally, in the kind of womb-like group life the majority of Japanese feel most comfortable leading. And if they don't actually lead it, they dream about it.

Seeing heroes and heroines suffer, one is often told, makes Japanese audiences feel *anshin*, literally 'peaceful in their hearts'. Not just Japanese, but people everywhere find it wonderfully reassuring to see that other people's problems, even in fantasy, are worse than their own. But Japanese audiences, especially enthusiasts of 'mother things', will not even tolerate a happy ending. Mother is a kind of scapegoat, for nobody's fate could possibly be worse than hers.

This too has something to do with traditional child-rearing techniques. It has been pointed out that small boys are allowed to express anger and frustration by using their mothers as punching bags, pummelling their breasts and tearing at their hair.[11] Desperate for some response, they find no resistance, like hitting a trampoline, which only increases the aggravation. Japanese mothers rarely punish directly or rationally: how could they, lacking a rational system themselves?

Education in the West is still influenced by a religious system of abstract moral values as well as reason, transcending – or being supposed to – the arbitrary vagueness of human relationships. This is still largely true even of people who have consciously rejected organized religion. The need for a moral and rational ideology is part of our culture, for better or for worse. In Japan people attach far more importance to human feelings and the hierarchy of relationships than to reason or any universal moral system. There is no God, outside or above society, watching us all. Instead there is a complex system of etiquette, rules of behaviour to fit specific social situations. Which is why many Japanese put in a foreign and thus unpredictable environment either panic, or dispense with rules altogether. Society itself is God: we are constantly watched by other people. Hell, as Sartre said, really is the others, although to many Japanese it seems more like Heaven.

Because feelings are more important than logic or reason, the laws of the Japanese home are as vague and as open to emotional manipulation as the laws of the country itself. This is exactly what the Japanese mother does: manipulate with her emotions. Bad behaviour does not result in a quick slap or a powerful telling-off, but in a sulking mother withholding her affection, retreating into her cave like the Sun Goddess, after appeasement, bribery and begging have failed. 'Okachan wa kirai yo', 'mother doesn't love you any more', is the often used threat. The other one is isolation: 'We'll send you away' or 'I don't want to see you again'. Because most children become addicted to maternal affection during those blissful early years, this method usually works perfectly.

So what happens in effect is that the mother sets herself up as a sacrificing scapegoat in order to make the child feel guilty, and when this does not work, threatens to withhold her affection. It is around these two themes that most 'mother things' revolve. We have already seen an example of the first: the audience feels guilty for the children's callous behaviour and produces the handkerchiefs when mama throws herself in front of a train.

An example of the second theme is a popular play called 'Mother Behind My Eyes' ('Mabuta no Haha'); this is a common expression for a long-lost mother: mother in the mind's eye, so to speak. 'Mother Behind My Eyes' used to be a stock favourite of travelling theatre troupes performing at country fairs and local variety halls. The first film version was made in 1931.

The story is about a young gambler called Chutaro and his lonely quest for his long-lost mother. They were separated during one of the epidemics that plagued Edo in the nineteenth century. Leading the hard life of a criminal outcast, he spends twenty years saving enough money to help his mother through her old age, should he ever find her again.

And as one would expect, after many adventures involving the murder of at least a dozen men – Chutaro is by then a practised swordsman – he does indeed hear where she is. It appears that after hard times working as a geisha, she now runs a prosperous shop in Edo. She has turned over a new leaf, as they say, and she want nothing and nobody to disturb her new prosperity. At this rather ill-timed point Chutaro, the gambler son, walks into her shop, shaking with emotion. He blurts out who he is, expecting a tearful welcome. Mother goes pale at first, then pulls herself together and refuses to recognize him. Now would he stop being a nuisance and get out of her shop. The hero breaks down, choking with grief.

Mother gets more and more agitated, treating her son like a blackmailer out for her money. Chutaro explodes in a peculiar staccato laugh, common with Japanese heroes in the grip of hysteria. He throws his savings down in front of her, apologizes for causing any inconvenience and walks out. As he leaves the room, very cool now, his mother, barely able to contain her emotions (she is 'crying inside' as the Japanese saying goes), gets up as if to stop him; then she stumbles and upsets the teapot; she hesitates a moment – will her mother's heart win after all? – but no, she turns and picks up the pot, still preferring order to disruption: even cheap genre films abound in this kind of quite sophisticated symbolism. Chutaro has gone. But his sister persuades his mother to go after him and by the time they catch up Chutaro has killed another dozen men: 'If none of you have parents, don't expect any mercy from me.' His mother and sister scream his name. But he hides behind a tree and speaks the famous lines that never fail to produce the handkerchiefs: 'How could my sister live with a no-good brother like me? I'd better not look at them. Whenever I want to see mother, I'll just shut my eyes, and there she'll be, right behind my eyelids.'

What is remarkable about this story is that Chutaro, despite obviously 'crying inside', never shows any resentment. On the contrary, knowing that his presence as a known gambler would damage his mother's business and his sister's chances of a good marriage, he makes his final exit. Turning against his mother would cause too much guilt. The real sacrifice, in this case, is his.

But sacrifices are never made quite for nothing. Mother's business might prosper, but she'll still suffer. Chutaro has made his point, like a slighted child vowing to kill itself to spite Mummy and Daddy. This kind of one-upmanship in guilt is very common in Japanese entertainment, although it is never presented in those terms of course: demonstrative suffering is shown as a sign of sincerity or earnest intentions. Both mothers and children indulge in it.

Emotional blackmail is of course not unknown in other cultures – the most famous example, celebrated and lamented in almost equal measure, being the Jewish mama. But in Japan people are especially defenceless against it, for there is nothing to fall back on, no stick to fight it with; not reason, certainly, for it is immune to that, and not humour either – there are no Japanese Woody Allens making fun of the Japanese mama. In the words of the psychiatrist Kawai Hayao: 'One can imagine how hard it is for a people who have never known a patriarchal religion to stand up and fight against the Great Mother.'[12]

Humour, especially the ironical kind, needs a certain distance, and this the clinging mother–child relationship clearly prevents. The immunity to reason is perhaps more serious. One could possibly argue that social etiquette is itself a rational system, resistant to emotional manipulation. But even the social rules are not really fixed by any laws. They are to a large extent governed by the gut feeling of what is appropriate in a certain situation.

The word gut, *hara*, is used in many cases where one would normally assume that the brain was involved rather than the stomach. *Haragei*, for example, literally 'the art of the gut', is the art of guessing other people's motives, of figuring out what is in another person's mind. Businessmen and politicians have to be good at this.

But far from being resented, all this emotional judo is considered by the Japanese to be a sign of warmth and tenderness, of a uniquely Japanese sensitivity. *Yasashii* (gentle, tender, soft) is how the Japanese describe both their mothers and themselves. This is contrasted with Western ways which are cold, blunt, even brutal to the Japanese mind. Reason, to many Japanese, is the exact opposite of sensitivity.

The golden age of the gentle, tender and soft 'mother things' in the cinema was the 1950s, an age when film, not television, was still the main family entertainment. Both 'Mother' and 'A Japanese Tragedy', as well as several versions of 'Mother Behind My Eyes' were made then. But the same stereotypes are now alive and well on television in so-called home-dramas. These are broadcast in serial form, usually in the morning, in between commercials for baby powder and washing detergents.

The typical home-drama is family orientated, traditional in outlook and often mawkishly folksy, usually set in romantic rusticity or cosy, warm-hearted urban quarters. To make it even more safely unreal, the action often takes place in the past when things were simpler and more traditional; long enough ago to seem faintly exotic, but not so long as to seem remote: the 1920s are ideal, though the immediate post-war period is popular too: there was an abundance of suffering war widows then.

It is usual for home-drama heroines to lose their husbands somewhere around the second or third episode. A common cause for this quick despatch is the Second World War. The men are seen off at the station with much tearful flag-waving and are never seen again. This serves a double purpose. It confirms the popular myth of the Japanese as the prime victims of the war, and the heroine can now devote herself fully to her brood. The critic Ishiko Junzo has pointed out that 'a fundamental principle of the Japanese mother-film is that the mother must sacrifice her womanhood; she can't fall in love, or get married again. She must live for her children and then die.'[13]

Few of these mothers become doctors or bank-managers: I, at least, have never seen one on television. The typical working widow mother runs a little restaurant, manages a public bath or a pub. These kinds of jobs offer plenty of scope for her maternal instincts: motherhood goes public, so to speak. She becomes everybody's favourite mama. Luxury and wealth, though common in home-dramas of another sort, are not usually part of the 'mother thing' fantasy: after all, the mother must suffer.

One of the most popular home-drama series, first shown on television in 1977, is called 'A Wandering Life' ('Sasurai no Tabi'): as we shall see later, wandering is part of the Japanese hero's condition. The heroine of this particular story is Ryoko, a seamstress in a humble dress-shop. She marries above her station into the wealthy Otani family, where her presence is much resented by her mother-in-law. The mother and son relationship being what it is in Japan, one can imagine the kind of jealousy unleashed by the presence of another woman. This is particularly dramatic when all parties live under the same roof; less common these days, but a convention still rigidly adhered to in home-dramas.

When the bullying by the jealous mother-in-law becomes too insufferable Ryoko is compelled to leave the house, leaving her husband behind. Like most husbands in these entertainments, he is a typical mother's boy, who does not lift a finger to protect his wife from maternal harrassment. What is more he gets a divorce and marries a girl personally picked by his mother.

Ryoko's ensuing wandering life is very much a three-handkerchief affair and the only thing to keep her going is the memory of her beloved son, Minoru. For him she can bear any hardship and humiliation. Her ex-husband, as one can imagine, plays little or no part in her emotional life. This makes the following twist in her unlucky fate interesting. He is running for parliament and Ryoko falls into the hands of a blackmailer threatening to ruin her ex-husband's career by exposing her unsavoury life. (Unlikely as it seems, this kind of thing does work in Japan.) Ryoko murders the man and is promptly arrested. Why did she do it? Surely not for the sake of her ex-husband. She gives the answer herself in a long emotional speech on how she could not let the villain destroy the image of the pure, beautiful mother behind her son Minoru's eyelids. Thus the truth about her wretched life could not be let out.

In court one of those wonderful coincidences that never cease to delight Japanese audiences occurs: her state-appointed defender is none other than her grown-up son Minoru! He hears the truth and grabs his mother's hands in a harrowing close-up, the camera panning from hands to tearful face, and then utters the final climactic words of the series: 'Okasan!', 'Mother!'

It is interesting to note the ratings of this programme. In the beginning when the heroine has just got married and her problems are still purely domestic, the ratings ran from 12 to 15 per cent, high enough. But when her life really goes to pieces and her wandering life begins, the ratings shot up to 19 per cent.[14] One really has to suffer to be popular in Japan.

This does not necessarily mean that most viewers are sufferers too, identifying with the ill-fated heroine. On the contrary, as one housewife said: 'I find it soothing (*anshin*) to watch this series, precisely because the heroine is so different from myself. If it were about somebody just like me, leading a peaceful, uneventful life, I probably wouldn't be watching.'[15]

The story is actually based on an English novel, written in 1910, called *Madame X, A Story of Mother Love.* The difference is considerable and highly revealing. In the original blue-eyed version, the wife gets tired of her husband who thinks of nothing but his career. She then leaves him voluntarily to lead her dissolute life. Later, realizing the wickedness of her ways, she begs him to take her back. He refuses, but after more time passes regrets his cold-heartedness. By then it is too late, however: she can no longer be found and both their lives are ruined.

The heroine of this Edwardian melodrama has a strong will of her own. Ryoko, on the other hand, is a passive victim of fate, which is exactly what makes her a typical Japanese heroine. Also, the fact that her husband thinks of nothing but his work, in Japan, would hardly be a reason for leaving him. On the contrary, it would be regarded as a source of stability, something to be encouraged, if not always in real life, certainly in a television drama.

Thus, in the Japanese serial, a wicked mother-in-law had to be invented. And the husband actually marrying another woman selected by his mother would have been hard to imagine even in Edwardian England. The mother-in-law, the passive, suffering heroine, the mother-hen-pecked husband, all are Japanese additions which could have been lifted straight out of a seventeenth-century Kabuki play.

This drama brings to mind another story entitled *Taki no Shiraito, the Water-Magician*, made into a film in 1933 by Mizoguchi Kenji. The story of Taki the water-magician was written by Izumi Kyoka around the turn of the century. For the first time in Japanese history it became possible in those days for sons of reasonably but not terribly-humble families drastically to improve their social positions by higher education. This still meant a drag on the family finances, however, so for the son to succeed, the rest of the family, especially the mothers and sisters, for whom there was little money left, had to make sacrifices.[16]

Moreover, climbing the social tree would frequently take these fortunate sons into a completely different world from the one they came from. Embarrassment about their rustic origins, which they would often wish to hide, could easily lead to just the kind of tragedies cinema-goers have delighted in crying about ever since. 'Taki no Shiraito, the Water-Magician' must be seen against this background.

After one of her performances of water-tricks in a provincial variety hall, Taki meets and falls in love with a penniless but ambitious young man. His dream is to study law at the Imperial University (now Tokyo University) which was then, and still is to a certain extent, a passport to success. Taki then provides all her earnings to fulfil his dream. Like the mothers of Japan she sacrifices everything for her man. And with such a sponsor, how could he fail?

He doesn't. But his life in the capital is so exciting that he gradually loses touch with his benefactress. This is painful enough, but because of her debts on account of him she gets into serious trouble with a brutal usurer, who treats her with the kind of sadism usually reserved for villains on the Kabuki stage. After much silent suffering, making her seem ever more heroic, things go too far and she kills him.

She is duly arrested and put up for trial. Once again coincidence proves to be without limits: her judge is none other than the man she supported for so long. His shock is as great as hers, for by now he had completely forgotten about her. Yet she feels no resentment at all. She proudly gazes up at the great man as he pronounces her death sentence in a trembling voice. (He is in fact redeemed by doing the only right thing: he commits suicide.)

Clearly Taki is more mother than lover. This is indeed very common in Japanese drama, starting with the romantic Kabuki plays in which the male lovers are often effeminate and helpless weaklings. In a sense Japanese love stories are all variations of the *haha mono*. The cult of the mama transcends its narrow genre to spill over into romantic melodrama. It has its roots – like Tanizaki's worship of the Virgin Mary – in the religious tradition.

The critic Sato Tadao sees in Mizoguchi's women 'the image of the Sun Goddess, which, as a form of woman worship has influenced Japanese thought since ancient times'.[17]

The wife of General Nogi, who bravely committed suicide with her husband out of loyalty to the Meiji emperor on the occasion of his death in 1912, wrote that the perfect Japanese wife ought to be her husband's 'guardian deity'. In adversity it is her duty to protect him, not the other way round.[18]

A magazine called *Young Lady* featured an article (January 1982) on 'how to make ourselves beautiful'. How, in other words, to attract men. An American or European magazine would then go on to tell the reader how to be sexually desirable, no doubt suggesting various puffs, creams and sprays. Not so with *Young Lady*. 'The most attractive women', it informs us, 'are women full of maternal love. Women without maternal love are the types men never want to marry . . . One has to look at men through the eyes of a mother.'

All Mizoguchi Kenji's films seem to support this notion. Only through the sacrifice of Taki could the young man become a successful judge. A young actor in 'The Story of the Last Chrysanthemum' ('Zangiku Monogatari', 1939) owes his career to the tireless devotion of the family maid, O-Toku. She dedicates her life to her lover's success. But his theatrical family will allow him to continue his career only if he gives up seeing the maid. As one would expect, he complies, and while the new star is born, O-Toku dies.

The son in 'Sansho the Bailiff' ('Sansho Dayu', 1954) manages to escape from a cruel and frightful slave-camp because his sister covers up for him, paying for his freedom with her own life. All the male characters in Mizoguchi's last film, 'Street of Shame' ('Akasenchitai', 1956) are kept in various ways by their women who work in a sordid brothel. This image is incidentally quite common in Kabuki plays, where wives are wont to show their devotion by selling themselves to 'the narrow and willowy streets' of shame.

Mizoguchi is often called a 'feminisuto' in Japan. As with all Japanese-English terms, one cannot be too careful with this. Mizoguchi was never a fighter for women's rights. There is no evidence that he seriously considered possible, or even thought desirable, a real change in the state of affairs he so movingly depicted in his films. It would be more accurate, as the American film critic Audie Bock pointed out, to define a feminisuto as a worshipper of women.[19] This Mizoguchi undoubtedly was.

Like Tanizaki, Mizoguchi used Buddhist as well as Christian symbols for his worship. The last scene of 'Women of the Night' ('Yoru no Onnatachi', 1948) for instance. The film has a typical Mizoguchi heroine: a ruined war widow. Rejected by her family and cheated by her friends, she ends up, like so many women just after the war, on the streets as a *pan-pan*, a whore specializing in members of the American occupation forces. Towards the end of the film she finds her sister involved in a territorial brawl with another gang of prostitutes. Bitten, slapped and kicked from all sides, the sisters embrace, screaming in misery. Slowly the camera pans up to reveal a faded image on a broken wall of the Madonna and child.

This is not cinematically the happiest of Mizoguchi's images perhaps. But it is a good illustration of the way in which foreign images are borrowed quite unselfconsciously to express Japanese feelings. Logically speaking Mizoguchi could have borrowed a more appropriate idol from the exotic West: Jesus Christ. In their willingness to bear their men's crosses, Mizoguchi's heroines are more like Christ than his virginal mother. Men, like sinners in Christian thought, are never truly worthy of this sacrifice. The women are abused, rejected, betrayed and degraded, but still they will suffer for their men, and ultimately forgive them, like Taki gazing up at her judge.

In this they are also like Kannon, the Buddhist goddess of mercy, who plays such a large part in Tanizaki's imagery, as indeed in the work of many male Japanese authors.[20] The embrace of the merciful goddess is the salvation of men. In this light, choosing the Madonna instead of Christ is wholly understandable. Woman's remission, like God's in the confessional, absolves men from their sins. Sin, in this context, is of course not sin against some holy ghost, but sin against the Mother whose sacrifice and devotion no son could ever hope to repay.

Mizoguchi's favourite actress, appearing in most of his later films, was Tanaka Kinuyo. It is said that Mizoguchi was in love with this petite, plump, classically beautiful woman: round face, small, cherry-like mouth, narrow eyes. Tanaka herself, no doubt rightly, maintained it was her image he loved rather than herself.

Let us compare her to more modern goddesses created by a contemporary worshipper of women, Imamura Shohei. The women in his films, which, as Japanese critics never fail to point out, veritably reek of mud, are just as motherly as Mizoguchi's heroines. Physically, they are even more so. His ideal woman, according to his own description, is 'of medium height and weight, light colouring, and smooth skin. The face of a woman who loves men. Maternal. A lukewarm feeling. Good genitals. Juicy.'[21] Moreover, says Imamura, she binds herself to men who are weaker than she is.[22]

Imamura has little time for Mizoguchi's women. He doesn't believe those self-sacrificing heroines really exist. But he is no fighter for female rights either, even though he, too, is often called a feminisuto. Not only are his heroines stronger than men, as indeed they are in Mizoguchi's films, but they beat them at their own game. And their power rests to a very large extent in the male addiction to mothers.

In 'Intentions of Murder' ('Akai Satsui', 1964), for example, we see how a weak whiner of a husband curls up in bed with his wife, burying his head in her voluminous breasts, murmuring the by now familiar words: ''kachan', 'Mummy'. In 'The Pornographers' ('Jinrui Gakku Nyumon', 1966), the eldest son, a healthy teenager, still sleeps with his mother. And her lover finds he is impotent with anyone but her, so that when ''kachan' dies, he has to make do with a plastic doll. And as a last piece of maternal symbolism, in the final shot of the film, he drifts off in his boat into the sea to disappear forever. (This is a parody by the author, Nosaka Akiyuki, of the last chapter of a seventeenth-century masterpiece by Ihara Saikaku, in which the lecherous hero, after a life of complete dissipation, drifts off in his boat in search of The Island of Women.)

Perhaps the most typical and I think the best Imamura film is 'Insect Woman' ('Nippon Konchuki', 1963). The beginning is set in Imamura's favourite territory, the cold, muddy and backward north-east of Japan, where superstition and age-old customs still survive. Tome, the heroine, played by Hidari Sachiko, is born into a family of impoverished peasants who discard her as one too many mouths to feed. She is forced to fend for herself in the big city, like so many girls from the country. We are shown with

Imamura's customary sense of irony, how this superstitious, uneducated, but extremely vital and tough peasant woman copes with the modern world. She drifts like an insect through bars, brothels and new religious cults, using men as she goes along.

Somehow she survives, writing her bad poems and praying to her local northern deities. But ultimately she is defeated by her own daughter, who, with the same utter lack of scruples as her mother, first seduces her mother's patron and then takes off with his money. Tome and her daughter bend all the social rules when and where it suits them. They are perhaps aided in this by the fact that, as we have noted before, there are no absolute moral rules in Japan. This was perceived quite accurately by Francis Ottiwell Adams, a nineteenth-century observer of the Japanese scene. In his *History of Japan* he wrote: 'It seems to me that the Japanese woman is chaste, not from a religious point of view, but because she is ordered to do so by her parents. It is not with her a matter of principle, it is a matter of obedience. I should be glad if the contrary could be proved.'

It cannot. This may have dismayed a nineteenth-century European, but it amuses Imamura, as it amused many authors of fiction during the Edo period, such as Ihara Saikaku. Imamura sees his heroines as symbols of Japanese life: the native, vital, one is almost tempted to say, innocent life still to be found in the rural areas of Japan. Not Kannon or the Madonna are Imamura's symbols, but the shamaness, the muddy goddess of the village. He uses this image over and over again, even in a documentary film ('A Man Vanishes', 'Ningen Johatsu', 1967). The hand-held cinema vérité scenes are punctuated by shots of old country women speaking to the spirits in thick, rustic accents, like the witches in 'Macbeth'.

Another film, 'Tales From a Southern Island' ('Kamigami no Fukaki Yokubo', 1968) shot on a tiny island in the Pacific, ends with a shamaness dancing on the tracks of a tourist train. We see her, but the camera-clicking tourists in their rainbow-coloured Bermuda shorts no longer can, blinded as they are by the modern world.

All Imamura's woman are shamanesses of a sort, in touch with the dark mysteries of nature, as links with the earliest gods. It throws an interesting light on modern Japanese history that Tanizaki and Mizoguchi, both born at the end of the last century preferred to use Christian as well as Buddhist images for their idols, while Imamura and other modern artists go back to the oldest native traditions. But then the older generations were not quite so obsessed with the search for 'Japaneseness'; they were more secure in their cultural identity than the post-war writers and directors who have literally had to pick up the pieces of national defeat. The work of Imamura, Shinoda, Shindo, and many others, can be seen as a search for Japanese roots, to use a fashionable word. Imamura especially has often been likened to an anthropologist, digging for meaning under the mud. When Japanese get obsessed with their native identity they invariably turn to Shinto and that automatically leads them to the matriarchal goddesses that are its backbone.

3

Holy Matrimony

After reaching a certain age, twenty-five, say, the first question one is asked by strangers on a train is whether one is married. If the answer is yes, the next question is how many children one has. For women the age is lower, and to answer both questions in the negative is to brand oneself as someone out of the ordinary. As for unmarried mothers, they are not only extraordinary, but at best to be pitied, at worst to be severely frowned upon. Japan is in many respects a profoundly traditional society. Marriage is one of those respects.

Marriage is the passport to respectability in most parts of the world, but the pressure is particularly relentless in Japan. To be fully regarded as a woman one has to be a married mother – no matter whether the husband is dead or alive – for only then can one be called *ichininmae*, a favourite expression meaning both 'adult' and 'respectable'. The popular media – newspapers, comics, films, magazines, television – help to drive this message home.

Take, for example, the way unmarried career women are depicted in television dramas. This is in itself a new development, incidentally, for unmarried women in fiction, pictorial or literary, used to be almost exclusively prostitutes, geisha, bar ladies and other members of the 'floating world' of nocturnal entertainment. Women now constitute about 40 per cent of the Japanese workforce.[1] Fifty-two per cent of all office workers are women, and 37·7 per cent of all sales personnel. The average wage for women, however, is only 59·4 per cent of the wages taken home by men and just 6·7 per cent of the women hold managerial posts. Work for women usually means looking charming, answering telephone calls politely and brewing the green tea that fuels the Japanese workforce. Most women, moreover, work before they get married or after their children have grown up, or at least gone to school.

The 'O.L.s' (office ladies) in television soap operas are different. They are generally single and lead superficially glamorous lives which few of the viewers could possibly afford to emulate. What one sees is the good life as dreamed by millions of *Cosmopolitan* readers. The heroines are fashion designers or well-paid secretaries at smart advertising agencies full of dashing young executives ripe for the plucking.

Okura Junko, heroine of 'The Dazzling Desert' ('Hanayaka na Koya') is of this kind. She is single, pretty, in her thirties and a successful designer. Everything, in short, that a modern girl would want to be. And, to be sure, according to government statistics an increasing number of girls want to remain single working women if they have not yet found Mr Right by the time they reach their late twenties.[2] But is Junko happy? No, and this is the point, she is miserable. Her life, as the title of the series implies, may be dazzling, but it is also a desert. At one point she laments that 'when a woman becomes like me, it's the end of everything'. This is of course a reassuring thought for the many housewives watching this kind of programme.

Marriage is essential to a woman's happiness. Love, on the other hand, seems less so. In the morality of the samurai (warrior) class in traditional Japan romance and matrimony were two completely separate things; personal feelings were irrelevant and sometimes even antagonistic to the interests of the clan. It was different among the vast peasant population in the countryside: they often did marry for love.[3] But modern Japan has been strongly influenced by the samurai mentality, and love, though increasingly desirable, is not yet deemed essential for a marriage to succeed.

One of the most haunting scenes of a traditional marriage comes into a film directed by Ozu Yasujiro. It is called 'Late Spring' ('Banshun'). The grown-up daughter insists on living with her widowed father. But he patiently explains that 'marriage is a necessary step in the course of a human life'. In the end she is half tricked into marrying somebody she has hardly ever met. We see her being tightly harnessed in her ceremonial kimono. There is no trace of joy in her face; all emotions are hidden under a mask of chalk-white make-up. The last shot of the film is of her father, all alone now, sitting in his chair, peeling a bitter-sweet fruit. Only a slight twitch in his throat gives his loneliness away. Such is life, Ozu implies, and there is great beauty in the melancholy inevitability of its passing.

This film was made in 1949 and Ozu, despite his great cinematic reputation, is considered to be very old-fashioned now. Things have changed, one is told. And so they have . . . but only to a certain extent. It is true that love marriages (*renai kekkon*) have become much more common and the effects of 'samuraization'⁴ are slowly wearing off. Television and cinema heroines who insist on their right to pick their own mates are even shown with a certain amount of approval. Even so, up to 50 per cent of all marriages in Japan are still arranged by parents and go-betweens (partly, perhaps, because boy-meets-girl situations are hard to come by in a society where the sexes still keep very much to themselves in work and play). One has the right, of course, to turn prospective partners down, but especially in conservative families there is a limit to this. Many girls, and indeed boys, still settle for the person their parents think most suitable. 'I don't dislike him' (or her), is enough for a start.

A fascinating insight into contemporary attitudes to marriage is offered by those great architectural sugar cakes, known as wedding ceremony palaces. These function as ceremonial conveyor belts rushing happy families from the initial ritual right through to the final banquet. So many people are fed through these institutions in the course of one day that the tables have to be cleared while the toasts are still being proposed. The only advantage of this unseemly haste is that long-winded speakers are sometimes hurried a little by the sight of another family nervously waiting to get in at the door.

Advertisements for these places are to be seen everywhere: in subway trains, buses, magazines, on television. Since they deal with a natural event in everybody's life, it seems perfectly logical that one would often find them right next to another advertisement recommending a 'nice, quiet cemetery'.

The texts for these commercials are remarkable. I remember

one in particular, written in bold characters under a large photograph of a dejected-looking boy dressed in a tight suit: 'Get married! The final act of filial piety'. One marries to please one's parents, to fulfil one's social obligations.

I do not wish to be too cynical about this. There is no reason to believe that traditionally arranged marriages, unburdened by romantic expectations, are any less likely to succeed than the romantic Western kind, where the wife has to be a Madonna and a whore as well. There are good reasons to assume that quite the opposite might be true. The divorce rate is certainly lower in Japan: about 1 per cent, compared to around 4 per cent in the U.S.A. and 2·5 per cent in Britain.[5]

This is not to say that romance is not pushed as an ideal at all. It is, especially in women's magazines. Being 'happee' with one's loved one, living in the lifelong glow of a 'romanchiku moodo' is perceived by many young girls as their goal in life. Unfortunately the contrast with reality in many cases could not be greater, for society is not yet geared to fulfil these dreams.

This explains, perhaps, why most divorce cases are brought to court in recent years through the complaints of wives rather than of husbands.[6] This is a dramatic change from pre-war Japan when husbands could still send their wives back home – often because of problems with possessive mothers – while wives had no such rights. And to be sent home meant disgrace to their families. Since 1948 husbands and wives are equals before the law and the economic clout of women in an industrial society has obviously increased. But old ways die hard. The idea that it is disgraceful for a woman to get divorced still appears strong, and is encouraged by the mass media – on the widely watched 'real life' programmes on television, for example.

These melancholy shows are broadcast in the mornings so that the maximum number of housewives can watch them. They feature 'real people' with 'real problems'. Wives who have walked out of disastrous marriages are hauled in front of the cameras and confronted for our amusement with their irate husbands. These often hang on pathetically to a couple of howling children who are terrified of all the shouting and screaming under the glare of studio spotlights. 'Look what you're doing to them!' roars the husband, pointing at the cowering kids; and he is vociferously backed by a panel of well-paid 'counsellors', usually showbiz personalities or pop psychiatrists who spend more time on television than in their offices. To the general approval of these television sages, the woman is usually bullied into resuming her miserable existence in the home, sobbing convulsively in cruel close-up.

Television, the most modern of the mass media, is also in many ways the most old-fashioned, precisely because it is so popular. Traditional values are both reassuring and unlikely to offend a large number of people. To be conservative shows good business sense. It must also be added here that the press, gutter and serious, very rarely attacks the basic values of the majority of people in Japan. It may attack the government from time to time, but it is nevertheless much less independent than the American or Western-European press. Far from subverting the basic assumptions upon which Japanese society is based, it sees itself rather as the Confucian guardian of the public status quo.

There is a type of story called *kanzen choaku*, literally 'reward the good, punish evil'. This would seem to contradict the idea that there is no such thing in Japanese thinking as absolute good and bad. Actually it does not. These moral tales are based upon mainly Confucian rules of conduct. They are usually set in the Edo period, when those rules were at their pinnacle, and the star is often a samurai dispensing a kind of inspired justice to all and sundry. Typically this justice has little to do with law books. Everything is dealt with, as they say in Japan, case by case. These wise samurai are almost obsolete in the cinema, but on television they live on in a remarkably pure form, as do so many relics from the past for the edification of the family.

The perfect example is a series called 'Chohichiro Tenka Gomen'. It is set in the eighteenth century and the hero is a wise samurai called Chohichiro. One typical instalment featured a woman who became a successful comb merchant in Edo. The snag is, she had to leave her husband and child behind in her village in order to succeed; and now she has succeeded she wants her child back. After a long and complicated search she finds her daughter, who either cannot or will not recognize her: the classic estranged parent–child situation.

The mother is in despair, but just then Chohichiro, the samurai hero, steps in. The woman tells him her sad story: how her husband spent all their money on drink; how their daughter fell ill, and how she came to the capital to earn money to save the child. 'Everything I did was for the child', she cries. A good 'mother thing' heroine, one would think. But the earnest warrior in his supreme wisdom decides to give her a piece of his mind: 'Either you behave like a good mother, or you will go to hell!' (Heroes in these entertainments tend to speak in booming exclamation marks.)

The story then goes on. It transpires that her chief clerk, an evil little man, wants to take over her business. With the help of a corrupt official and several other shady characters, he kidnaps his employer's child. The woman is then forced to hand over the deeds of her business in exchange. Once this dirty deed is done, the villains decide to kill the mother and daughter, for, as the saying goes, they know too much. But before this can happen, in comes the hero once again, like a *deus ex machina*.

What follows is a classic cliché of period dramas: the hero reveals his true identity as a relative of the Shogun. In a flamboyant Kabuki-like gesture he whips his kimono open to reveal his illustrious family crest. Immediately the villains fall to the ground, knocking their heads in the dust like grovelling dogs. This is feudal theatre at its best! The shining prince, however, shows no mercy. He makes them stand up and fight to their deaths, one by one. And with a deft flick here and a well-timed swipe there, heads roll all over the screen.

This hour-long drama ends with a final homily from the hero to the mother: 'I trust you'll mend your ways and become a true mother from now on!' She promises, deeply moved, and as if by some miracle the child then recognizes her mother for the first time. 'Okasan!' ('Mother!'), she squeals, and rushes into her arms. Though we see the drunken father, he is never more than an insignificant figure shuffling in the background. Good motherhood has nothing whatsoever to do with him whether he is drunk or sober, good or bad.

Of course television is but an imperfect mirror of society. Not every Japanese conforms to the strict Confucian morality advocated in this kind of drama. More and more women are filling other roles besides motherhood. But even if the national mass media do not reflect what is real, they do offer a picture of what is proper, just as Hollywood did until recently in America.

This does not stop with fiction. Real people in the camera eye are made to conform publicly to moral stereotypes in a way that comes very close to Hollywood in the 1940s and 1950s. This is especially true of those television super-stars manufactured to appeal to the very young: the *talentos*, a Japanese-English term meaning a performer without one specific talent, like an instant Jack-of-all-arts with a pretty face. *Talentos* sing and dance in variety shows, act in teenage movies, smile a great deal, and do as they are told by an army of producers, advertisers and various assorted middlemen.

Talentos are products of advertising companies using the most sophisticated marketing techniques. They rarely last long, but while they are around, their ubiquitous and inescapable presence makes them a major social influence. Everything they say or do is immediately transmitted to millions of fans through gossip magazines and television shows. What they say is carefully programmed by the people who created them. It never veers from the most conservative social morality: how wonderful it is to be Japanese, how glad they are for all the help from their seniors, how hard work is the prime virtue of the Japanese people and finally how they would love to get married and raise a family. Even known homosexuals – though this is never openly stated – are constantly linked in the popular press to various suitable partners in a 'will they, or won't they' game, right until the final decision that they will.

There are of course one or two successful entertainers who remain single, but they are careful to show themselves suitably repentant. At every public performance they stress with consummate professional skill how much happier they would have been as ordinary married people. Meanwhile their popularity keeps on rising.

The reaction to scandals, when they become public (the many tabloids make sure that they do), is equally predictable. Obviously Japanese love reading juicy stories as much as anybody. But the punishments meted out to offending *talentos* are curious. One female *talento*, after being questioned – not even arrested – about smoking pot with friends in a hotel-room, found all her contracts cancelled, including a lucrative tampon commercial she starred in. This would have been quite conceivable in Hollywood in the 1940s: Robert Mitchum, too, was arrested for smoking pot. But the following scene has an unmistakably

Japanese flavour: the *talento* was made to go through a humiliating public apology on television, something like those self-criticism sessions in China during the Cultural Revolution, telling us how truly sorry she was, and how frightful the effects of pot smoking are. Only after this tearful demonstration of sincerity and good intentions did the wrath of the public-spirited media abate and she was let back into the tampon advertisements and the sing-along shows.

Sagara Naomi, another female singer, was not so lucky. One ill-fated day her lesbian lover told all in a television talk show. Why she did it nobody knows, but as a result Sagara was barred from appearing on television as long as the incident remained in the admittedly fickle public memory. Sagara's problem was not, I think, due to any innate wickedness of lesbian love. Homosexuality as such was never a sin in Japan. The problem was that she did not keep her friend under control. She let down the façade of propriety, she caused embarrassment, she rocked the social boat, and of course, she happened to be single. Nobody seems to care much about what people do in private, as long as they conform in public. After all, it is perfectly acceptable for a Japanese prime minister to keep several mistresses, as long as he is not a bachelor, in which case he would never have become prime minister in the first place.

In a way the *talentos* in Japan fulfil the function of royalty: they are models of propriety as well as entertainers; bubble-gum royals, as it were. The *talento* world even had its own prince Charles and princess Diana: Yamaguchi Momoe, the girl and Miura Tomokazu, the boy. She, a singer/actress with cute good looks; he, a handsome actor of average, but not more, ability. Both were hugely popular, especially after being cast together in films as the romantic couple.

They were known in the heady summer of 1980 as the 'Goruden Combi' (Golden Combination). They were the most virtuous, most handsome, most polite, most quintessentially Japanese couple of the decade. When they decided, with or without the prompting of their producers, to get married, the mass media — and thus the rest of the nation — went berserk. Not a day went by without some T.V. special, 'Goruden Combi' issue or exclusive interview. It was a true royal bubble-gum wedding: she wanted to retire, his career had never really taken off, so why not go for some big money in the end? Reality is beside the point here: what matters is what is proper and lucrative.

Everybody got into the act: his mother, Momoe's first schoolteacher, his best friend, her sister. There was even a real 'mother thing' sob story about her abandoned mother who sacrificed everything for her children: Momoe had a good cry over this on television at least twice every week. The national broadcasting company, NHK, devoted two evening-long specials to the impending event. Newspapers and magazines outdid each other with long studies about her skills as a housewife and his favourite dishes. Momoe herself wrote a book, published in great haste, about the proper role of women in Japanese society. I stopped counting the number of 'sayonara (goodbye) concerts'.

What was most impressive of all, however, was the decision by Yamaguchi Momoe, a much bigger star than her fiancé, to give up her lucrative career for ever, in order 'to look after Tomokazu'. She did the right thing. It was the most improving, uplifting, truly proper event of the decade. This was two years ago. His film career is virtually at a standstill, though he still manages to cut a dash in commercials for men's clothes and cigarettes. The magazines are speculating now about her 'come backu consato'.

4

Demon Woman

There comes a point in every man's life when he realizes, sometimes with considerable dismay, that women's needs and desires go beyond the simply maternal. The fact that women have sexual desires, for instance, is a delight to some, but a source of intense anxiety to others. Both reactions are of course as common in Japan as anywhere else. But for a country internationally known as a paradise of guiltless erotic fun – geisha girls, mixed bathing and so on – anxiety plays a remarkably large part in its popular culture.

Once again we sense the grip of the matriarch. This is evident, for example, in the work of Terayama Shuji, poet, playwright, photographer and avant garde film-maker. He was obsessed, in his work at least, with his mother. One scene which appears in a number of his works is of a young, pretty boy seduced by a sluttish older woman, the caricature of a whore. This is then followed by some expression of unbridled aggression against the mother: choruses belting out, 'please die, mother!' or, in one of his books, photographs of Terayama's own mother, torn to bits or framed under shattered glass.[1] This seems to be symptomatic of most of his work.

So many modern and traditional artists show a similar preoccupation that one can only assume that it reflects something deeply embedded in Japanese culture. Woman, it appears, is not readily forgiven for her fall from grace. She is worshipped as a maternal goddess, but feared as a demon. When the maternal mask is ripped off, a frightening spirit is revealed.

This is a common theme in folk beliefs as well as classical literature. A famous play, performed both in the No and the Kabuki theatre, entitled 'Dojoji',[2] is about one of these demon women, called Kiyohime. She falls in love with a young priest. But since he has taken his vows of celibacy, he tries to escape from her advances. Her pursuit gets more and more desperate until finally she turns into a hissing serpent. The terrified priest then hides under a great bell. But in the climactic scene the serpent coils itself around the bell and destroys it as well as the poor priest with the deadly flames issuing from her fangs.

Victorian Englishmen also insisted on a dichotomy between the pure woman and the sexual savage, but that had less to do with the dominating mother-figure than with the morality of the period which denied sexuality to 'respectable' ladies. This was never the case in Japan. As exemplified by the goddess Izanami, purity and pollution can exist in the same person. This same principle can be seen with the Tantric Indian deities who appear as beautiful women inspiring the life-force in men, or as ogres decorated with garlands of dead corpses.

The process of pure female turning into demon is described in modern literature too. For examples let us turn once more to Tanizaki Junichiro who was something of an expert on the subject. When he was twenty-five in 1910, he wrote 'The Tattooer' ('Shisei'),[3] a short story about a tattoo artist obsessed with the idea of finding the perfect woman as a canvas, as it were, for his art. When he does find such a woman, a young geisha with 'exquisitely chiselled toes', he drugs her in his studio and, 'pouring his soul into the ink, he sinks it into her skin'. When she wakes up, she sees to her horror a great black spider covering her back and 'with each shuddering breath, the spider's legs stirred as if they were alive'. Henceforth, the artist tells her, all men will be her victims.

The foot with its 'exquisitely chiselled toes, nails like the iridescent shells along the shore at Enoshima, a pearl-like rounded heel, skin so lustrous that it seemed bathed in the limpid waters of a mountain spring' becomes a weapon to be 'nourished by men's blood and to trample on their bodies'.

Mishima Yukio wrote about Tanizaki's fascination for the demon woman, the metaphysical *femme fatale*, that when 'the pure love for the mother is confused with sexual desire an immediate metamorphosis takes place. She becomes a typical Tanizaki woman, such as the girl in "The Tattooer". Her beautiful body houses a dark, cruel and evil element. If we examine this more closely, it is clear that this is not a particular evil inherent in women. Rather it is an evil desired by men; a reflection of masculine lust.'[4]

The typical Tanizaki hero worships the feet that trample on him. The more they trample, the more he worships. This erotic game escalates further and further, sometimes resulting in actual death, which no doubt adds to the *frisson*. This is especially true of his later characters, such as the old professor in 'The Key' ('Kagi', 1956) or Utsugi Tokunosuke in 'Diary of a Mad Old Man' ('Futen Rojin Nikki', 1962), both in their seventies and neither of them up to the cruel temptations of their female idols.

Sex literally is a dance of death. Each time Utsugi's daughter-in-law Satsuko allows the old man to lick her feet, as a special favour, his blood pressure shoots up to dangerous heights. After almost meeting his end at one of these sessions, he writes in his diary:

> The thought of really dying did frighten me. I tried to calm myself down, telling myself not to get excited. The strange thing is, however, that I never stopped sucking her feet, I couldn't stop. The more I sought to stop, the harder I sucked, like an idiot. Thinking I was going to die, I still kept on sucking. Fear and excitement and pleasure came in turns.

The mad old man wants to continue the game even after his death. Instead of the more usual effigy of Kannon, the goddess of mercy, on his grave he plans to have his daughter-in-law's feet cast in stone to trample on him forever. Thus he shall 'feel the full weight of her body, and the pain, and the velvety smoothness of her feet'.

The hero of an earlier story ('Aguri', 1922) has similar fantasies about his wicked temptress. He imagines his own death and how his spirit will then meet his lover, showing off her gorgeous legs in silk stockings and garters:

> 'I'll hug that old corpse as hard as hard as I can,' she will say, 'hug it till his bones crack, and he screams: "Stop! I can't stand

it any more!" If he doesn't give in, I'll find a way to seduce him. I'll love him till his withered skin is torn to shreds, till his last drop of blood is squeezed out, till his dry bones fall apart. Then even a ghost ought to be satisfied.'[5]

Georges Bataille has said that eroticism is the joy of life pushed to the point of death.[6] There are shades of this in Tanizaki's work, but his imagery comes closer to the tradition also found in India, China and Tibet of the life-force being drained by demon-like passion: the ultimate union of eros and thanatos. Traditionally, though, it is often the female demon, not the male victim, who is depicted as a skeleton. One thinks, for example, of a print by Kunisada of a samurai making love to a horrible skeleton in a graveyard, under the illusion that it is his wife. In another Kunisada print, entitled 'Hell of Great Heat', we see the Hell of a libertine with his grotesquely extended penis being eaten away by evil-looking spirits with vulvas instead of heads.

The most modern example of man being consumed by female passion is Oshima Nagisa's film 'Realm of the Senses' ('Ai No Korrida', 1976). A love affair between a gangster and a prostitute accelerates in an ever-tightening coil of passion culminating in violent death. Sex becomes the lovers' whole claustrophobic universe and after strangling her lover during a shuddering climax, the girl cuts off his penis as the ultimate gesture of possession. It is a beautiful but frightening film perfectly expressing that anxious–sensuous ambivalence which is so much part of the Japanese psyche.

Tanizaki was an unusual individual, yet at the same time representative of his culture and times. None the less the typical Tanizaki temptress, or the 'Eternal Woman', as he often called her, is far removed from the pure Japanese mother; or, for that matter, from the pure, virginal young girls Kawabata favoured in his novels.

The Tanizaki Venus is indeed young, though hardly innocent; she is usually rather vulgar, an ex-nightclub dancer or a waitress, and thoroughly modern in her tastes, in a word, 'Westernized'. But never Western. The hero in 'Aguri' dreams of his mistress as 'a sculpture of the "Woman" under the kimono . . . He would strip off that shapeless, unbecoming garment, reveal that naked "Woman" for an instant, and then dress her in Western clothes

. . . Like a dream come true.'

Like most of his countrymen, Tanizaki felt ambivalent about the West and its women. He had a taste for things Occidental, but always from a distance. He lived in a foreign quarter of Yokohama for a time. He even took English lessons and tried to learn dancing.[7] But he never actually went to the West. Like many intellectuals he preferred his ideals to be pure and unsullied by too much reality.

He once wrote in an essay entitled 'Love and Sex' ('Ai to Shikijo') that Occidental women are best seen at a distance. Western women, according to Tanizaki, are better proportioned than Japanese, but 'they are disappointing when one gets too close and sees how coarse and hairy their skins are'. He concluded that Western women are to be looked at, admired even, but not to be touched. This sums up rather well, I think, the common attitude of Japanese intellectuals to the West.

Feelings of superiority and inferiority towards the West are strangely mixed in Japan, especially during Tanizaki's lifetime, when the economic decline of the Western world was not quite so apparent as it is today. The main protagonist in 'A Fool's Love' ('Chijin no Ai'), an as yet untranslated masterpiece, explains how he would love to marry a Western woman if only he had the money or the social opportunity. But, he confesses, 'even if I did have the money, I have no confidence in my appearance; I'm small, I'm dark-skinned, and my teeth stick out in all directions.' So he settles for a Western-looking Japanese.

An aesthetic fascination for the West is still evident in modern Japan. Fashion magazines use blondes from Sweden and California to show Japanese-designed clothes; Caucasian dummies stand stiffly in Japanese shop-windows; students decorate their dormitory walls with *Playboy* magazine pin-ups. On the other hand, like Tanizaki, they seem to favour more traditionally Japanese types, plump and maternal, as girlfriends and wives.

This aesthetic schizophrenia was particularly strong during the Meiji period, when Tanizaki grew up. Japan wanted to be or at least look like a modern state. And to be modern in those days, in aesthetics as well as politics and economics, was to be Western. Tanizaki's *femmes fatales* had to be influenced by the West. The romantic idea of the *femme fatale* is largely European, and it enjoyed a special vogue in the nineteenth century. The examples of females using their demonic powers over men in Japanese literature are, by and large, just that: demonic – jealous spirits, vengeful ghosts, fox-women and serpents.

The cruel temptress using only her earthly powers is rarer and the adoration of her almost non-existent. There is no Salome in Japanese mythology and no Dietrich or Mae West in its cinema. Tanizaki hinted at this when he wrote that 'the greatest influence we received from Western literature was the liberation of love, and indeed even of sexual desire.'[8] According to Tanizaki sexual love in pre-modern Japanese literature had never been treated as a serious subject. Hitherto, he thought, it had been mostly play or suicidal sacrifice. Whether he was right about this or not (it is debatable), is not the point. What is interesting is that in his own mind the influence from the West was linked to his masterly analysis of the libido. He was also certainly aware of the romantic trends in nineteenth-century European literature, of which he was quite fond, in which the destructive powers of 'das ewig Weibliche' played such an important part.

But, as we have seen, creating the eternal female, in Tanizaki's novels, is a Frankenstinian business. One of his most Frankenstinian creations is Naomi, the girl in 'A Fool's Love' ('Chijin no Ai', 1924). Naomi starts life as a waitress in a seedy area of Tokyo, 'the name of which is enough for most readers to guess at her background'. Her creator, Joji, is a thrifty, mousy engineer at an electrical company. The only woman in his life, apart from Naomi, is his mother. Joji decides to adopt this fifteen-year-old waitress with a face like Mary Pickford's, and dreams of turning her into a 'dashing, modern woman one can take anywhere without feeling ashamed'. He tries to teach her English, they attend dancing classes together and he dresses her in costly Western clothes. But as usual the creator is doomed to be engulfed by the forces he has unleashed. Naomi becomes a pampered goddess, changing foreign lovers as often as new clothes, while her benefactor is reduced to being her grovelling slave, his will utterly shattered, licking the feet that kick him in the face.

The character of Naomi is said to have been based on Tanizaki's sister-in-law, with whom he was infatuated for a time, without, it appears, much success. But she is also a caricature of the modern Japanese woman, the so-called *moga* (*modan garu* = modern girl), the flapper of the naughty 1920s, dancing the wicked nights away. The *succès de scandale* of the book was such that the type of behaviour exemplified by Naomi, and widely imitated by others, became known as Naomism.

Naomism essentially meant a breakdown of traditional restraints. The 'Woman' was revealed under the kimono. Raw passion was unleashed. Westernization, especially before the war, was in some ways like the opening of a fascinating can of worms. Hence, the death of the mother in Tanizaki's work and the birth of the wicked temptress can be read as a metaphor of the loss of the traditional Japanese past. The West, as attractive as it is illusory, is a stain on this mythical, irretrievable past. The flowering of extreme nationalism, resulting in the doomed militarist adventure, came very soon after the golden age of Naomism.

Naomi was born less than twenty years after a woman much like her: Rosa Frohlich in Heinrich Mann's novel *Professor Unrat*, better known as Lola-Lola in Von Sternberg's film 'The Blue Angel'. I doubt if Tanizaki was aware of it, but the two women are remarkably alike. Both are beautiful, vulgar temptresses, whose sexual powers drive their pathetic male slaves to the edge of insanity. Both, in their time, signalled a breakdown of their respective old worlds: bourgeois, small-town Germany and traditional Japan.

Fear of female power need not necessarily result in male masochism: slavery can just as easily turn into aggression. This can be more or less disguised, as in Mizoguchi's films. The violent degradation of his women is painted with such loving care that it seems like a kind of aesthetic revenge. In this sense Mizoguchi was like that other great sensualist of the early cinema, Erich von Stroheim, the infamous Hollywood German of the 1920s.

Von Stroheim, under his campy dictatorial façade, was a moralist. His films are about the way people are corrupted by money and power and the humiliations they inflict on each other because of it. His moral indignation, like Mizoguchi's, was no doubt genuine, but one cannot help feeling that it was superseded by his aestheticism. Corruption is also erotic; it is bad, of course, but fascinatingly and beautifully so.

Mizoguchi's attitude to women was equally ambivalent. In his own life he was quite a philanderer, particularly in the red-light districts of his beloved Kyoto. Like Von Stroheim, he had the reputation of humiliating women. And it is said that his wife died of the syphilis he gave her. There is a well-known story that he once broke down in a V.D. clinic in a room full of prostitutes, telling them it was all his fault, begging their pardon over and over again. If the story is not true, it ought to be, for it seems so typical of the man. He both adored and hated women and above all he wanted them to forgive him for their humiliation.

He also had a profoundly religious streak, carrying the votive idol of the Buddhist saint Nichiren with him to film festivals.[9] Mizoguchi's aesthetic is infused with what the Japanese call *mono no aware*, the pathos of things, or *lacrimae rerum*. It is a melancholy, even tragic sensibility inspired by the Buddhist resignation to the suffering of life. Yes, life is sad, but what can one do about it? And after all, is that sadness not rather beautiful too? This attitude is behind most traditional Japanese art. In Mizoguchi's work the victimized woman, prostrated on the floor (his favourite image), suffering the full cruelty of life, thus becomes a symbol of great and melancholy beauty.

But aggression is by no means always this guarded or beautiful. Modern Japanese pornography is overwhelmingly sadistic, as anyone can find out by spending five minutes in any Japanese bookshop. This is not a new phenomenon. Some of the most extreme examples of aesthetic cruelty are to be found in the so-called decadent art of the late Edo period (mid-nineteenth century), in the woodblock prints of Kuniyoshi, and especially in those of his pupil Yoshitoshi, or in the grotesquely violent paintings by Ekin. They shared an artistic fondness for tortured women. One of the most telling images by Yoshitoshi is of a pregnant woman suspended upside down over a fire, while an old hag is sharpening her knife to slit her stomach open. In an almost identical print by the same artist we see a man actually slashing a hanging woman to pieces.

This form of torture is something of a cliché in Japanese art – and, it seems, in reality: it is first mentioned in the Nihonshoki, an eighth-century chronicle of Japanese history. Apparently in A.D. 500 the emperor Buretsu 'had the belly of a pregnant woman opened for an inspection of the womb'. In the

Kabuki play 'Hitori Tabi Gojusantsugi' by Tsuruya Namboku, a pregnant woman is tortured, cut open and her child is tossed up in the air. This form of violence is perhaps the most extreme expression of anger at having lost the pure Arcadia of early childhood. It is also a transgression of one of the strictest taboos. In an utterly perverse manner the transition between life and death is stood on its head.

Aesthetic cruelty, in Japan as elsewhere, is a way of relieving fear, of exorcizing the demons. Because female passion is thought to be more demonic than the weaker, male variety – it is she, after all, who harbours the secret of life – and because of her basic impurity and her capacity to lead men so dangerously astray, it is Woman who has to suffer most.

Judging from what is readily available I cannot think of many countries more inundated with pornography than Japan: not the hardest, perhaps, but the most. The smallest neighbourhood bookshops are well stocked with pornographic magazines, comics and books. There are vending machines, conveniently located on street corners, offering a large variety of porno-comics and 'dirty pictures'. One of the largest surviving companies of the once great Japanese film industry now produces nothing but soft porn – except for the occasional film for children – at the rate of one new picture a month.

In the early nature-worshipping stage of Japanese history there was no pornography. Pornography cannot exist with natural innocence. The phalluses and vulvas carved out of wood or stone were, and sometimes still are, magical objects to be used in rituals promoting good crops and female fertility. Significantly the first examples of what could perhaps be called pornography, such as obscene drawings, go back to around the tenth century, when Buddhist morality had already had several centuries to make its impact felt.[10] These drawings of monks indulging in all manner of mischief and abbots entertaining aristocratic ladies may well have been part of a popular reaction to what was still essentially a foreign creed. They also suggest social satire rather than purely erotic titillation. Certainly the fact that these early erotic drawings were called *warai-e* (comical pictures) does not point to a strong sense of sin, however hellish Buddhist warnings may have been.

The tension between the earthy, hedonistic side of Japanese

culture and an imported morality imposed by the authorities (in medieval Japan the clergy played a strong political role), was at its height during the Edo period (1615–1867). This time it was not Buddhism but Confucianism that the government deemed to be most effective in keeping the populace under control.

The people in the cities found an outlet in the Kabuki-culture of the licensed quarters: the theatres, teahouses and brothels. Pornography played a vital part in this. Most popular artists, including the most famous, such as Utamaro or Hokusai, made many erotic pictures and a large number of authors wrote erotica. Many pornographic images satirized the stuffy Confucian classics in the same way that tenth-century erotica made fun of Buddhism.[11] Nevertheless, anything that could conceivably be construed as criticism of the government, however oblique, was strictly forbidden.

Pornography under the rule of the Tokugawas was not only a secretive hobby of a socially frustrated upper-class, as was the case in Victorian England or Imperial China, but also a spontaneous expression of a people whose spontaneity was suppressed in every other way. Hence certain Japanese critics and scholars like to present the Kabuki-culture as a form of political protest. This is dubious. Political protest needs an ideology, whether political, religious or both. This the Kabuki world certainly never had. It is true, though, that despite their wealth, merchants, artisans and even samurai, who suffered more than anybody from the constraints of Confucian morality, were politically muzzled. And so, in a sense, pornography and violent entertainment took on a subversive meaning far beyond its original intentions.

Even now a large number of critics, film-makers, writers and political activists see pornography as a subversive weapon against the authorities. And yet again a foreign religion plays a part in this. Since the nineteenth century Christianity has cast its shadow on official morality. Not that Japanese politicians and law-makers are Christians, but the anti-obscenity laws passed since the Meiji restoration in 1868 have certainly been influenced by a desire to appear 'civilized' in Western eyes.

Thus pornography still sometimes becomes mixed up with an odd kind of paranoid nationalism. There was a famous case, for instance, involving a film ('Black Snow', 'Kuroi Yuki', 1965) directed by Takechi Tetsuji. The film is about an impotent young man who gets his kicks by shooting American soldiers, and making love with a loaded gun. The connection between the American occupation and Japanese impotence is in fact quite a common theme in the work of artists who went through that period; indeed, one gets the impression that losing the war had a most traumatic physiological effect. In any event, Takechi's film was originally banned for its pornographic content and he was even sued by the Tokyo Metropolitan police. Eventually he won his case, but not before the Japanese intelligentsia had made a huge fuss about it.

Takechi saw his film as a political statement against 'American Imperialism', a popular target in those heady days. He still describes himself as a *minzokkushugisha*, literally an ethnic nationalist, a position that has strong racialist overtones. This is evident in the film. Not only does the young hero murder a G.I., but it has to be a black G.I. (This, incidentally, has become a standard cliché: whenever G.I.s are shown in Japanese porno films, invariably in the act of outrageously raping Japanese maidens, they are very often blacks to make the outrage seem even worse.)

Takechi, who also regards film editing in ethnic terms – 'Japanese editing must reflect our unique spiritual values' – described the attack on his work in wholly traditional terms:

The censors are getting tough about 'Black Snow'. I admit there are many nude scenes in the film, but they are psychological nude scenes symbolizing the defencelessness of the Japanese people in the face of the American invasion. Prompted by the CIA and the U.S. Army they say my film is immoral. This is of course an old story that has been going on for centuries. When they suppressed Kabuki plays during the Edo period, forbidding women to act, because of prostitution, and young actors, because of homosexuality, they said it was to preserve public morals. In fact it was a matter of rank political suppression.[12]

It seems ironic that once again foreigners are involved and blamed. But what is interesting here is not that 'Black Snow' is an eloquent political statement – which it is not – but that it should be regarded as such both by the author and the authorities. The same is true of Oshima's 'Realm of the Senses' ('Ai No Korrida'), a much better film. Using the not unreasonable slogan, 'what's wrong with obscenity?' Oshima has been putting up a courageous fight in the law courts for years. Thus a film entirely about sex has again become a political issue. And even entirely commercial porno films are often regarded on university campuses and in late-night cafés as subversive statements.

It is unlikely that Japanese intellectuals, the so-called 'interi', really believe that soft porn producers are political activists. But it is certain that pornographic books, films and comics are regarded as weapons in the continuing tug of war between the 'muddy' culture of the people (with the 'interi' as their self-appointed representatives) and the authorities who are trying to stamp it out.

A typical example of this on-going moral struggle is the great pubic hair debate. Rape, sadism, torture, all this is permissible in popular entertainment, but the official line is drawn at the showing of pubic hair. This is more reminiscent of schoolmasters measuring the length of their pupils' unruly mops than an indication of any deep moral conviction.

The rule is constantly being tested by film directors, photographers and artists, by no means all in the porno trade, who stretch it to its absurd limits: woman in comic books crouch down awkwardly in front of men, who spout great shafts of empty space into willing female mouths and hands, suspended somewhere in mid-air; girls are photographed wearing the sheerest of see-through panties, hiding absolutely nothing, or they simply shave the offending hair off, which, for some reason, makes it all more acceptable. The latest round in this curious contest seems to have been won by 'the people', for the government has announced that 'there will be about a 5 per cent reduction in the number of black dots and squares that are painted on pictures that the authorities consider to be harmful to public morals.'

In many Western porn movies, even of the crudest kind, it is at least sometimes suggested that mutual enjoyment is part of the sex act. In Japan this is rarely the case: either the female is an innocent victim of rape, or she is a compulsive man-eating ogress consumed by her sexual savagery. One often leads to the other:

defiled innocence becomes man-eating ogress. Either way, she is punished for taking off her maternal mask. What is truly remarkable, however, is that after all that she often ends up putting it on again.

A fascinating example is a 'political' pornographic film jointly directed by Wakamatsu Koji and Adachi Masao, who later fled to the Middle-East because of his alleged links with the Japanese 'Red Army' terrorists. The film has a 'message', but it is entirely symptomatic of commercial erotica in Japan. It is entitled 'When the Foetus Goes Poaching' ('Taiji ga Mitsuryu Suru Toki', 1966). In it a manager of a department store lures one of his salesgirls to his flat. There he immediately proceeds to tie her hands and feet to his bed, after which he tortures her with candles, whips and even a razor. Throughout this messy ceremony he wears pure white gloves.

Just as it becomes too unbearable to watch (though it did not seem to faze the Japanese watching it with me), the scene turns into an illusion: the concrete wall of the bedroom becomes like a great big womb, sucking the manager inside. He screams, 'Okasan!' ('Mother!'). The girl, blood pouring from a mass of wounds, then sings him the sweetest lullaby until the man, exhausted by his labour, falls asleep like a baby.

In a review of this film the critic and German literature scholar Tanemura Suehiro, a somewhat flowery 'interi' with a taste for the macabre, called this torture session a 'purification ceremony'. 'Purified by the whip, the woman, in a sea of blood, changes into an unborn foetus. Trussed up in ropes, like an animal being consumed by a snake, she goes through the spasms of birth.'[13] By so punishing or 'purifying' the sexual female, the hero presumably regains his 'sweetly, dimly white dreamworld' of the maternal bosom. (A very similar process is at work at many Shinto festivals. They also start off with often painful purification ceremonies and end in a crawling mass of naked bodies, without ego or identity, crushed together in a pitch-black shrine.)

Before sexuality can be purified it must first manifest itself. In Japanese pornography this usually means rape. The victims are symbols of innocence: schoolgirls in uniform, nurses, just-married housewives and so on. These women *always* fall in love with their rapists. Or perhaps love is not the right word: 'They are betrayed by their bodies' is how the film distributors put it in their publicity handouts. They become addicted to the forbidden fruit. They are polluted, or rather, their inherent impurity manifests itself.

This pollution is often shown at the beginning of the film in a very literal way: the female victim is dragged through a rice-field, for example, or thrown into a rubbish dump or sent into the streets naked. In short, exactly the sort of thing that goes on at the start of a Shinto ceremony, when men roll in the mud or run through the village naked.

Very few women in the Japanese world of porno become savages of their own free will. Their impurity, as was the case with Izanami, is simply a consequence of nature. It is no sin: they cannot help it, but neither can they escape it, for it is in their blood. This is the meaning of the following English language synopsis handed out by a company of soft porn producers: 'This is the story of three sisters. They becom [*sic*] sluts, not so much out of their own free wills, but more at the mercy of their lascivious blood of their parents that runs through their blood.'[14] Or this one: 'No matter how chaste a girl like Natsuko may be, once she is raped, the traumatic experience is apt to change her whole life.' Understandably so, one thinks, but then the pamphlet goes on: 'Violently assaulted in an elevator, Natsuko had sobbed convulsively back in her room over the loss of her virginity. Then to her friends' amazement, she changes completely. Natsuko goes after all the men she thinks she can hook.'[15]

In the case of blondes (all foreign ladies are fair-haired in this fantasy world) it is even more clear cut: the blue-eyed ones need not even be raped for their savagery to manifest itself. In one of the many erotic comic-books on sale – millions are sold every week – I once saw the following story: a fair-haired foreign woman living in a suburban apartment block seduces every healthy Japanese boy she can find: the milkman, the postman, the laundry boy; nobody, but nobody is safe from this man-eating tigress. Finally they decide something must be done and they ambush the woman, tie her to a tree and then torture her. 'Oh!' she cries (foreigners always cry 'Oh!' in Japanese comics), 'in my country it is quite usual to do what I did.' The boys are naturally horrified and torture her even more.

Actual intercourse in films is usually a joyless affair of spasmodic motions filmed behind a chair or a flower-vase to avoid those wicked genitals from coming into view. Although the victim is naked, the man is usually fully clothed, rarely taking his trousers down below the upper thighs. Sometimes there is no need to take the trousers down at all: whips, candles, pistols and shoe-horns do nature's job just as well.

After seeing the umpteenth shoe-horn scene it becomes clear what these films are really all about; what anxiety in particular is being exorcized: a desperate fear of masculine inadequacy.[16] Not that this is even hidden by the pornographers. Porno in Japan is remarkably honest about its intentions. But the realism of these anxious entertainments goes further. The assault is often followed by an agonized confession by the rapist that this is the only way he can get any satisfaction. This is the cue for the maternal instinct to reassert itself, and the victims end up comforting the aggressors.

Natsuko falls in love with the rapist in the elevator, who turns out to be an impotent lorry-driver. Junko, a just-married housewife, takes care of a thief who enters her flat and violates her with a jack-knife. The sex scenes following the male confessions seem to be lifted straight out of the 'mother things'. Well, almost . . .

As if possessed, the men throw their arms around their former victims, frantically sucking their breasts, dribbling and drooling and smacking their lips. Love scenes are traditionally called *nureba*, wet scenes. Sensual experience in Japan is often associated with water, the most maternal of symbols. Thus in comics and films the climactic moments of sex scenes are often followed by shots of crashing waves or cascading, foaming waterfalls. Both are standard clichés of the genre. And a favourite trick to make love seem even wetter – and more infantile – is to pour some liquid such as beer, rice-wine, or best of all, milk over the woman's breasts so that the man can slither and slobber over it.

The combination of cruelty and adoration, of sentimental sadism, as it were, in 'mother things' and Mizoguchi's films, is also quite evident in porno. Not surprisingly, the most popular porno stars combine the savage and the maternal. The most celebrated example is a woman called Tani Naomi. This actress, who decided only recently that enough was enough, spent almost her entire career being tied up, beaten with whips and shoe-horned by impotent brutes. Like the mother heroines in television dramas, the more she suffered, the more popular she became. Fans and critics alike waxed lyrical in their praise of the 'sweet look in her eyes' while being tortured with some horrible instrument.

Tani Naomi even looked like a Japanese mother, her ample breasts tucked into a matronly kimono. She was the ideal object for men to take their anxieties out on, like the patient mother being pummelled by her sons. She was the Mother Goddess in bondage, the passive cross-bearer of masculine inadequacy.

One sometimes wonders who the real victims in these entertainments are. Is it, in the final analysis, really the woman who suffers most? Physically, undoubtedly so. Mentally, I am not so sure. If we take the average husband of the rape victims for example: he is always depicted as a passive weed, the sort of person left in the corner at parties; the typical 'salaryman' who spends his off hours in porno cinemas or reading porno comics in rush-hour commuter trains, pushed together with people just like him, hiding their faces in similar literature, sometimes using the stifling congestion to feel up some hapless young secretary, too meek to protest. (This furtive form of violation is very common in Japan and the anonymous assailant, the so-called *chikan*, is a popular figure in porno fantasies.)

So are the male readers not really the victims? Twenty-six-year-old Shimako in the film 'Hot Skin of the Love Hunter' has an impotent husband and, says the publicity folder, 'her nights are unbelievably long'. As soon as she is assaulted by another man, she turns into a nymphomaniac fury with an insatiable taste for the whip.

One senses the masochism of the inadequate cuckold, and by implication of many people in the audience. The female victims in these fantasies often submit to section managers and office chiefs to save their husbands' jobs or to save them from bankruptcy. Impotence and money problems are intimately connected in these stories, as they are in real life. The real aggressors are of course just the type of people who make life difficult for the kind of 'salarymen' (white-collar workers) who form the majority of the audience. What makes it even more piquant is the fact that the fantasy wives rather enjoy being violated by these brutes and in the more passionate scenes they are wont to shout, 'Oh, you're so much better than my weakling of a husband!'

Of course these fantasies are not uniquely Japanese. One need only look at the letters column of a British or American nude magazine to know that. What is striking is the frequency of the same stereotypes and the hysteria with which they are presented. The combination of almost suffocating physical intimacy during childhood and the social repression that follows; the idealization of the mother and the trauma at the first discovery of female sexuality; all this could occur anywhere, but nowhere, it seems, is the shock quite so devastating to so many people as in Japan.

5

The Human Work of Art

Love of nature is generally regarded as the basis of Japanese aesthetics. In China and Japan, one is told, man blends with nature; there is no dichotomy, such as exists in the West, where man is inclined to oppose the forces of nature. This argument is frequently supported by pointing to traditional scrolls or ink drawings in which man claims only a modest, sometimes almost invisible place. Natural scenery is not simply a backdrop for depicting man; no, man is part of the natural scene.

In art and daily life Japanese like to use natural images to express human emotions. Japanese novelists are masters at weaving natural metaphors and images into the fabric of their stories. And letters and postcards written by a Japanese always begin with a short description of the season.

The traditional Japanese house is not built like a stone fortress against the elements, as is often the case elsewhere. Instead it is a flimsy-looking wooden building, which can be opened on all sides. It looks as impermanent as the seasons themselves.

In traditional paintings there is no fixed view or vanishing point. One looks downwards at the scene and the higher up in the picture the objects are, the farther away the scene. This gives the illusion of depth, but it is not a three-dimensional illusion; there are no shadows, nothing stands on its own: man, house, nature, all are blended into one.

This concept of the world has its roots both in the Shinto tradition and the Buddhist religion: in Shinto everything in nature is potentially sacred. In the Buddhist view human beings are only one element in the natural cycle of life and death. One could come back in the next life as a frog or a mosquito.

Man is an inseparable part of nature. But does this make him natural? Let us try another analogy: nature is a fertile mother giving us our food and drink. But, and this is the snag, it can also contain terrible forces of destruction; it can suddenly break loose in devastating earthquakes, murderous typhoons and floods. Like woman, that other mysterious force liable to erupt in frightful passions, nature must be tamed, or at least controlled.

The Japanese attitude to nature is not therefore simply a matter of love, for it is tinged with a deep fear of the unpredictable forces it can unleash. It is worshipped, yes, but only after it has been reshaped by human hands. All those beautiful gardens 'naturally' blending with Japanese homes are entirely man-made. Nothing wild is left to grow – some of the most prized gardens are made entirely of stones. Japanese love of nature does not extend to nature in the raw, for which they seem to feel an abhorrence.

This includes, of course, human nature. Baudelaire's maxim, 'la femme est naturelle, c'est à dire abominable', echoes traditional Japanese sentiments exactly. People, especially women, have to be redecorated as it were, ritualized and as far as humanly possible, turned into works of art. Of course form plays a large part in what any of us do, anywhere in the world, and for similar reasons. Moreover, certain sections of Western societies have shown – and sometimes continue to show – a similar obsession with style. But, to say the least, many cultures, including those of China and Korea, Japan's closest neighbours, leave more room for individual spontaneity than is the rule in Japan.

The traditional Japanese aesthetic is often expressed in an artificial and rather anonymous kind of beauty. In his novel *Some Prefer Nettles* (*Tade o Kuu Mushi*, 1928) Tanizaki describes this with reference to the puppet theatre:

The real O-Haru [name of a courtesan and character in the puppet play] who lived in the seventeenth century, would have been just like a doll; and even if she weren't really, that is the way people would have imagined her to be in the theatre. The ideal beauty in those days was far too modest to show her individuality. This doll is more than enough, for anything distinguishing her from others would be too much. In short, this puppet version of O-Haru is the perfect image of the 'eternal woman' of Japanese tradition.

There is another doll-woman in the same Tanizaki novel called O-Hisa. She is the mistress of an old rake of impeccable taste in Kyoto. Or, rather, as his son-in-law, Kaname, puts it, she is 'one of the antiques in his collection'. The old man dresses her up in old silk kimonos, 'heavy and stiff as strands of chain'. She is allowed to see only traditional puppet plays and eat insubstantial Japanese delicacies. She is refined and cultivated as the old man's 'principal treasure'. Kaname is slightly envious of his father-in-law. Thinking of his own messy problems, he sees 'the type O-Hisa' as an escape. 'Surely one does better to fall in love with the sort of woman one can cherish as a doll . . . the old man's life seemed to suggest a profound spiritual peace reached without training or effort. If only he could follow the old man's example, Kaname thought.'

The aesthetic of the human doll is carried to its extreme consequence in Kawabata Yasunari's novel, *House of the Sleeping Beauties* (*Nemureru Bijo*, 1961). Young girls in an expensive and rather specialized brothel are drugged into a deep sleep to serve as silent and wholly passive sleeping partners for wealthy old men. 'For the old men who paid all that money, it was absolute bliss to lie next to one of those girls. Because they were not allowed to wake the girl, they had no need to feel ashamed of the inadequacies of old age. Furthermore, they could give free rein to all their fantasies and memories of women they had known.'

Several times in the book Kawabata compares these sleeping beauties to Buddhist deities, offering salvation and forgiving the old men for their sins. 'Perhaps she is the incarnation of Buddha,' thinks the old man, 'It is possible. After all there are tales of Buddha appearing in the guise of a woman of pleasure, a prostitute.' Not only are these drugged girls – and the Buddha – doll-like, seemingly without personal identities like enigmatic Buddhist sculptures; but they are also virginal and pure. They can be approached erotically, but they are ultimately un-assailable, for they are innocent sleeping objects. Only through such pure innocence, Kawabata seems to say, is salvation and reconciliation with death possible.

A comparable situation occurs in a recent film by Wakamatsu Koji entitled 'Pool Without Water' ('Mizu no Nai Puru', 1982). A young ticket collector at a subway station finds the perfect way to rape young women. He creeps up to their homes at night and sprays chloroform into their rooms, using a hypodermic. When they are suitably drugged he has his peculiar will with them. In one scene he arranges three naked girls, all fast asleep, arround a festively laid dinner table. He carefully makes up their faces with lipstick and rouge. The ghostly beauty of this strange, silent tableau is punctuated by the occasional flash of his polaroid camera. This is not an exceptionally bizarre film in Japan. The unknown rapist is such a common figure in Japanese entertainments that the fantasy of complete anonymity must run very deep indeed. One certainly senses a strong sympathy for the anonymous assailant in this film. In the last freeze-frame he sticks his tongue out at us: he has cocked a snook at the world. There is a possible social explanation for this: it is hard to be alone in Japan, in a traditional home well nigh impossible. And the complexity of human relationships, fraught with duties and obligations can be hard to take in a society where social face counts for so much.

On the other hand there is a general horror of loneliness, of being cut off from the physical intimacy of the others. The answer seems to be the anonymity of the crowd. People are soothed by being with others without having actually to communicate with them: hence the thousands of expressionless faces one sees on an average day in Tokyo, mesmerized by pinball machines (*pachinko*), sitting in long, silent rows like drugged assembly-line workers. Hence, also, the fantasy of the anonymous rapist.

The predilection for doll-women is evident in many other, less perverse ways too. They are a popular feature of modern department stores, for example, where they are especially trained to be as puppet-like as possible. The elevator girls, smartly dressed in uniforms and pure white gloves, greet the customers in artificial falsetto voices followed by ritual arm movements, like toy soldiers, up and down, left and right, always in the same way, indicating the direction of the lifts.

Not only are these girls drilled to sound like female impersonators on the stage, but the precision of the ceremonial bow is practised as a fine art. I was once shown round a training centre by a proud personnel manager. He explained how the girls are taught the perfect bow by a machine. It is a stainless-steel contraption standing in the middle of a spotless room. A steel bar in their backs pushed the girls into the desired angle: 15 degrees, 30 or 45, all minutely registered on a digital screen. 'This isn't just for newcomers, you know,' the manager assured me, prodding a young employee with a stick, 'senior employees like to use it too from time to time, to get in a bit of bowing practice.' Some stores actually went one step further, and, as an economy measure, decided to introduce real dolls instead of living ones. It did not work: customers complained that it lacked the human touch.

Television is a remarkably rich showcase for doll-women. Late night shows, for instance, feature so-called 'mascotte-girls' whose only function is to sit in a chair, blink provocatively at the camera and remain absolutely silent. One sees this type of thing in the West too: perched on top of cars at trade shows, for example. But bikinied beauties on Western television at least *pretend* to serve some function, if only to hand props to a quiz master. In Japan they are simply there, passive and pretty.

Teenage *talentos* are often dolls. They are choreographed, directed and drilled to such a degree that any spontaneity that might have been there to begin with stands little chance of surviving. Every move, every gesture, every smile, every phrase is the result of thorough training. The most extreme example in recent years has been a singing duo called 'Pink Lady', two leggy girls whose dizzy heights of popularity lasted for about three years. Not only did they sing and dance in perfect unison, they would even speak in unison, and always in elevator-girl falsettos.

This went on for several years. But then, very occasionally, a dim light of emerging humanity started to shine through the plastic façade: a small inkling that 'Pink Lady' were actually human beings and not just clever robots. It was precisely at that point that they started to lose their goddess-like status with the very young. When the dolls came sufficiently to life to turn down an appearance in the highly prestigious annual New Year television extravaganza, the end of their fame was assured.

Obviously many so-called 'personalities' on, say, American television are as carefully rehearsed and as far removed from their supposedly 'real selves' as the Japanese. The act is different, however: in the U.S.A. people train to seem natural, informal, in a word, real. One acts 'naturally'; people are not supposed to see that it is all fake. T.V. performers are, after all, personalities.

In Japan it tends to be the other way round. People are not interested so much in 'real selves' and no attempts are made to hide the fake. On the contrary, artificiality is often appreciated for its own sake. Performers do not try to seem informal or real, for it is the form, the art of faking, if you like, that is the whole point of the exercise. This is not to say that professional television performers in Japan all behave like anonymous undertakers. Quite the reverse is often true: television can be a licence to carry on outrageously — screaming and screeching like manic clowns — for it is not the real world. This, needless to say, is as artificial as the formal school.

If we take the traditional puppet theatre as an example, the cultural difference will be clear. In Western theatres the manipulators remain hidden in order to make the puppets seem as real as possible. In Japan the puppeteers stand on stage with the puppets: there is no reason to hide them. People want to see them so they can appreciate their skills, just as the earliest Japanese cinema audiences were as fascinated by the projector as by the flickering images on the screen. Now, both the American personalities and the Japanese talentos may be puppets, but the average American audience does not want to be made aware of this, while the Japanese do.

The same principle applies to social life. The more formal a society, the more obvious the roles people play. In this respect the Japanese are quite scrutable. Acting, that is, presenting oneself consciously in a certain prescribed way, is part of social life everywhere. But an increasing number of people in the West are so obsessed with appearing 'genuine' that they fool themselves they are not acting, that they are, well . . . real. Carried to its extremes, rudeness is seen as a commendably honest way of 'being oneself'. In Japan it is still in most cases a necessity to subordinate personal inclinations to the social form. Being a polite people, most Japanese spend most of their time acting.

Most of them of course realize this. The gap between the public and the private persona is often striking. As soon as the elevator girl is off duty, the pitch of her voice drops several octaves: she becomes a different person. Obviously Japanese have individual personalities like everybody else. But personal feelings are reserved for those (often alcoholic) occasions when intimacy is called for. Feelings vented at those times may often seem excessively sentimental, but then that too is another form of acting.

All this does make life in Japan seem highly theatrical to the outsider. Even the way people dress often appears a little stagey. Japanese, on the whole, like to be identified and categorized according to their group or occupation, rather than simply as individuals. No Japanese cook worth his salt would want to be seen without his tall white hat; 'interis' (intellectuals) sport berets and sunglasses, like 1920s exiles on the Left Bank of Paris. And gangsters wear loud pin-striped suits over their tattooed bodies. In brief, everybody is dressed for his or her part: even vagrants look like stage tramps in their impossible rags and with their hair hanging down to their waists in knotty ropes.

This tendency to conform to stylized patterns is perhaps most visible in the traditional arts. These patterns, or forms, are called *kata*. The Kabuki theatre, for example, is based on *kata*: a series of traditional postures and movements learnt from an early age by mimicking one's masters. Because of this the choreography, even down to the smallest details, of every stage role has remained unchanged for centuries, apart from slight personal additions by famous actors which are only noticeable to connoisseurs of the art. Significantly many of these postures and gestures in Kabuki were lifted straight from the puppet theatre.

But *kata* come in more modern guises too. A Japanese cook, unlike a Frenchman or an Italian, does not as a rule invent his own recipes. Instead, after years of imitating the movements of his master (quite literally, for Japanese cooking is more a question of skilful cutting and slicing than of mixing different ingredients), he learns the *kata* of his trade. Preparing raw tuna is essentially learnt in the same way one learns, say, karate kicks: by endless mimicking of patterns.

Kata, whether they are a matter of cutting fish, throwing a judo opponent, arranging flowers or indeed social acting, should ideally become second nature. *Karada de oboeru* is the term for this: to learn with the body, just like a child learns to swim, or even to bow, when it is still strapped to its mother's back. This sometimes goes together with considerable bullying by masters and seniors, which is considered a kind of mental training in itself, rather like fagging in old British public schools. Only a pupil who can stand this for a very long time can ever aspire to being a master. Naturally an apprentice cook who has spent three years of his life learning the perfect way to slap a ball of rice into his left hand will be the last one to debunk this laborious method of learning: he has been through the mill too long and too rigorously.

Conscious thought is considered to be an impediment on the way to perfection. A Japanese master never explains anything. The question why one does something is irrelevant. It is the form that counts. One constantly sees businessmen on crowded station platforms practising the motions of a golf-swing, or students endlessly repeating a baseball throw, just the movements, that is. Baseball and golf are hardly traditional Japanese arts, or very spiritual activities, but the way they are learnt is entirely traditional. The idea is that if one perfects the prescribed motions, one will, as if by some mystical force, hit the ball automatically, just like the famous Zen archer hitting the bull's eye with his eyes closed, after having spent years just straining his bow. One is almost tempted to say that ideally the form masters the individual instead of the other way round.

A well-known Japanese cultural critic has made a clear distinction between this type of *kata* culture, which he calls the 'Way of Art' (*geido*), and a more playful, popular culture, stressing content rather than form. The 'Way of Art', according to this critic, is 'strongly religious and suffused with the aristocratic mentality of the warrior class. The other type, at the peak of its development, escapes from religion and is based on the playful spirit (*asobi no seishin*) of the common people.'

A similar distinction could be made in most countries, but is it really valid? The answer must be: only partly. There is obviously a difference between aristocratic Art and popular 'play'. But the two traditions do influence and feed off each other, and it is doubtful whether it can truly be claimed that one is the art of form and the other of content. It is certainly striking how the Japanese remain bound to the rules of *kata* even in their most popular and playful pursuits.

6

The Art of Prostitution

The clearest case of life and theatre overlapping is the greatest doll-woman of all time, that much misunderstood symbol of Japan: the geisha. She is surely the ultimate human work of art. An art that is – or was – popular and playful, as well as highly aesthetic. And as such she is symbolic of the Japanese sense of beauty. Everything she does is stylized according to strict aesthetic rules. Her 'real self' (if there is such a thing) is carefully concealed (if that is the word) behind her professional persona. Like Kabuki actors and sumo wrestlers she usually bears the name of some illustrious predecessor; and even her facial features are hardly recognizable under a thick layer of make-up, as white as the rice it is made of.

The traditional geisha still exists, but fewer and fewer girls are still prepared or economically forced to put up with the rigours and restrictions of the geisha life. As an institution its significance has gradually diminished to the point that only a tiny minority of Japanese males has ever seen the inside of a traditional teahouse. Like so many classical arts *geisha asobi*, literally 'playing with geisha', has become a very expensive hobby for a small number of people who can afford it: mostly politicians and business tycoons who use the teahouses as discreet places in which to divide the spoils of the Economic Miracle.

I was once told by an ex-geisha in Kyoto that most customers don't know the rules of *geisha asobi* any more. Geisha who have been trained in traditional repartee – rather stilted at the best of times – get blank stares, making the whole thing rather a one-sided affair, like an Elizabethan costume play performed for incomprehending football supporters. What started as a theatricalized version of life has now become pure theatre. The mannerisms that were once quite *de rigueur* are fixed for ever in a ghostly fashion show. It is as if geisha parties are preserved as living reminders of the traditional past, like costly time-machines. (They are in fact very costly indeed; a visit to a geisha party, after the necessary introductions – otherwise one would not even get through the door – could cost more than $500 a head.)

The fate of the geisha party is much like that of the Kabuki theatre. In the olden days, the popular theatre audiences, thoroughly familiar with both the actors and the plays, knew exactly when to shout encouraging and often ribald witticisms at the stage. For this too was bound to rules, to *kata*. Nowadays every theatre employs an official claque, strategically placed amongst the audience, to shout out the actors' names at the appropriate climactic moments. This is to create a semblance of the old atmosphere. Meanwhile visiting groups from the countryside try to follow the plays with recorded explanations plugged into their ears. Still, the fact that these institutions have lost much of their vitality is beside the point. The mentality that helped to shape them is still there, albeit in an often vulgarized version.

Nightclub hostesses and bar ladies have taken the place of geisha and courtesans and the traditional 'floating world', familiar to admirers of Japanese prints, has become the '*mizu shobai*', the 'water business'. Certainly the importance of women as entertaining works of art remains undiminished, socially as well as artistically. In the following chapters I shall deal with the changing image of, for the lack of a better expression, female entertainers. In order to understand their significance in modern society, it is necessary to give a brief sketch of their history. If you are wondering what real people are doing in a book about fantasies, remember that the women of the Japanese water business *are* fantasies, alive, but still fantasies.

It is not always easy to distinguish between pure entertainers and prostitutes. Even now, one is told, some hostesses in modern nightclubs are prostitutes and others are not. As with so much in Japanese life, it all depends. The geisha certainly is not a prostitute, even though it used to be customary for her employers to sell her virginity for a great deal of money to a particularly favoured client. This is no longer done. The geisha is an entertainer, pure and simple, but she is part of an old tradition in which prostitution plays a vital role.

Prostitutes were popular playmates of Heian nobles in the tenth and eleventh centuries. During the Kamakura period (1185–1333), the Golden Age of the samurai, girls were especially trained in many skills apart from the obvious erotic ones to serve the upper echelon of the warrior class, including the emperor himself, who, one may add, had little else to do but 'play' with girls.

It was in the sixteenth century that the military ruler Hideyoshi decreed that prostitution would henceforth be confined to special licensed areas. This marked the beginning of a unique culture which continued to flourish until the late nineteenth century and its influence is still felt today. Never in the history of mankind have prostitutes played such a prominent and important part in the culture of a nation as the courtesans of Edo.

From the seventeenth century onwards the licensed brothels were salons for the richest and most powerful people in Japan, as well as inspiring playwrights, poets, print artists, writers and musicians. Many a song that started in a brothel sounding a plaintive note about the vicissitudes of a courtesan's life three hundred years ago is still being performed, most likely by a respectable middle-aged matron with a taste for the classics.

The world of prostitutes was as hierarchical as the rest of Japanese society. There were many ranks between the top courtesan, the *tayu*, and the common whore, the *joro* or the *yuna*, who plied her trade at public baths. The *tayu* was a highly accomplished woman, though usually of humble birth. A famous *tayu* called Takao, living in the latter half of the eighteenth century, is said to have been a master of flower arranging, the tea ceremony, poetry, various musical instruments, art, card games, and incense smelling – a highly prized skill since Heian times.[1]

Not only was the *tayu* a great artiste, she was also a great work of art. The grand entrance of a famous courtesan in a teahouse, followed by her entourage of jesters, apprentices and sycophants, would be a series of elaborate dramatic poses, rather like an old-time Hollywood goddess slinking her way down a spotlit staircase. The effect was highly theatrical, like a piece of performance art. In the words of the American scholar Donald Shively: 'The presentation of a customer's first meeting with a courtesan, its protocol and characteristic banter, is indeed an ultimate refinement of the prostitute-accosting skits popular in primitive Kabuki.'[2]

From the very beginning theatre and prostitution were intimately connected. Travelling entertainers, often dancers or Buddhist story-tellers, were frequently prostitutes as well. The legendary O-Kuni, the alleged foundress of the first Kabuki troupe, is said to have combined these functions very profitably. She was officially a *miko*, a shamaness belonging to a shrine; but her performances, dressed as a man, were erotic advertisements for further dalliance after the show.

The authorities, fearing disorder, tried to put a stop to this by forbidding actresses to appear on the stage. The result was that young boys simply took their places in the favours of wealthy patrons. The cynical observer of the Kubuki scene in the seventeenth century, Ihara Saikaku, remarked that 'truly nothing in the world is more painful than the necessity of making a living under these circumstances. All too closely do the actor and the courtesan resemble each other in their hopeless fates.'[3]

Reality and fantasy in the pleasure quarters of Edo, Osaka and Kyoto tended to be confused. Real-life intrigues, scandals and tragic love affairs were almost immediately worked into plays performed in the Kabuki theatres. In erotic prints (*shunga*) famous actors were depicted in amorous poses with equally celebrated prostitutes, though they were rarely recognizable individuals. Rather they were idealized versions of real people, bearing professional names of famous forebears. (This habit is still common, even when there is no connection with the honourable ancestor at all: I have seen third-rate entertainers in sordid variety halls proudly bearing the names of great Kabuki families.)

Prostitutes in the seventeenth century were appraised like actresses by professional critics. The so-called *joro hyobanki* were critical guidebooks to the various pleasure quarters, with detailed reviews of the accomplishments of their denizens. In concept and design these reviews were very similar to the critical booklets about actors. To be sure, these actor booklets were at first almost wholly concerned with the physical charms of the performers, rather than with their artistic expertise. Even so, prostitutes were definitely regarded as artists, whose entertainment was as theatrical as the theatre they tried to emulate. To quote Donald Shively once more: 'If Kabuki was unexpectedly erotic, the brothel could be described as a theatre of love, where country girls masqueraded as sophisticated beauties and lowly merchants assumed the airs of men of affairs.'⁴

People had few moral compunctions about playing this game. As long as men did their duty and provided for their families in a way that would not shame their ancestors, they were free to indulge in sensual pleasures, provided they could afford them of course. A man's family life and his love life were two different things. After all, his wife was chosen for other than romantic reasons. And sex as such was no sin. Thus, as long as playing with prostitutes remained just that, playing, there was no objection. This, despite the official proscription of prostitution since 1958, is by and large still the case.

'Play' was perhaps more important than sex *per se*. One still sees Japanese businessmen spend their companies' fortunes in Tokyo nightclubs on nothing but risqué repartee with hostesses. This kind of professional social intercourse has a long tradition in the Far East. During the Tang dynasty (618–906) in China, for example, wealthy gentlemen, scholars and poets all surrounded themselves with highly educated courtesans.⁵

And those who could afford it had at least three or four wives at home. According to Confucian rules of morality it was a man's duty to keep them all sexually satisfied. But apart from producing children, preferably sons, and running the household, these respectable matrons had little to offer in the way of social excitement. They were, on the whole, illiterate and ignorant of the world outside, isolated as they were in the back rooms of the home. So, for more stimulating female company Chinese gentlemen had to turn to the courtesans, who could hold their own in any conversation, besides being accomplished dancers and singers. The best teahouses were artistic salons, rather than places for sex; one could go to cheap brothels for that, and those were mainly for men who could not afford several wives. The relationship between the courtesans and their patrons was bound by strict rules of etiquette. Even if a sexual liaison did develop – elegant banter could not satisfy everybody all the time – this had to be preceded by an elaborate courtship: the exchange of love poems, rejections, secret meetings and finally, a great deal of money.

One cannot help feeling that the actual sex act must have been something of an anti-climax. For, again, sex was not really the point. It was the elegant flirtation, the refined courtship, in short the 'play' between man and woman, romance as high art, that thrilled the rakes of ancient China. The same seems to have applied to the Japanese during the Heian period, lasting from 794 until 1185; or, to be more precise, to the small aristocracy of Heian Japan imitating the elegant lifestyle of Tang China. But then the aristocracy *was* Heian culture, the rest of the people being far too poor to play any games.

Promiscuity was part of court life. This may seem surprising when one considers that men and women of noble birth hardly saw each other. The ladies were hidden away in the women's quarters and they would communicate with their lovers through poems passed on by trusted go-betweens. Even when lovers were in the same room, the women would often be sitting behind a screen. And at night, when most trysts took place, it must have been so dark that physical intimacy can hardly have been a great visual experience. Nevertheless, if 'The Tale of Genji' or 'The Pillow Book', two contemporary chronicles of court life, are anything to go by, Heian aristocrats entertained each other in bed with great frequency and a steady change of partners. But, as in Tang China, the rules of the game were intricate and strict. Everything was done with style and decorum. Also, the game was never allowed to interfere with family duties.

The hierarchy among married women (it was a polygamous society) had to be respected, especially the position of the first wife. Rank and class were of the utmost importance in choosing a marriage partner, for the power of a family was largely a matter of judicious marriages. Marriage was, in other words, a political institution. But, though men and women were much freer to indulge in sensual pleasures than they were to be in later ages, there was no tradition in Japan of courtly love. Love as an abstract ideal, severed from purely sexual attraction, did not really exist at all until recently. Homosexual love is a possible exception.

Ivan Morris has observed:

> The absence of any ideal of courtly love involving fealty, protection, and romantic languishing, and the acceptance of a high degree of promiscuity, frequently gave a flippant, rather heartless air to the relations between the men and women of Murasaki's world. One has the impression that, for all the elegant sentiments expressed in the poems, the love affairs of the time, especially at court, were rarely imbued with any real feeling, and that often they were mere exercises in seduction.[6]

In other words, it was a game, an *asobi*, but it was saved from degenerating into something crass and sordid by the dominant part played by taste.[7] The emotional high point of a love affair was perhaps not so much the night spent in passion as the obligatory, elegant poem composed according to strict aesthetic conventions the morning after. These extremely clichéd efforts rarely made any references to love or even the loved one. Instead they mentioned tear-stained kimono sleeves at the sight of dawn or the cruel crowing of the cock announcing the time to say farewell. One refined Heian gallant even sent his lady-friend the feather of one of these spoilsport birds, attaching the following poem:

> Now he is dead —
> That heartless bird
> who broke the dark night's peace with his shrill cry
> Yet dawn, alas, will always come
> to end true lovers' joys.[8]

It was as if people had affairs in order to heave elegant sighs about the melancholy fleetingness of life. Obviously they must have had feelings, but these were largely sublimated by aesthetic ritual and social ceremony. Human passion and its physical expression were not controlled by an abstract moral code, whether of chivalry or sin, but by aesthetics, by decorum for its own sake. Love was a kind of art for art's sake, an exquisite piece of theatre. Emotions which could not be sublimated in this way were poured into melancholy diaries by court ladies, whose literary elegance has never been surpassed.

The 'floating world' of the pleasure quarters during the Edo period was in many ways a continuation of the two traditions described above: the Confucian double standard and the play-acting of the Heian court. The need for professional female company arose from similar conditions to those in ancient China. Although the Japanese were by and large monogamous, the influence of Confucian morality was strong and 'the cultural accomplishments of the higher class of prostitute far exceeded those of the townsman's wife'.[9]

The manners and mores of the Edo-period brothels were inspired by and often a direct imitation of Heian court life. Prostitutes borrowed the names of noble ladies in 'The Tale of Genji'.[10] Guidebooks to the prostitutes' quarters, such as the Togensho compiled in 1655, were written in the classic style of the Genji as well as other famous traditional works. Though bordering on satire, this kind of publication exuded an atmosphere of high aristocratic taste.

Of course it was all an elaborate fantasy, for there were basic differences between the decadent life of the Heian aristocracy and the pleasure areas of the Edo period. For one thing, the latter were in a true sense democratic. This seems paradoxical in an age which left little room for class mobility. In fact playing in the brothels and theatres was one of the few ways in which people could free themselves from the stifling class restrictions of their time. Not only were the licensed areas patronized by all classes, from samurai down to lowly merchants, much to the annoyance of the government, but the plays performed there were a pastiche of society itself.

In the theatre, outcasts — actors were forced to live in ghettoes — acted the parts of swaggering samurai and elegant court ladies. They would dress up in the most outrageous finery, outdoing the aristocracy in sheer brilliance. In short, they broke one of the most serious taboos of their time by imitating the style of a higher class. The pleasure quarters were literally a stage where people could act the parts forbidden to them in daily life. This was almost subversive in a society based to such a large extent on the style of outward appearances. These actors have been described as religious scapegoats, breaking taboos in order to purify them.[11] One of the traditional functions of the feast, after all, is the ritual breaking of taboos.

The aristocracy of the brothels consisted mostly of peasant girls who would paint their dark skins white as a sign of nobility and cover up their rustic accents with an artificial language based on the polite forms of the Kyoto dialect, full of flamboyant phrases and elaborate verb-endings.[12] One had to be well versed in the manners and mores of the brothel, even as a customer, or else be ridiculed as an ignorant bumpkin, which to the Edo playboy was a fate worse than death.

It was far from easy to win the favours of a high-class *tayu*. She had to be courted, and just as in the Heian court, this was a matter bound by strict rules of etiquette. A clumsy provincial, ignorant of the rules, stood as little chance with a *tayu* as his modern counterpart would with a top fashion model.

The guidebooks, described earlier in this chapter, were to initiate the common man in these complex rules, as well as to titillate his vicarious fancies. Even when they later turned into a purely literary genre, the so-called *sharebon*, they never quite lost their didactic function. The authors of these books, particularly popular during the eighteenth century, were often intellectual members of the samurai class, and connoisseurs of brothel life. The ideal of every dandy in those days was to be a *tsu*, a man of savoir faire, an aficionado of brothel etiquette. So obsessed were they with the minutiae of low-life elegance that their books are almost unintelligible today.

The typical *sharebon* story usually revolves around a *tsu* and a bumpkin, often posing as a *tsu*. The comedy is always at the expense of the bumbling boor who does not know the rules. But just knowing them is not quite enough either. This is the moral of a famous work entitled *The Rake's Patois* (*Yushi Hogen*), published in 1770 and written by a gentleman signing himself as 'Just An Old Man' ('Tada no jiji'). It is about a father taking his son to a brothel for the first time, a not unusual initiation into the pleasures of adult life. The father, a flashy bore, proudly flaunts his intimate knowledge of brothel manners. The son is gentle, modest and polite to the courtesans. Needless to say, it is to him and not his blustering father that one of the girls extends the honour of spending the night in love. A real *tsu* knows how to please the prostitutes.

The market for erotic guidebooks is far from exhausted: a modern book called *A Textbook for Night-Life* (*Yoru no Kyokasho*) became a best-seller. It carefully and patiently informs us just how to disport ourselves in night-clubs, bars and 'cabarets' (cheap night-clubs) without making a fool of ourselves. This is the way, for example, to hold a conversation with a bar-hostess:

> Everybody resembles someone else. This is particularly true of hostesses who use the same make-up techniques as actors and entertainers. Now, when you meet a hostess for the first time, you don't just blurt out that she looks like a certain famous singer. Everybody does that. What you do, is talk about that singer in the most glowing terms, how sexy she is and so on. Then, as nonchalantly as you can, you let it slip how much your hostess resembles the star.

The practised *tsu*, then as now, like the courtesans, would affect an aristocratic nonchalance. He would stick to the formal rules of behaviour, but in a slightly off-hand way, never visibly doing his best. This is the kind of elegance the Japanese call *iki*, variously and never quite accurately translated as 'dashing' or 'chic'.[13] *Iki* is helped by the patina of age and hard-won experience. It is also visible in the details of dress: the nonchalantly-tied sash of a kimono or a bold design just bordering on vulgarity. *Iki* is a way of playing around with the rules without ever quite transgressing them. It is an aesthetic directly derived from life in the brothels.

There was, however, one rule of the demi-monde which could not be broken; and this was more or less the same as in the Heian court: the play had to remain exactly that — romance, not sex, was the forbidden fruit in these quarters.[14] It was thought to be highly uncivilized, uncouth even, to fall in love. The courtesan, after all, had to remain a work of art, a fantasy without a real personal identity. 'A sincere courtesan is as rare as a square egg', was a popular expression in the Edo pleasure quarters.[15] This was not meant as a put-down, it simply meant that courtesans were artistes.

Prostitutes and actors were the fashion-leaders and super-stars of their time. Consequently the successful actor could be quite wealthy and even mix with the high and mighty. But they were also at the bottom end of the social hierarchy. The Yoshiwara, the biggest old licensed quarter in Tokyo, now filled with garish massage parlours, is still flanked on one side by the ghetto for *burakumin*, religiously polluted outcasts comparable to the Indian untouchables. In a sense consorting with outcasts might have given people a liberating *frisson*. Indians made love to temple girls for the same reason. But when play became personal and serious it was a direct threat to the class system. There was also the danger that falling for a courtesan would lead to financial ruin, a serious crime in an increasingly mercantile society.

An example of how seriously the government took the dangers of social pollution is the Ejima–Ikushima affair. Ejima (1681–1741) was a high-ranking lady-in-waiting. She had been the secret mistress of a celebrated Kabuki actor named Ikushima for nine years before they were both arrested at a drunken after-theatre party. This had the unfortunate result of making their affair public and everybody involved was severely punished: some with death, others, like Ikushima, with banishment to an isolated island. His theatre was razed and all other Kabuki theatres were closed for three months.

Play, but not love. That at least was the ideal. But was it always like that in real life? To what extent were the women of the pleasure quarters really living dolls? Surely the affected nonchalance of even the most elegant dandies and courtesans had its limits. No matter what the rules of the fantasy were, they were still human beings. Clearly sometimes people must have fallen in love and spontaneous feelings were sometimes expressed, despite the social dangers; not all was flippant repartee. The tension between forbidden feelings and fantasy, between acceptable sensuality and illicit love, in brief, between play and reality, was an important theme of popular drama and fiction in pre-modern Japan. While abiding by the rules of their frivolous games, the courtesans and their merry-making paramours had to face one totally unfrivolous question: how to live in Tokugawa society without losing one's humanity.

Perhaps the majority of writers of fiction gave this little thought at all, for they rarely went deeper than the elegant surface of artificial eroticism. But two writers, both living in the seventeeth century, did, in their own rather different ways: the playwright Chikamatsu Monzaemon (1653–1725) and the poet and novelist Ihara Saikaku (1642–93). Chikamatsu was the son of a samurai and Saikaku (he is always known by his first name) was born into a family of merchants. Neither was strictly a man of Edo, for they lived in Osaka and Kyoto respectively at a time when Edo was little but an up-and-coming provincial town. But both are still considered to be the greatest writers of fiction of the Edo period and both reflect the mentality of many Japanese towards prostitutes even to this day.

Saikaku, the merchant's son, is the typical townsman with the morality of a ribald shopkeeper. As long as business keeps ticking over and the bills are paid on time, what one does with the rest of one's time is nobody else's business. Saikaku's stories, unlike those by writers following the aristocratic tradition, are mostly about people who have to work for a living. Typically money itself plays a progressively important part in his work. Once he wrote that 'money is the townsman's pedigree, whatever his birth or lineage. No matter how splendid a man's ancestors, if he lacks money he is worse off than a monkey-showman.'[16] His most famous picaresque novel was *The Life of an Amorous Woman* (1686) upon which Mizoguchi based his classic film 'Saikaku Ichidai Onna', literally 'The Life of a Saikaku Woman' but generally know in the West as 'The Life of O-Haru'. The story, written in the first person as a parody of a Buddhist confession, is about a highly educated young lady of noble birth called O-Haru, who ends up as a common street-walker hiding her ruined looks in the dark. When she fails to attract men even then, she retires as a Buddhist nun. But she calls her lonely retreat 'Hut of Fleshly Pleasures' and she still ties her kimono sash in front in the rakish way of a courtesan. And as she relates her story of degradation to two male visitors, she burns sweet incense reminding them more of teahouses than temples.

It is interesting to compare the original O-Haru, Saikaku's version that is, and O-Haru in Mizoguchi's film. The original story is a tale of self-indulgence. Saikaku was too cynical and too much a man of his times to paint her as a victim of society – though, unlike most of his contemporaries, he had no illusions about the darker side of prostitution. Just like most of his amorous characters, O-Haru is no better than she ought to be. Several times in the story she has the option of settling down to a life of bland respectability and each time she chooses the more appealing life of debauchery. It is, as they say in the porno industry, in her blood.

One story, in particular, shows the difference with Mizoguchi's film treatment. Saikaku relates how O-Haru, exhausted by the brothel life, seeks employment as a respectable housemaid, pretending to be innocence itself. But soon she cannot stand hearing 'the screens rattling' every time her ardent employer makes love to his wife and she seduces him on a day of religious observance, 'making him forget all about Buddhism'. The story ends with O-Haru running through the streets of Kyoto, stark naked, singing 'I want a man! Oh, I want a man!'

Mizoguchi's O-Haru, on the other hand, is the tragic victim of a succession of brutish, lecherous males. She is the one to be seduced by her boss in the most degrading manner, and running around the streets naked, mad with desire, would have been unthinkable for his angelic heroine, even had it been allowed by the censors. While Saikaku's story pokes fun at the Buddhist confession tale, Mizoguchi ends his film with O-Haru going from door to door as a seriously repentant nun. Saikaku's cynical mockery has been replaced by the melancholy resignation of a true Buddhist.

Saikaku's *Life of an Amorous Woman* is a satire, not of society itself – that would have been far too dangerous – but of the absurdity of people in search of pleasure, ever more pleasure. The irony is a universal psychological truth: the further one carries one's sensual pursuit, the more elusive satisfaction proves to be. Saikaku's characters come alive through their very weakness. But Saikaku never shows contempt. They may be frivolous, self-indulgent fools, but they are unmistakably human fools.

Mizoguchi's faithful script-writer, Yoda Yoshikata, who wrote the film script of O-Haru, has often said that the Japanese title for the film should not have been 'Life of a Saikaku Woman' but 'Life of a Chikamatsu Woman'. There is much to be said for this. Mizoguchi's ambivalent moralism comes much closer to the spirit of the great samurai's son. Chikamatsu Monzaemon was more of a moralist than Saikaku. Members of the warrior class despised the business of money making, though some were to prove remarkably good at it. The way Chikamatsu made his living, as a playwright for the plebeian puppet theatre, was considered shameful indeed. This cannot but have contributed to an attitude of ambivalence. Although he lived amongst the merchant class and wrote about their affairs, with some compassion even, he was never quite one of them: he remained an outsider. His tone is quite different from Saikaku's amused cynicism. His plays, written in the romantic yet realistic style favoured by the Osaka merchant class, are often dramatizations of rather pathetic love affairs between clerks and prostitutes, usually based on newsworthy contemporary scandals. These affairs are often sordid and the characters insignificant, simple-minded even, especially the men: clerks, shopkeepers or lowly traders making a mess of things. But in the end they manage to rise above their banality; they seem dignified even, often by saving their honour in the classic samurai way, by killing themselves. The most important thing, however, is that love does transcend mere sexual infatuation: it may destroy its proponents in the end, but it is real, not just play.

One of Chikamatsu's most popular dramas is 'Double Suicide at Sonezaki', written in 1703, and since made into many films. The last cinematic version, using puppets instead of actors, was made as recently as 1981. The play revolves around Tokubei, a lowly shop-assistant who falls in love with an equally humble prostitute called O-Hatsu. For this reason he refuses to marry a girl chosen for him by his uncle. Thus he has to return the girl's dowry. Foolishly the good-natured clerk lends this money to Kuheiji, a classic villain. When he asks for it back, Tokubei is beaten up by Kuheiji's henchmen, after which he escapes, hiding under O-Hatsu's kimono. The villain Kuheiji then visits O-Hatsu's brothel to enjoy her for himself. While her price is being discussed, Tokubei, hiding under the porch, grabs one of O-Hatsu's feet and drags it across his throat. This gruesome signal is not lost on her and after everybody has gone to sleep, the lovers escape to the woods of Sonezaki carrying a razor blade which sparkles in the moonlight.

Then the ordinary affair of the simple clerk and the prostitute becomes a real tragedy. Accompanied by the plaintive notes of the three-stringed *samisen* they make their last exit along the ramp (*hanamichi*) jutting into the audience at a right angle from the stage. While the sad victims of passion desperately hold on to each other, and the theatre claque shouts out the actors' names, the singers at the side of the stage sing their melancholy farewell song:

Farewell to this world and to the night farewell
We who walk the road that leads to death, to what
    should it be likened?
To the frost by the road that leads to the graveyard
Vanishing with each step we take ahead:
How sad is this dream of a dream![17]

What follows is a cruel scene in which he slashes his lover to death before killing himself. There was no other way out.

The play is best seen in the puppet theatre, for which it was originally written. The puppets manipulated by the puppeteers dressed in black, suggest perfectly the hopelessness of the individual in a society where the assertion of personal will and spontaneity can lead only to catastrophe. Not for nothing are most of Chikamatsu's heroes weak men, for it is they, rather than swaggering tough guys, who truly bring home the powerlessness of humans in the hands of fate.

Tokubei, the insignificant clerk, is transformed by his love, even though, as is often the case in Edo drama and doubtless in reality too, his lover is a prostitute. The only way pure love can be proved is by the ultimate sacrifice. Death is the price one pays for following one's feelings, for not just playing.

Self-destructing heroes and heroines are also like safety valves in a closed society. They put up a last stand for individual feelings and will, but by destroying themselves, as aesthetically and ceremoniously as possible, they ensure that order is always restored in the end.

'Double Suicide at Sonezaki', as the first of a series of romantic suicide plays, enjoyed a huge public success. The effect was comparable to that of Goethe's 'Junge Werther': romantic suicide became a fashionable thing to do: together, of course, never alone. The authorities strongly disapproved. Not only was the glorification of personal feelings, specifically love, bad for public morals, but suicide was after all a privilege of the warrior class, not to be frivolously indulged in by mere tradesmen and prostitutes. And in 1736 a law was passed against love scenes on the stage.

Dying for each other as the ultimate union, if not in this life, then at least in the next, is nevertheless still deeply ingrained in Japanese culture: pop songs celebrate it, films melodramatize it, and young girls swoon at the idea of romantic authors throwing themselves into rivers together with their loved ones.[18] In a recent film, Tani Naomi, the eternally suffering porno star, played a country geisha on the run with her demented and murderous lover. Instead of running the risk of his being caught and thus being separated for ever, they decide to die together. In the end we see him hanging from a rope, still holding her brains in his hands. And while the camera lovingly pans along her mutilated corpse, their voices echo eerily in the background, as if straight from the depths of Hell:

'You're mine for ever now!'
'Yes . . . I'm yours, only yours!'
'Finally we're one . . .'

Despite the government's attempts to ban love on the stage, and the aesthetic and social resistance against it in the licensed areas, love actually became an increasingly popular subject in Edo-period fiction, particularly during the nineteenth century. What is interesting is that the so-called *ninjobon* (human feelings stories) written by such authors as Tamenaga Shunsui (1790–1843) feature the same social stereotypes as Chikamatsu's plays: feeble, effeminate men and strong maternal prostitutes. In the *ninjobon* love always entails sacrifice by the women. One has the impression even that sacrificial mother-love is the only alternative to impersonal eroticism; when a man is not a *tsu*, a sensual connoisseur of play, he is a pampered weakling dependent on his lover and passive as a child.

A good example of the latter is Tanjiro, the young hero of Tamenaga Shunsui's story, *Colours of Spring: The Plum Calendar* (*Shunshoku Umegoyomi*), written in 1832. There are two women in Tanjiro's life: a geisha called Yonehachi and a prostitute named O-Cho. A salient detail of the hero's early life is that he was adopted and raised in a brothel. O-Cho and Yonehachi are fiercely jealous of each other. In one typical scene both ladies vow to marry him and take care of him for the rest of his life. At another point in the story Tanjiro takes money from O-Cho, is officially kept by Yonehachi, and has an affair with a third geisha. The episode ends with all three women happily pampering him. To ask what these wordly-wise women could possibly see in such a man is to misunderstand the nature of maternal love: they love him *because* he is a weak and presumably pretty boy; and he loves prostitutes for the same reason.

The kind of sentiments described above still haunt the popular imagination in our own time. *Enka*, the sentimental drinking songs people sing in bars, flushed with too much drink, eyes half closed in maudlin melancholy, and voices vibrating with dramatic emotion, are suffused with them. 'Love Suicide of a Shinjuku Woman' is one example:

> Never mind how hard my life is,
> I can take anything, if it's for your sake
> I may be just a bar-lady, two years older than you
> I wanted to pay for your education
> But you hit me when I got home late
> You couldn't write your novel
> You took to drinking hard
>
> Let us now die together, in this room
> Where I had dreams of becoming a good wife
> Tomorrow might never come
> Let me pour our last cup of tea
>
> Love suicide of a Shinjuku woman
> Few will have seen it in the papers
> But life was warm that night with my white arms around
>   your neck.

During the Edo period many writers and artists immersed themselves in a very narrow world. They spent much of their creative lives as chroniclers of the manners and mores within a delicate goldfish-bowl; or, rather, a goldfish-bowl within a goldfish-bowl, for Japan itself was almost completely isolated for three centuries. In the latter half of the nineteenth century, when Japan had finally opened her doors to the rest of the world, this bowl was shattered. What had been the elegant centre of the world became a provincial relic of the past.

By the 1870s Kabuki had in effect ceased to be a contemporary theatre. In 1872 the greatest Kabuki actor of his time, Ichikawa Danjuro, dressed in white tie and tails as a sign of civilization, made the following speech: 'The theatre of recent years has drunk up filth and smelled of the coarse and the mean. It has disregarded the beautiful principle of rewarding good and chastising evil. It has fallen into mannerisms and distortions and has steadily been flowing downhill . . . I have resolved to clean away the decay.'[19]

The ensuing fate of Kabuki theatre was ironic in the extreme: after being purified of its 'coarser' aspects, this theatre of outcasts and riverside prostitutes steadily became an official repository of tradition. During the Second World War it even became the expression of militarist patriotism.

In the heady days of the early Meiji Restoration, at the end of the last century, exciting new ideas floated around about the new status of women in society and writers of fiction were encouraged to write about other women besides ladies of pleasure. The general creed was that Japan had to become 'respectable', 'modern', and above all, 'Western'. All these aspirations – and they were no more than that – were summed up by the slogan of the age: Enlightenment and Civilization (*Bunmei Kaika*).

Old traditions die hard, none the less, no matter how many castles are torn down to appear advanced and progressive. This is as true of fiction as it is of prostitutes. Lefcadio Hearn wrote in 1895 that:

> as a general rule, where passionate love is the theme in Japanese literature of the best class, it is not that sort of love which leads to the establishment of family relations. It is quite another kind of love – a sort of love about which the Oriental is not prudish at all – the *mayoi*, or infatuation of passion, inspired by merely physical attraction; and its heroines are not the daughters of refined families, but mostly hetarae, or professional dancing girls.[20]

If this was true of 'literature of the best class', it was so much more so of less elevated genres. And by and large it is still true, despite the appearance in fiction, film and theatre of other types of women, too. As works of art the ladies of pleasure may have lost much of their traditional refinement. But they are still very important, as social life still takes place largely outside the family home. They are by no means always prostitutes, but in so far as they still offer, for a price, romance, as well as maternal solace, they are figures of a common fantasy. Moreover, one feels that many Japanese artists are still often searching for another goldfish-bowl on the fringes of society, a world within a world: and it is here, in the 'water business', that they frequently find it.

There are two authors in particular, both born in the late nineteenth century, who exemplify the half-traditional, half-modern attitude to prostitutes still shared by many Japanese: Nagai Kafu and Higuchi Ichiyo. Kafu, as he is always known, was one of the great eccentrics of his time. Almost his entire life was spent in the company of strippers, prostitutes, geisha and chorus-girls. Born into a respectable family of landowners and bureaucrats, he became professor of French literature when he was only 31 years old, establishing himself as a superb translator of Baudelaire and Verlaine, as well as publishing many essays and short stories. But a few years after all these honours came his way, he turned his back on them. He professed to hate writers, journalists, academics, relatives – everybody, in fact, except a number of female entertainers with whom he had relationships which were generally as short-lived as they were presumably passionate.[21]

Kafu had a romantic, elegiac imagination which led him into a life-long chase of the ever-shortening shadows of the Edo period, mostly to be found among the demi-monde of prostitution. His life, beginning in 1879 and ending messily in the solitude of his rented room in 1959, neatly encompasses the period during which modern Japan was built. Thus his images of strippers and prostitutes are reminders of the past as well as increasingly vulgar symbols of Japan as it has become.

According to the critic Kato Shuichi, writing about the Meiji period, 'the alienation of the artist drove him either into a nostalgic yearning for the culture of the Edo period, or into an infatuation with the West'.[22] Kafu went through both stages. In 1903, under pressure from his father, who disapproved of his son's nocturnal habits, Kafu sailed off to the U.S.A., bound for the doubtful pleasures of Kalamazoo, Michigan.

Kalamazoo was hardly to his taste. He felt more at home in the opium dens and brothels of New York's Chinatown. In *Leaves From a Journal of a Western Voyage* (*Sayu Nishisho*), published in

1917, he wrote of the ladies he encountered there: 'I do not hesitate to call them my own dear sisters. I do not ask for light or help. I only await the day when I, too, shall be able to offer myself to a grain of opium.' And about the place he wrote: 'A monotonous Oriental melody was constantly repeated. Overcome by the stench and the heat I stood for a while and thought ah what harmony, what balance! Never before had I heard the music of human degradation and collapse so poignantly . . . '[23] He went on to say: 'I love Chinatown. It is a treasury of *The Flowers of Evil*. I only fear that the so-called humanitarians will one day tear down this world-apart-from-the-world . . . ' (*Notes on Chinatown, Chinatown no Ki*, 1907.)

Although shades of a second-rate Baudelaire are to be heard in this romantic straining by the youthful Kafu, one can also detect the voice of the typical man of Meiji: 'world-apart-from-the-world' – the smelly sanctuary where everything is in harmony, just as it was in the licensed quarters of Edo; he had caught a glimpse of his ideal goldfish-bowl.

There was also no doubt a 'nostalgie de la boue' involved in Kafu's romantic reveries. The young bourgeois reacting against his family of earnest bureaucrats and industrious businessmen. His father, who was both a progressive businessman and a strict Confucian moralist, insisting on filial obedience, represented everything that Kafu loathed; like the period itself, he was stuffily old-fashioned and crassly modern at the same time.

There was another reason for Kafu's self-imposed isolation amongst the prostitutes of his city. One must take into account the often suffocating nature of Japanese society with its relentless pressures to conform. This is as true of literary circles, if not more so, as of a bourgeois family. Isolation is often the only way to achieve the necessary distance between oneself and society. Kafu's solution to the alienation of the artist was indeed similar to that of Baudelaire and other so-called 'decadents' in late-nineteenth-century France. He chose the marginal 'world-apart-from-the-world' as a kind of exile. In the brothels and teahouses he could be anonymous. He would be left alone there, something which is quite easy to achieve in London or Paris (where it is also tolerated more), but well-nigh impossible in huge, but provincial Tokyo.

He even entertained fantasies of being part of this world, in the same way as his literary heroes of the Edo period had been. In *Strange Tale from East of the River* (*Bokuto Kidan*), written in 1937, the narrator, a writer much like Kafu himself, becomes a frequent visitor to a certain prostitute called O-yuki. He pretends to be a writer of 'secret books', thinking that 'women who live in the shade feel neither hostility not fear, but rather affection and pity when they encounter men who must shun the public gaze.' He goes on to compare O-yuki to 'the geisha at the lonely wayside station who did not hesitate to give money to a gambler and smuggler . . . '

In the same story, the writer explains his fascination for prostitutes:

In Tokyo, and even in the Occident, I have known almost no society except that of courtesans . . . I might here quote a passage from *Unfinished Dream* [a novel by Kafu himself]: 'He frequented the pleasure quarters with such enthusiasm that ten years was as a day; for he knew only too well that they were the quarters of darkness and unrighteousness. And had the world come to praise the profligate as loyal servant and pious son, he would have declined, even at the cost of selling his property, to hear the voice of praise. Indignation at the hypocritical vanity of proper wives and at the fraud of the just and open society was the force that sent him speeding in the other direction, toward what was from the start taken for dark and unrighteous. There was more happiness in finding the remains of a beautifully woven pattern among castaway rags than in finding spatters and stains on a wall proclaimed immaculate. Sometimes in the halls of the righteous droppings from cows and rats are to be seen, and sometimes in the depths of corruption flowers of human sympathy and fruits of perfumed tears are to be found and gathered.[24]

This is the true voice of Kafu, spiced just a little with Baudelairean hyperbole. The 'quarters of darkness and unright-eousness', of 'castaway rags' and 'perfumed tears' were a refuge from the growing vulgarity and stifling conformity of a rapidly industrializing Japan which was starting to resemble Detroit and Birmingham more than old Edo.

It was a refuge from his age and his immediate social

environment. Like Chinatown, the Yoshiwara or red-light area east of the River Sumida offered him a last glimpse of a kind of harmony that would be lost for ever.

> There was a sad, plaintive harmony in the life and scenes of the Yoshiwara, like that of Edo plays and ballads . . . But time passed, and the noise and glare of the frantic modern city destroyed the old harmony. The pace of life changed. I believe that the Edo mood still remained in the Tokyo of thirty years ago. Its last, lingering notes were to be caught in the Yoshiwara. (*Housefly in Winter*, 1935)[25]

Kafu loved his native city, Tokyo. It is hard to detect a similar depth of feeling for his women. His attitude seems entirely traditional, in so far as the women in his stories are either mothers, or dolls. Men play with them, or else are fed by them, just as Jukichi in *Flowers in the Shade* (*Hikage no Hana*, 1934), who is kept by a succession of ladies of doubtful occupations, one of whom, O-Chiyo, he actually forces back into prostitution. Men such as this (remember also Tanjiro in *The Plum Calendar*) are not so much pimps as male mistresses tickling maternal fancies.

And even O-Chiyo is more a puppet than a human being. There was one thing Kafu insisted on in his heroines, however: the talent to invoke nostalgia, to remind him of the past. It is as if he could not experience anything as being real if it lacked a literary precedent. His favourite adventures, literary as well as real, tended to remind him of Kabuki plays. And his favourite kind of woman, such as O-Yuki in *A Strange Tale from East of the River*, is a 'skilful yet inarticulate artist with the power to summon the past'.

This is how he describes O-Yuki, meeting the male protagonist for the first time, sheltering from a rainstorm (in itself a well-worn cliché of Edo-period romances):

> She stood up and changed into an unlined summer kimono with a pattern printed low on the skirt – it had been draped over the rack beside her. The undersash in fine reddish stripes, was knotted in front, and the heaviness of the knot seemed to balance the almost too large silver-threaded chignon. At that moment to me she was the courtesan of thirty years before.[26]

The prostitute, however lowly, played much the same role in Kafu's imagination as she had for centuries in the Japanese arts: she was an ideal, a mirage, a kind of conductor for aesthetic reveries. Her personality was much less important than the atmosphere she invoked; her hairdo and kimono more important than her face. She reminds one in fact of those courtesans in the woodblock prints Kafu loved: of those women without faces, or, more correctly, those women who all share the same face: a vague sketch, just enough for a dream.

Higuchi Ichiyo, the first important female writer Japan had seen for centuries, was less of a dreamer. She was born in 1872 and died, tragically, just twenty-four years later, of consumption. This early death, reminding one most poignantly of the evanescence of all earthly things, would most likely have secured Ichiyo's place as a romantic Japanese heroine even if her literary talents had not been as great as they were.

Unlike the voyeuristic Kafu who always made sure he lived in more salubrious quarters than those he frequented at night, Ichiyo actually lived on the border of the Yoshiwara. This was not so much a matter of choice – she obviously never played at being the Edo brothel-creeper – as of several financial disasters in her family which compelled her to live in not-so-genteel poverty. None the less, she turned her misfortune into a virtue and wrote about the world of prostitutes in a way that has not yet been rivalled.

She was as disillusioned about the world she saw around her as Kafu. But she never let nostalgia for the old world cloud her judgment. Kafu was a romantic, Ichiyo was more an elegant cynic in the style of Saikaku, whose writings had a profound influence on her work.[27] Her own life as a woman in an age that promised emancipation without really following it through, may have had something to do with this. She wrote in her diary that 'in this floating world of ours no one cares about anybody else. I used to believe in people. I actually thought it was possible to improve the world. But I was too naive, I deceived myself. Time and time again those I trusted disappointed me and now I don't have much faith in anything.'[28]

She never thought of prostitutes as reminders of the good old days. To her they were symbols of broken dreams, but they were real people too, with individual personalities, something that

Kafu's ladies never were. Her most famous story of the pleasure quarter is called *Takekurabe*, variously translated as *Growing Up* and *Child's Play*. It was written in 1895 and later made into a superb film. The story is about several children growing up around the Yoshiwara, 'where lights flicker in the moat, dark as the dye that blackens the smiles of the Yoshiwara beauties'. Her ironical descriptions of the quarter do not attempt to disguise its sordidness:

> It's one thing to see a woman of a certain age who favours gaudy patterns, or a sash cut immoderately wide. It's quite another to see these barefaced girls of fifteen or sixteen, all decked out in flashy clothes and blowing bladder cherries, which everybody knows are used as contraceptives. But that's what kind of neighbourhood it is. A trollop who yesterday went by the name of some heroine in 'The Tale of Genji' at one of the third-rate houses along the ditch, today runs off with a thug . . . [29]

One of the main characters in the story is a young girl called Midori, 'a winsome girl, exuberant, soft spoken'. Her elder sister was purchased by a prestigious brothel of the quarter and her success ensures that Midori is never strapped for pocket money. In and out of the brothel all the time, Midori soon learns the ways of the floating world, but in the beginning it all seems like innocent fun, child's play really, with her friends, Shota, leader of the main-street gang and Nobu, the son of the priest.

As she grows up, however, she feels increasingly awkward: 'How was she to explain it? If they would just leave her alone . . . If only she could go on playing house forever, with her dolls for companions, then she'd be happy again.' She begins to understand, very vaguely at first, why she was always treated so kindly by the proprietor of her sister's establishment.

One day Shota sees her in front of the teahouse with 'coloured ribbons in her hair and tortoise-shell combs and flowered hairpins. The whole effect was as bright and stately as a Kyoto doll.' A neighbourhood boy remarks that she looks even prettier than her sister, but he certainly hopes she will not end up like her. 'What do you mean?' Shota replies, 'That would be wonderful! Next year I'm going to open a shop, and after I save some money I'll buy her for a night!'[30]

'He didn't understand things,' is Ichiyo's wry comment.

Midori, alas, does. That is her tragedy. Her childhood dreams slowly come apart. She has to accept her fate. None of this is directly stated by Ichiyo. All is implied. The last image of the story is typical of her style: it is indeed the sort of image Japanese artists have used for centuries, and still do, even in popular modern films (the line between hoary cliché and high art is a fine one): 'One frosty morning, a paper narcissus lay inside the gate. No one knew what it was doing there, but Midori took a fancy to it, for some reason, and put it in a bud vase. It was perfect she thought, and yet almost sad in its crisp, solitary shape.'

Growing Up is not a criticism of prostitution as such. Ichiyo was too cynical and too detached for straight social criticism, and she was certainly no prude. If it is against anything, it is against the lack of freedom to choose one's own destiny in Japanese society. What is truly tragic is the way people are bound to fate; all the more so because the Meiji restoration, in its early years, had promised change.[31] But soon society became almost as rigid as it had been under the Tokugawas. Ichiyo's response is a combination of Saikaku's irony and a Heian sense of pathos.

Troubled Water (*Nigorie*), also written in 1895, actually takes us inside an even lower kind of brothel than the one for which Midori was destined. Ichiyo's description of some of its inhabitants is hardly inviting: 'She was a woman of perhaps twenty-seven, perhaps thirty. She had plucked her eyebrows and painted a dark line in their place and had outlined her widow's peak in black. A thick layer of powder covered her face. Her lips were rouged a shade of crimson so deep they lost their charm and suggested more a man-eating dog than a courtesan.'

The story is about one prostitute in particular: Oriki, the number one attraction at the Kikunoi House. A merchant named Genshichi is so devoted to her services that he spends all his money on her, ruining his business and leaving his family destitute. She has another admirer called Yuki Tomonosuke, a wealthy, suave playboy, who is 'different from other men'. He becomes her confidant, listening patiently to all her woes. She tells him about all the men she has to be nice to, and how they sometimes propose to marry her. But she doubts that would be the answer. Tomonosuke, though, is not like that; she really likes him:

'When I don't see you for a day, I miss you. But if you asked me to be your wife, I don't know . . . I doubt it would work, and, yet, when we're not together . . . In a word, I suppose you could say I'm fickle. And what do you think made me this way? Three generations of failure, that's what.'[32]

Like Midori, and almost every Japanese heroine or hero, she cannot escape her fate.

How she hated her life! She never wanted to hear another human voice, or any sound at all . . . How long would she be stuck in this hopeless situation, where everything was absurd and worthless and cruel . . . 'I have no choice,' she whispered. 'I will have to cross the bridge by myself. My father fell treading it. They say my grandfather stumbled too. I was born with the curse of many generations . . . Oh, it doesn't matter any more what happens — I haven't the slightest idea what will become of me — I might as well go on as Oriki of the Kikunoi . . . With my station in life and my calling and my fate, I'm not an ordinary person any more. It's a mistake to think I am. It only adds to my suffering. It's all so hopeless and discouraging. What am I doing standing here? Why did I come here? Stupid! Crazy! I don't even know myself,' she sighed. 'I'd better get back.'[33]

This is the voice of Oriki of the Kikunoi. It is also the sort of thing one hears 'salarymen' say on a drunken evening; it is what their wives, pushed into marriages with men they hardly knew, often say. It is, in fact, what many Japanese are liable to say in their more melancholy moods.

Choice of one's destiny, though doubtless wider than it was in Ichiyo's time, is still subject to severe limitations. People in Japan, more than in any Western country, are still ruled by the demands of their social environment. This is, in effect, what is meant by fate — the pressure to conform to expectations. Although the prostitute, in her self-abandonment, is in a sense freer than the rest of us, she is also the most dramatic victim of this predicament. It is this paradox that speaks so vividly to the Japanese imagination: she is a sacrificing mother, a victim of fate and free from the usual social conventions, all at the same time.

In 1950, a much younger writer called Yoshiyuki Junnosuke, carrying on the tradition of brothel literature, had a very similar point of view. In *Street of Primary Colours* (*Genshoku no Machi*) a prostitute named Akemi tries but fails to escape her fate. The quarter itself has changed considerably since Ichiyo's days, along similar lines to Japan itself:

> Both sides of the main street were inundated with strong, garish colours. A red neon light flickered inside a heart-shaped fluorescent tube. Pink curtains hung down from doorways of Western-style houses in front of which several women with bright red nails and lips were listlessly hanging about . . .
>
> Painted lips moved rapidly up and down; white teeth reflected the neon lights. Bare arms stretched out to grab arms, coats, and even hats of men strolling by. Making meaningless sounds and cracking silly jokes, the men stopped to take a better look at the women: everyone to his own taste. They would then be taken inside, or they would disentangle themselves and walk on to the next place . . .
>
> The relationships in the area were quite clear. As far as the women were concerned, however pretty and naive they might have looked, they still bore the marks of their profession. The men would look at them without even wondering whether they would respond to their advances; they would simply be calculating how much pleasure they could get for their cash . . .
>
> Some people were attracted to these streets by a certain sense of freedom. The girl called Akemi who lived in one of the houses there was one of them. Or, rather, her position made it impossible for her to find freedom anywhere else. This, at least, was how she rationalized her actions . . .

In fact Akemi falls into the same trap that had claimed so many of her literary – and no doubt real – predecessors for centuries: she falls in love – with an employee of a shipping company, named Motogi Hideo. She experiences her first orgasm with him. Unfortunately, however, 'Motogi Hideo lost interest as soon as he saw that Akemi had ordinary emotions like everybody else'. In other words, she stopped being simply an image, a popular piece of art with painted lips.

Akemi conforms to another classic convention too: she tries to commit suicide with the man she loves. In an attempt to drown them both, she drags him overboard at a launching party. They are saved, however, and when Akemi comes to her senses and sees everybody staring at her, 'she knows she'll return to those streets again'.

Higuchi Ichiyo's story, *Troubled Water*, ends with a murder of passion as well but a 'successful' one. Oriki of the Kikunoi is found by gossiping neighbours:

> . . . slashed across the back, down from the shoulder. There were bruises on her cheek and cuts on her neck. She had wounds all over! Obviously she tried to flee, and that's when he killed her.
>
> He, on the other hand, did a splendid job of it! Hara-kiri and the whole business. Who would have thought he had it in him? . . . He died like a man. Went out in a blaze of glory.
>
> What a loss to the Kikunoi.
>
> Yes. Think of all the men she attracted! To let all those customers slip through your fingers![34]

Love is the death of the courtesan. In the case of Chikamatsu's seventeenth-century heroines, their deaths were at least made to seem noble, demonstrating the purity of their love. Even the most hopeless cases could still be redeemed by sacrificial beauty. In modern Japan this beauty has somehow lost its bloom. The sordidness of reality is harder to escape.

But why this tyranny of fate? Why is there this deep sense of tragedy in everything these heroines do? Oriki is held back by the failures of her ancestors. She cannot imagine herself in any situation but the one she finds herself in. And there is nothing she can do about it.

Yoshiyuki, like Ichiyo, an author of rare psychological insight, comes to a conclusion which, again, could serve as a metaphor for the Japanese way of life:

The reason they always return to the streets must be sought in the women themselves . . . As long as their consciousness is not severed from their environment, that is, from their way of life, living by selling their bodies, such words as freedom and bondage are irrelevant. There are plenty of stories of idealistic men attempting to change this consciousness. But these attempts must always end in failure.

The same thing could be said about most Japanese. While they remain in Japan, their lives and the way they define themselves are impossible to separate from their Japaneseness. The personal is often indistinguishable from the collective. In practice this may be true of most people in the world, but in the West at least one has the idea – perhaps the illusion – of being an individual amongst other individuals, together but separate, like islands in a sea of islands.

In Japan one's identity seems to be defined to a greater extent by the social environment and one is responsible to that environment only. This could be a motorcycle company, a baseball team, a theatre group, or even the entire country; all depending on the time and place. The point is that one cannot really exist separately from these groups without risking severe psychological problems. Writers, because of the nature of their work, are sometimes forced to take this risk. This is one way of explaining the many suicides of authors in recent times.

It also explains why it appears to be so difficult for many Japanese to return to the national fold once they have left it for any length of time. Alienation in Japan is a very high price to pay. Not conforming to the expected pattern means essentially that one does not exist at all. This is why Japanese companies abroad often discourage their Japanese employees from mixing with the 'natives' (*genchijin*) too much. For, to turn Yoshiyuki's sentence round, separating one's consciousness from the Japanese way of life makes such words as freedom and bondage at once extremely relevant.

From midnight on 31 March 1958, public prostitution was officially banned for the first time in Japanese history. Fifty-five thousand girls (not counting the many unregistered prostitutes) all over the country found themselves out of a job. The first reaction to the new law was rather charming and very Japanese:

just before the midnight deadline prostitutes and their customers all over Tokyo began singing 'Auld Lang Syne', a hugely popular song in Japan, appropriated for those deliciously sad occasions, so dearly beloved by the Japanese people, of saying goodbye.

This was of course not quite the end of prostitution. In many parts of the country it simply went on as before. Even in Tokyo the streets were only really 'cleaned up' just before the Olympic Games in 1964 to make a civilized and enlightened impression on the world. Whether the foreign visitors were pleased with this measure history does not tell.

Whether the anti-prostitution law is good or bad does not concern us here. Suffice it to say that the steady economic development of Japan made a system of virtual slavery an embarrassing anachronism. It also showed the power of crusading female pressure groups – who were largely responsible for the new law – in Japanese politics. It did not mean, however, that a fundamental change had taken place in people's attitudes to sex. In fact, despite the new law, the image of women of pleasure in popular culture has hardly changed at all.

Bar and club hostesses, still an indispensible part of Japanese social life, serve a similar function to the courtesans of Edo. The top-ranking ones dispense their favours neither easily nor cheaply and they are still the much publicized companions of famous actors and showbiz personalities. They specialize in skilled entertaining and a rather artificial bawdy banter, which would perhaps not set most Western men alight, but is highly appreciated in Japan. But most important of all, from the lowliest masseuse to the top-flight geisha, they serve to put the Japanese male at ease, to make him forget the tensions of collective company life, to soothe his masculine anxieties, to indulge his whims and flatter his social pride. They are, perhaps increasingly, highly trained mothers.

Pure prostitution exists, too, of course. But many newly affluent Japanese now go to Bangkok, Taipei and Manila in highly organized tours, like hungry wolf-packs. They set off armed with golf clubs which they leave at the airports to be collected on the way home, so as not to seem too blatant about the purpose of their trip.

But one does not have to go as far as Manila. The cold letter of the law is one thing in Japan, and human reality quite another. As

long as a degree of discretion is observed – and perhaps the right
people are paid off – much is allowed to go on unimpeded. The
massage parlour, for instance, the *toruko*, short for Turkish bath,
is simply a continuation of an old tradition combining the
bathhouse with the brothel: the attendants used to be called *yuna*,
bath girls, and now they are known as *torukojo*, Turkish bath
girls.

At first sight these places hardly remind one of the romantic
past. There are no girls any more, attracting customers to their
establishments by tapping them coyly on the shoulder with the
long stems of their pipes, whispering risqué witticisms. *Torukos*,
announcing themselves in loud neon lights, are instead fronted
by young men in suits shouting at the taxis cruising by. For prices
up to $200 one is offered a *furu kosu* (full course), lasting about 90
minutes. The 'course' comprises a wash, a soapy massage, and a
series of sudsy sexual acrobatics, during which the man remains
quite passive. The *torukojo* is after all a skilled entertainer; and she
goes about her business with the same dedication as a
flower-arranger. When the performance is over, she bows and
politely thanks the customer for his patronage, handing him her
business card.

Apart from the ceremonious behaviour, which is simply the
Japanese way, there are several interesting parallels with the
past. In the first place many modern *torukos* are situated in the old
licensed areas: the brothels have simply been rebuilt to
accommodate a large number of baths. Not only that, but some
establishments even bear the same names as illustrious Edo
teahouses, in the same way that variety-hall entertainers
sometimes borrow the names of great Kabuki actors.

It is the emphasis on fantasy, however, and the attitude to the
women that has hardly changed at all. If the brothels of the Edo
period borrowed their fantasies from the tenth-century world of
Prince Genji, the massage parlours draw from all the images in
the modern world. The architecture is usually an indication of the
type of illusion for sale. Some *torukos* have entrances built to
resemble jumbo jets with wooshing jet noises switched on as one
steps inside. The girls are of course dressed as stewardesses.
Other places have façades resembling banks, featuring girls in
company uniforms. There are 'Young Rady' schools with girls in
tennis outfits, greeting the customers in the hall with rackets

under their arms. There are hospitals with nurses, Chinese pavilions, American discos, and even a place with a jungle full of Janes in leopard-skins waiting for Tarzan to turn up. Perhaps the most bizarre of all are the fake-Japanese castles where kimonoed attendants kow-tow in front of the entrance and say 'welcome home, my lord'.

Many of these fantasies are universal, but the limitless energy and the innocent openness with which the Japanese try to fulfil them is perhaps unique in the world. It is not surprising that the Turkish bath girls are treated a little like actresses, just as their sisters of the Edo period were. There is even a rigorous ranking system with girls competing to be 'numba one'.

Another tradition still persisting is the detailed guide with information about the habits, prices and relative values of the many massage parlours. There are professional critics, called 'torukologists', who pontificate on late-night television shows, offering us the benefit of their expertise. Popular magazines and newspapers print weekly reports on new faces at the local *torukos*, and reviews of the current 'numba ones':

> Miss Akiko: service time, one hour and twenty minutes; price: 40.000 yen ($150) Height: 175 cm. Weight: 49 k. Proportions: 83–56–85. She is a hard worker with special oral skills. Very good at creating a romantic mood. 'I'm proud of our place,' she says, 'and I enjoy working hard to make it prosper.'
> Miss Miwa: 90 minutes. $180. Height 160 cm. Weight 51 k. She has great confidence in her work since she came to the Yoshiwara. She likes all kind of hard play. 'We have a very clean place,' says this refreshing city girl, 'and in the right mood there is no end to the service I provide. We take great pride in our good manners.'[35]

Finally a Miss Yuki, 83–59–86, informs us that her establishment specializes in a 'Japanese mood': 'We do our best to behave with the traditional delicacy and good manners we Japanese are accustomed to.'

If one removed the references to the precise nature of their business, these could be reviews of workers in an automobile plant or the staff of a chainstore: 'good manners', 'prosperity of our company' . . . It is a far cry from the dry 'call Annie for French lessons' in a British tobacconist's window or the lewd advertisements in Western porno magazines. The *torukojo* somehow manages to envelop her trade with a sense of duty and decorum.

A large number of men, one is told, go to the *toruko* to be babied. There are even certain establishments where the customers literally dress up in diapers so that they can make a mess and cry for mama.[36] Mama then cleans up and bathes them, clucking and cooing in baby-talk. These places are somewhat specialized, however, and though perhaps symptomatic, not common enough to be representative.

One does not have to go that far, though, to see the mother-figure looming. In *The Pornographers*, a novel by Nosaka Akiyuki, láter made into a film by Imamura Shohei, there is a hilarious description of a visit to a *toruko* by one of the main characters:

> 'You lie down on one of those massage tables like a baby. You then close your eyes without thinking of anything, leaving everything to the woman. It doesn't matter what she looks like or what she's thinking. With her fingers she looks for the most sensitive spot on your body, a spot you didn't even know yourself, that your own wife didn't even know. That's the best part of the "special treatment". Only the man feels good with the "special". The woman isn't allowed to feel anything. In short, it's as if you're treated by your own mother . . . Mother love is, how shall I put it, well, you know, service, sacrifice. All this is a bit cruel. When you climax, the woman must pretend to be shocked and then wipe you clean. At that moment she really is your mother. You wrap your arms around her. She won't mind what you do, just like a mother and child.'

Mother and child. That, once again, is the primal element. But fantasy women are not necessarily divided into mothers and whores: they can be one and the same; the whore often really is the Madonna. Not for nothing are prostitutes traditionally sometimes compared to Buddhist deities, such as Kannon, the Goddess of Mercy.

There is a widely read comic-strip by a celebrated comic artist called Kamimura Kazuo. It first appeared in 1977, but the story actually takes place in a Tokyo brothel area of the early 1950s and thus it is filled with nostalgia. The main character is Sachiko, the sweetest of maternal prostitutes. Like most suffering heroines Sachiko lost her parents soon after she was born. She was also raped by a big, bad American soldier during the occupation: this cliché is almost a required badge of courage, like a duelling scar on a pre-war German Korps Student: no fate could possibly be worse, so the heroine starts off with the reader's deepest sympathy.

In her more melancholy moments, Sachiko likes to think of her parents and she sings her favourite song:

> I'm the blooming flower of the red-light quarter
> If the moon were a mirror
> I'd stand in front of it
> So my dear lost parents could see me once again.

Sachiko is a good woman and like many sensible Japanese girls, she combines the practical with the maternal. She takes on students at reduced rates and even does their dirty washing for them, reasoning that 'of all the students who use my body now, at least one will end up as a company director and then surely he will take care of me'.

One day a student arrives, asking for the madam, a sour-faced woman always thinking of money. Sachiko offers the boy a cup of tea in her room and tells him all about the madam. He gets more and more agitated until in a fit of hysterics he bursts out: 'It's her! It's her! After fifteen years, I've found her! Mother! Mother!'

The following scene is identical to the one in 'Mother Behind My Eyes': the student, like Chutaro in the play, is delirious. He howls and cries but his mother refuses to recognize him, telling him to leave at once. How dare he play tricks on an old woman, obviously trying to get at her money. Again like Chutaro, the boy laughs hysterically and screams: 'How could I have been so stupid, spending all these years looking for nothing, all for nothing!' Perhaps the author did not steal this scene consciously, but it does show that the horrifying possibility of maternal rejection works again and again.

Sachiko comes to the rescue. She takes him to her room and whispers in her sweetest voice: 'I'll be your mother instead. That's what I live for.' She proceeds to spread her legs as wide as

they will go, inches in front of his tear-streaked face, just like in the striptease-parlour. 'Take a good look,' she coos, 'this is what they call a man's home. I'm your home, my dear boy, I'm your mother.'

'Oh,' he murmurs, and breaking into baby-talk, he asks, 'can I suck your breasts, Mummy?' The story ends with a close-up of Sachiko's breast cradling his sleeping head. Sachiko ponders: 'That night the old madam's son came in my body. Now he's sound asleep, looking so serene. At that moment I was happy too; perhaps one day I too shall be a mother . . . '

Sachiko's Happiness (*Sachiko no Sachi*), for that is the title of this comic, is a serious work. The point is not to titillate so much as to move. It is a tearjerker, a three-handkerchief comic-book. It is read in Japan, not just by the young, but also by highly educated adults. It is certainly not thought to be strange in any way that the sentimental heroine is a prostitute; on the contrary, it is deemed quite appropriate.

Real sexuality would upset the pure, suffering-mother image. Sachiko has sex, of course, for that is the prostitute's trade, but, as Nosaka's character said, she does not feel anything. Sex is just an instrument to make men feel good.

In another Sachiko comic an elegant kimonoed lady turns up at the brothel. She very politely asks the madam whether she could possibly work at the brothel for nothing. She would be happy to hand over her earnings. All she is interested in is the sex. The madam is naturally delighted with this arrangement. And the elegant lady gets carpenters and decorators to turn her shabby room into a veritable palace of pleasure.

Sachiko and the other girls are so upset by this turn of events that they decide to go on strike. But the newcomer proves to be insatiable. She has one rule only: she refuses to see any man more than once. This is too much to bear for one particular client who is driven half insane with frustration. Things then take the inevitable nasty turn: the man rushes into her mirrored boudoir and stabs her hysterically with a huge kitchen knife. Her gory death is depicted in all the graphic detail the Japanese comic reader is accustomed to: in a series of illustrations we see the knife go in and out, in and out, blood staining the double page like a horrible Rorschach test. The lady dies with an angelic smile fixed on her elegant face.

The passionate forces she unleashed have run their course and everything reverts back to normal again. The prostitutes get back to work. 'I never want to be like that woman,' thinks Sachiko, 'I never want to see that female Hell.'

Sachiko is anything but sexy, the opposite of the *femme fatale*. It is her maternal sweetness, her *yasashisa*, that makes her a popular heroine. There are examples of this phenomenon in real life too, which takes us back to the striptease parlour once again. In the early 1970s there was a sudden vogue for a stripper called Ichijo Sayuri, a pleasant, but unremarkable-looking woman from Osaka. At the height of her fame she was suddenly arrested on obscenity charges. Her exposure on stage was no different from

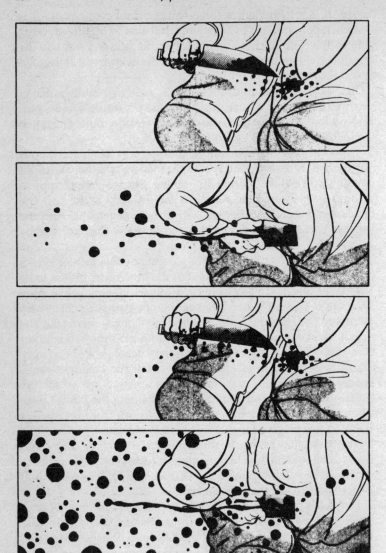

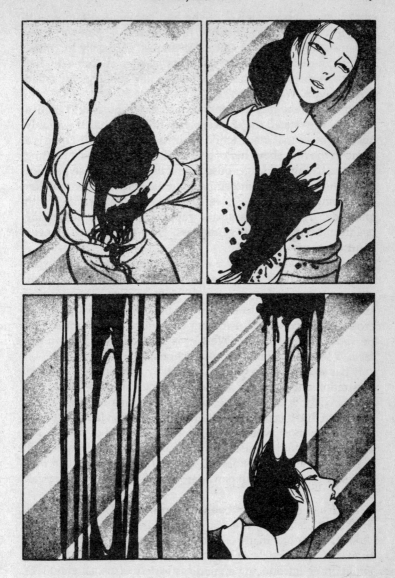

any other stripteaseuse's, but she had become too famous – it was all too public, the boat had been rocked. The news of her arrest was received with storms of protest, especially in 'interi' circles: journalists, writers and film-makers all came to her defence. A modish director even made a film about her life called 'Ichijo Sayuri–Wet Desire.'

Why was there this tremendous surge of popularity? I think a film reviewer stated the answer when he wrote that 'it was only her sweetness that made Ichijo Sayuri so much loved. There is a scene in the film about her of a truck-driver wildly masturbating while watching Ichijo's exposed genitals in a striptease parlour. She leans over to him and enquires in the kindest voice whether he is doing all right. "Yes, yes!" he answers, his eyes filled with gratitude. This tenuous sexual rapport turns into something beautiful because of her gentleness. Now the authorities even want to rob us of that.'[37]

It is as if 'the authorities' are like a Victorian father taking the good mother away from the people. The rules of society are always threatening the innocent child at play. This view of sexuality might help to explain the constant, almost palpable, erotic tension in Japan. Far from the cynical knowingness that pervades sexuality in the West, it is an adolescent tension one feels, a knot of insoluble contradictions.

It has existed for centuries, this itchy combination of social frustration and innocent sensuality; of pervading sexuality and deep anxiety. It is, of course, partly due to the universal human condition, but it is perhaps felt more extremely in Japan, which is at once the most natural and the most artificial of places. The Japanese are both intensely physical and extremely fastidious. It is the extreme character of these contradictions rather than their uniqueness that makes Japan as erotomanic as it so often appears to be.

The frustration has probably grown worse. The social brakes are still there, while the traditional outlets – for men at least; women never had many outlets – have become less available. In the last few years clever businessmen have capitalized on this situation by introducing an endless variety of sexual gimmicks. One in particular appears both typical of traditional attitudes and of contemporary society. The leading role is played by yet another version of the Japanese doll-woman.

This fantasy woman is the star of the *nopan kissa*:[38] nopan is an abbreviation of 'no pants', and kissa, short for *kissaten*, means coffee shop; in other words, a coffee shop where the waitresses wear no underclothes. The craze for this caught on in the summer of 1980, starting in Osaka, home of the lucrative gimmick. Within a few months every Japanese city was full of them, not just around the less salubrious railway stations, where one might expect them, but in the most fashionable shopping areas. They are decorated on the outside with pin-ups from magazines, polaroid pictures of the bare-bottomed waitresses, dingy neon lights and large posters with details of the specialities of the house: 'Stewardesses with no pants!', 'Porno video on the premises!' All this to drink a cup of coffee.

The customer is ushered inside by a young man in patent leather shoes and a cheap satin kimono draped over his Western-style suit. 'Welcome to our shop!' he shouts through a plastic megaphone. Inside the visitor is courteously greeted by two plump girls, naked apart from their minuscule skirts and two dainty ribbons wrapped around their necks like Christmas presents. 'Welcome inside', they pipe in perfect unison.

The decor is remarkable. Not only are there the usual pin-ups on the walls, porn comics on the coffee-tables and beeping, buzzing invader games for those who might get bored with staring at the waitresses' legs, but suspended from the ceiling are at least a dozen inflated condoms like balloons at a children's birthday party. The walls are further embellished with various articles of female underwear, such as stockings, panties and garter belts. There is also a sign that reads: 'Do not speak to the waitresses. Do not touch them. Do not bother them in any way'.

The customers pay about $7 for one cup of coffee. Is there perhaps more to this than meets the eye? Not necessarily. What meets the eye in Japan is often all there is. Japan is, after all, as Roland Barthes observed, the empire of signs, the land of the empty gesture, the symbol, the detail that stands for the whole. The fetishist ikon is so powerful that the real thing becomes superfluous.

There is something childlike about these men ensconced in the sticky imitation-leather chairs of the *nopan kissa*: sitting in groups, dressed in suits and ties, most of them in their thirties, giggling nervously, bobbing their heads up and down like yo-yos every time a waitress bends down to serve a cup of coffee. Bothering the girls seems to be the last thing on their minds.

The climax, if that is the word to use, of the visit is an auction of one of the girls' panties. The girl, fully dressed now, climbs up on one of the tables, looking faintly bored with it all, like a life model in an art class. The men cluster round, jostling each other for the best vantage point.

While a male employee shouts through a microphone, the girl slowly peels her clothes off, until she is only in her panties. The bidding then goes higher and higher and the voice through the microphone gets progressively louder. Finally the winner is allowed, for a considerable fee, to slide the panties off the girl's goose-pimpled legs, all the time nervously glancing over his shoulder at his friends, who are still nudging and pushing each other.

The men pay for their coffee and file out of the shop. One of the girls stands by the exit and one by one the men are invited lightly to squeeze one of her breasts, almost brushing the cash-register, just once. All the girls make a bow and say in mechanical unison: 'Thank you for patronizing our shop. We do hope we will have the pleasure of your company again.'

It might not quite match the aristocratic style of the Heian court, or the elegance of the floating world in Edo, or even the dashing teahouse of Meiji, but it does prove that even at the summit of sexual exploitation the Japanese have not quite lost their sense of manners and decorum.

7

The Third Sex

In the spring of 1914 Kobayashi Ichizo, former director of the Hankyu Railways, built a paradise on earth; about fifty miles from Osaka, in a sleepy hot springs resort called Takarazuka. It is rather a special kind of paradise, for its only inhabitants are girls, young girls. Its main attraction is the Takarazuka Young Girls Opera Company.

Kobayashi built the first theatre in a large swimming pool appropriately named Paradise. Because every collective venture in Japan needs a slogan Kobayashi thought of one too: 'Kiyoku Tadashiku Utsukushiku'. Pure Righteous Beautiful. And to this day the all-girl revue consists of pure, righteous and beautiful girls from the best families in the land. They live a cloistered existence in Takarazuka, segregated as much as possible from the sordid reality of the world outside. They are the official angels of paradise.

The angels are actually called 'students', never actresses, dancers or, perish the thought, showgirls. They are taken on at a very early age, usually around fourteen, after strict selection. Then, living in the Violet Dormitory, strictly off-limits for men, they are taught all the necessary skills of respectable young Japanese ladies, such as flower-arranging or the tea ceremony, as well as singing and dancing.

If one of the students should want to get married, she is automatically expelled from paradise. A married woman can be righteous and no doubt beautiful, but not pure. Takarazuka is pure virgin territory. The oldest star, a woman in her seventies, is not called 'The Eternal Virgin' for nothing.

One of the first things to strike the visitor to Takarazuka is the overwhelming predominance of pink. To reach the theatre the visitor crosses a pink bridge; the theatre itself is pink, and so is the foyer, and the halls to the dressing room, the cable cars that travel high over the 'street of flowers', the lunch boxes in the restaurants; and most of the girls in the audience are dressed in pink. If one can make the comparison without sounding blasphemous, the inside of the Takarazuka theatre reminds one of the pink interiors of Japanese striptease parlours; it has the same womb-like quality.

The architecture of paradise is interesting too: a kind of Disneyland Swiss village: little chalets and chocolate-box houses bearing such names as Ladies' Inn, Ladybird Café and, perhaps most apt of all, Illusion.

Apart from the wartime years, during which the Takarazuka stage was filled with pure, beautiful and righteous girls in army uniforms singing the praises of Japanese guns and brotherhood in Asia, the company has specialized in romantic musical revues, home grown as well as such foreign favourites as 'Gone With the Wind' and 'Romeo and Juliet'.

There are of course no men in the troupe. This is one of the outstanding features of the Takarazuka style; the girls playing the male parts are the stars, adored by fans all over the country. All Takarazuka members wear their hair short like freshly scrubbed schoolboys and it is the dream of every one of them to get to play a man. The 'male' stars are so popular that fans staged a protest demonstration when one of their idols was required to play Scarlett O'Hara: 'They've turned Maru into a woman!' they screamed.

Watching the Takarazuka students rehearse the male roles is a fascinating experience. It is all based on *kata*, formal patterns, just like in the Kabuki theatre. A series of formalized masculine postures is rehearsed over and over again until the girls get it just right. The older girls act as models and drill instructors for the younger ones. Apparently many of these postures were originally developed in the 1950s when senior members of the troupe diligently copied poses from Marlon Brando movies.

What is behind all this? Why this enthusiasm for transvestite

above left Female with a monkey face on an old fertility stone

above right Fertility goddess with a male symbol

Stone phallus and vagina

Dance of The Dread Female of Heaven in the *Nihon Tanjo* (*Birth of Japan*), made in 1955 by Inagaki Hiroshi

Striptease, Japanese style

top left The lovers in Mizoguchi's *Taki no Shiraito* (*The Water Musicians*)

top right Chutaro being rejected by his mother in *Mother Behind My Eyes*

below left The Mother of Japan (Mochizuki Yuko) trying to retrieve her son in *Japanese Tragedy*

below right Imamura Shohei's favourite woman, Hidari Sachiko, in *Insect Woman*

Mother and son (*The Golden Boy* and *Mountain Mother*) in a print by Utamaro, 1796–9

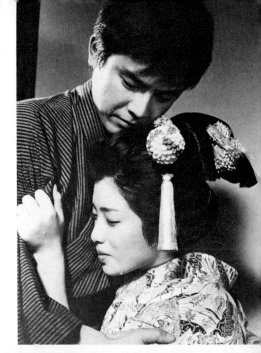

Yamaguchi Momoe and Miura Tomokazu, the 'Goruden Combi', in one of their romantic films (*Shunkincho*)

Pathos in a 'homu dorama', entitled *O-nesan* (*Sister*)

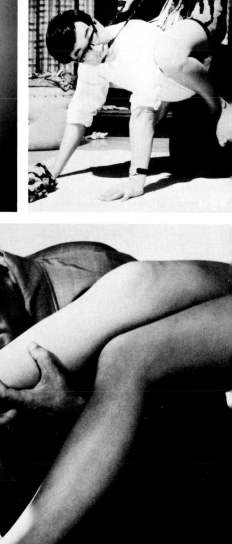

top left The threatening female

top right Naomi dominating
her slavish benefactor in a film of
Tanizaki's *A Fool's Love*.
Directed by Masumura Yasuzo
in 1967

bottom left The old man
worshipping his daughter-in-law's
feet in a film of Tanizaki's
Diary of a Madman. Directed in
1962 by Kimura Keigo

right Typical torture scene in a
run-of-the-mill porn film
(*Onna Ukiyoburo*)

below Tani Naomi being
tortured again in *Nawa to Hada*
(*Rope and Skin*)

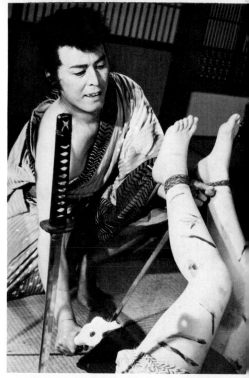

An Edo-period courtesan in a print by Utamaro, about 1796

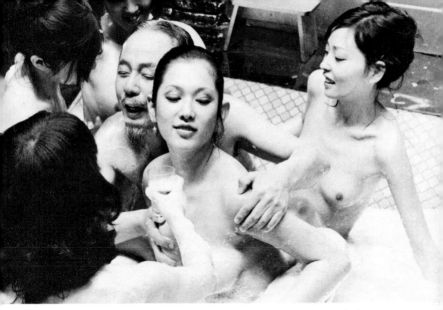

Scene in a 'Toruko' massage parlour in a porn film, appropriately entitled
Toruko

Modern Japanese amusing themselves at a geisha party in a long-forgotten
film

above left Female stars playing the romantic male leads in the Takarazuka version of *Rose of Versailles*

above right Tamasaburo, the most popular young *onnagata*, playing an Edo-period courtesan in full regalia

Romance in the Takarazuka theatre

The young Yoshitsune as a fighting *bishonen* in a picture by Takabatake Kasho

Young Kirokku in a fighting mood in Suzuki Seijun's *Elegy to Fighting*

Miyamoto Musashi, the archetypal hero of the Hard School, in Inagaki Hiroshi's *Ketto Ganryujima* (*Final Duel on Ganryu Island*) 1955

Kamikaze pilots waiting for departure in *Aa Tokubetsu Kogekitai* (*Ah, The Special Attack Forces*)

The assassination attempt on Moronao in Inagaki Hiroshi's 1962 film *Chushingura* (*Tale of the Forty-seven Ronin*)

大映作品宣伝案内

1965
April

left Ichikawa Raizo as a tattooed yakuza hero

top left Sugawara Bunta shooting his opponent in the stomach in *Fighting Without Nobility*

top right Takakura Ken purifying his sword with *saké*

bottom right Sugawara Bunta, the nihilist hero

below Death of the *oyabun*.
The man in the suit (a rare occurrence) is Tsuruta Koji. The man on the extreme right is Takakura Ken

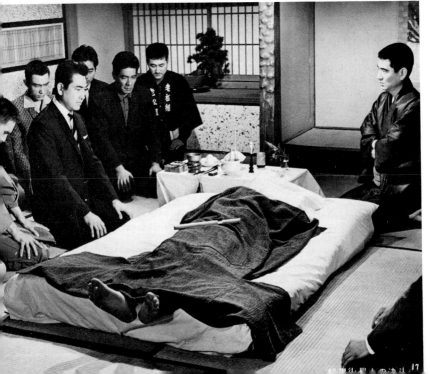

いれずみ突撃隊 A-

Good old Tora-san

Crowds queuing to see the newest Tora-san film

theatre? I asked a Takarazuka producer (the producers, directors, composers and choreographers, typically, are all males). He answered that it was surely healthier for young girls to idolize Takarazuka stars than those long-haired pop groups. Besides, he thought, girls of that age feel safer that way: 'They are too bashful to scream and shout at real men, even if they felt so inclined.' This is possible. But then he raised another, to me more fundamental point: 'It's a bit different these days, but before the war it was hard to find boys beautiful enough to suit the ideals of our audience.'

Not beautiful enough; in other words, no real man can ever be as beautiful as a woman playing a man, just as no woman is quite as stunning as a skilful female impersonator. This goes to the heart of Japanese aesthetics and just like the geisha, the female work of art, it is based on the principle of depersonalization.

As is the case in most cultures, the tradition of theatrical transvestism goes back a very long way in Japan. And like the theatre itself it has religious origins. When the Sun Goddess met her unruly brother Susanoo, she dressed up in male clothes. Cross-dressing certainly played a part in sacred rites and festivals. Female shrine dancers (*aruki miko*), who were often also prostitutes, dressed up as males, just as during the Edo period male geishas were trained in feminine arts.[1]

Sexual ambivalence is an important element in the Buddhist tradition too, as Lévi-Strauss explains in *Tristes Tropiques*: '[Buddhism] expresses a placid femininity which seems to have been freed from the battle of the sexes, a femininity which is also suggested by the temple priests whose shaven heads make them indistinguishable from the nuns, with whom they form a kind of third sex . . . ' Buddhist sculpture often expresses a kind of androgyny, transcending the sexes.[2] Kannon (Kuan Yin in China, Avalokiteshvara in India), the Goddess of Mercy, actually changed her sex. She started off as a god in India and in time, gradually moving further east, she became a goddess.

Sexual confusion was an integral part of the earliest Kabuki theatre. A seventeenth-century Confucian scholar, Hayashi Razan (1583–1657), remarked indignantly that 'the men wear women's clothing; the women wear men's clothing, cut their hair and wear a man's topknot, have swords at their sides, and carry purses.'[3] Out of this confusion, helped by the fact that after 1629 female players were banned by the government, grew what is perhaps the highest art of female impersonation in the world: the *onnagata*.

The *onnagata* in the Kabuki theatre does not attempt to impersonate a specific woman so much as an idealized version of Woman, such as one sees in woodblock prints. He is able to stylize the ideal Woman, precisely because he is a man. Even if he lives his daily life as a woman, which some *onnagata* used to do, he still remains a man. The sexual tension and the distance necessary to his art stay whatever he does, short of an operation, which, in any case, was rather difficult to arrange in the seventeenth century.

The ideal is to make the sexual transition seem as effortless as possible. In the words of the great master of these roles, Yoshisawa Ayame (1673–1729): 'If [the actor] tries deliberately to make his interpretation elegant, it will not be pleasing. For this reason, if he does not live his normal life as if he were a woman, it will not be possible for him to be called a skilful *onnagata*.'[4] He also said that 'if an actress were to appear on stage she could not express ideal feminine beauty, for she could only rely on the exploitation of her physical characteristics, and therefore not express the synthetic ideal. The ideal woman can only be expressed by an actor.'[5]

Goethe was an admirer of castrati artists for the same reason: ' . . . a double pleasure is given in that these persons are not women, but only represent women. The young men have studied the properties of the sex in its being and behaviour; they know them thoroughly and reproduce them like an artist; they represent not themselves, but a nature absolutely foreign to them.'[6]

This kind of skill has little to do with age. I have seen an actor in his seventies playing the young wife of a warrior, who was acted a trifle bashfully by his own son. Because of his complete command over the technique of female role playing, he could still create the illusion of female beauty. It is a very artificial beauty, of course, but this is precisely the point: 'the synthetic ideal'.

Influenced by nineteenth-century European ideas about naturalism, attempts have been made in the past to have women play female roles in the Kabuki theatre. It simply did not work: they looked too natural; they lacked the beauty of artifice; the only way they could achieve the desired effect was to imitate men impersonating women.

An important point about female and male impersonation in Japan and elsewhere in Asia, is that it rarely becomes caricature; it is never a send-up in the way that, say, Barry Humphries is or drag shows in pubs are. One must, of course, bear in mind that transvestite acting was a serious art in Europe too until the dawn of Reason put a stop to it in the seventeenth century.[7]

There is a nightclub in Tokyo run by a famous female impersonator called Miwa Akihiro. The customers are seated in rococo chairs under a crystal chandelier in front of an onyx fireplace amidst marble statues of nude boys and vases filled with peacock feathers. The atmosphere is utterly serious. 'Madame will be arriving presently', whispers one of the waiters dressed in a red velvet dinner jacket. And so she does, looking glamorous in her low-necked evening dress.

As she sings her usual repertoire of French chansons in Japanese in the warbling style of the 1930s, the people are visibly moved. 'Oh, she's looking lovely tonight', says an elderly gentleman to his wife. And a tear rolls down the scarred cheek of a tough-looking character immediately recognizable as a member of the gangster community.

To a Western observer all this is the highest of Camp. To many Japanese it is simply beautiful. Camp rests on a sense of irony; the irony of a serious attempt to reach an impossible ideal, the gap between human inadequacy and the grandiose goal.[8] Camp is always 'too much', 'too fantastic', 'fancy a man trying to look like a woman'. It is often said that the Japanese lack a sense of irony. As a general statement this is probably true. To a Westerner with a Camp sense of humour much in Japanese culture, from the plastic flowers in the streets to the electronic bird noises in department stores and, yes, even the Takarazuka theatre, seems Camp. The point is, though, that there is no gap between attempt and ideal in Miwa's club or the Kabuki theatre or the Takarazuka: people do not pretend that the ideal has anything to do with reality. They enjoy seeing Lady Macbeth played by a famous Kabuki star, precisely because it is more artificial, thus more skilful, in a word, more beautiful.

It is a universal truism that sexual attraction is enhanced by a certain amount of ambivalence. The true 100 per cent he-man is usually a little ridiculous rather than devastating. Japan, in particular, has a tradition of rather girlish heart-throbs. The *jeune premier* in romantic Kabuki dramas is usually a pale, slim youth who invites maternal protection. The attraction of ambivalence appears to be as strong as ever. According to a recent poll in a woman's magazine the two 'sexiest stars' of 1981 were Tamasaburo, a Kabuki actor specializing in female roles, and Sawada Kenji, a pop singer who likes to perform in semi-drag, more female than male.

There are social reasons too for the popularity of transvestite acting. Like everywhere else, learning to play the role of one's sex is part of social training in Japan. In fact one is constantly reminded of one's gender and is expected to behave accordingly. But not as soon as one is born; first comes that state of grace, the safe, warm, maternal world of early childhood when no role-playing is demanded quite yet and no real distinctions exist. In the words of the psychiatrist Kawai Hayao, 'there is no distinction in the all-enveloping world of the mother between man and god, good and bad, man and woman'.[9] This explains, in his opinion, why it seems so hard for many Japanese to escape from this world, to become adults.

The sexual ambivalence of the Takarazuka theatre and the girls' comic-books upon which many of its plays are based are manifestations of this. The critic Imaizumi Fumiko believes that the evident desire not to be female is often misunderstood as a kind of worship of men. Girls do not want to be men, she thinks, but 'their deepest desire is to be neither male nor female – in short, they wish to be sexless'.[10] This is not because of some innate fear of the female condition, some biological taboo, but, according to Imaizumi, because they realize that becoming an adult woman means playing a subservient role in life. 'They take on this role, knowing that in fact the difference between women and men is really a matter of appearances. And because of this, they also feel that reality and dreams can be reversed simply by changing those appearances.'[11]

This would certainly help to explain the phenomenal success of the most popular girls' comic ever staged by the Takarazuka. Called 'Rose of Versailles' it was later made into an atrocious film strictly for the Japanese market by the French director Jacques Demy. Young Japanese girls showed more taste than the producers, however, for the film was a disaster, unlike the play and the comic.

In this story the roles are indeed reversed: the hero/heroine called Oscar is born a girl not long before the French Revolution, but she is raised as a boy to succeed in a family of generals. Thus this androgynous fair-haired soldier becomes part of Marie-Antoinette's personal bodyguard. The tale ends with Oscar somewhat incongruously dying for the Revolution. But this piece of Republican sentiment inserted by the authoress, Ikeda Riyoko, for the edification of her readers, cannot be the main reason for the popularity of the work. More important by far is the ambiguous love life of the heroine.

Growing up as a boy, her best childhood companion is André, the son of her nanny. After she helps him out of a nasty situation when he almost kills Marie-Antoinette, his loyalty knows no bounds: in true samurai fashion he vows to die for her if necessary.

But, despite living like a man, Oscar falls in love with a Swedish nobleman named Von Felsen and she spends one romantic night dancing with him, wearing a dress. Still, once in drag, always in drag, and she soon changes back into her military uniform. Besides, Von Felsen is already in love with Marie-Antoinette.

But then André, in his turn, declares his ardent love – for Oscar, not Von Felsen – repeating his willingness, his desire even, to die for her. Moved by this demonstration of sincerity Oscar 'throws off her aristocratic cloak and reveals her beautiful self'. On stage the chorus goes: 'I love you for your nobility, your purity, your beauty, your friendly smile, your white face [sic], your shining blue eyes. I love you and I want to die . . . '

Of course this will not do, she being an aristocrat and he a humble groom. The dénouement is classic Kabuki: first André is conveniently shot during a fight between the rebels and the troops. But the most splendid death is reserved for the true hero/heroine: Oscar, fair hair waving, blue eyes flashing, storms the Bastille and is struck down by a great big cannon ball, 'blood colouring her breast red as the rose of Versailles'.

In the grand finale André, standing tall in a chariot drawn by Pegasus snorting clouds of dry ice, pulls Oscar's spirit on board and side by side the ill-fated lovers ascend to a spectacular

Heaven, where their love will burn in eternity. The entire cast assembled at the pearly gates, hardly visible now because of the flashing lights and the dry ice, erupts in the following boisterous finale:

> In the flashing golden light
> The guardsman's uniform burns red
> Fair hair waving, she takes the reins of the chariot.
> Ah, those blue eyes, ah, the waving fair hair.

This may sound like a piece of Nazi propaganda staged by Leni Riefenstahl. And indeed the popularity among young Japanese girls of late Visconti films, Helmut Berger and the extravagant posturing of David Bowie, does seem to point to a taste for the Teutonic bizarre. I once asked a Takarazuka actress what had attracted her to this type of theatre. *Akogare*, she replied, a word usually translated as 'yearning', 'longing' or even 'adoration'. It is used for people, places and ideals that seem impossibly far away, such as for example *akogare no Pari*, Paris of our dreams. It is the idealization of the unattainable, something like building paradise fifty miles from Osaka.

Possibly modern young girls look at fantasy European aristocrats in the same way that Edo audiences watched swaggering samurai on the Kabuki stage: far away and imbued with special powers. But to see this simply as a form of power worship, as some people do, is to miss the point. For there is a streak of deep pessimism running through this, or at least a tragic sense of *mono no aware*, the pathos of things.

The heroes never win. Kabuki samurai almost invariably end up getting killed or else killing themselves. Oscar and André can be lovers only in Heaven, never in this sad, evanescent world of ours, just like Chikamatsu's tragic heroes and heroines more than three hundred years ago. As the end poem of another girls' comic says: 'Look at the dreams of young girls, who grow up: they are like castles of glass.' Growing up inevitably means tragedy.

The young girl's dream, then, is to go as far away as possible, sexually, emotionally, geographically, from everyday reality: in outer space or in fantastic pseudo-European palaces, or even a combination of both, such as in 'The Adventures of Puppy From the Star Called Mill'. The sets of this play are pure Takarazuka paradise: eighteenth-century French ballrooms in a grand palace filled with tall, long-legged, short-cropped girls in blonde wigs, Donau monarchy guardsmen's uniforms and speaking in artificial mannish voices – Erich von Stroheim in Japanese teenager land.

The adults in this piece are all corrupt, deceitful and calculating. The young girls suffer terribly, but are rescued in the end by two androgynous extra-terrestrials, who can make time stand still and wear pendants with which they can see through people's hearts. This causes havoc, for unspoken thoughts become known to all and as one of the E.T.s points out: 'The people in this world live by cheating each other. They know they are being cheated, and so they cheat others. That is their way of life.'

The despair about growing up and the hostility to the adult world are remarkable for their intensity. The Takarazuka heroines echo the sentiments of Midori, the young girl destined to be a prostitute in Higuchi Ichiyo's 'Growing Up': 'If only she could go on playing house forever with her dolls for companions, then she'd be happy again. Oh, she hated, hated, hated this growing up.'

Although the Peter Pan syndrome of wanting to remain young for ever is certainly universal, growing up is perhaps even harder than usual in a world of contradictory values. We have already noted that marriage is a necessary condition of Japanese adulthood. In traditionally arranged marriages suitability still takes precedence over love. At the same time fashionable magazines for the young preach the relatively new gospel of romance. So what is a poor girl to do? In a sense every girl who conforms to tradition finds herself in Midori's predicament. The Takarazuka theatre tends to attract such girls and its answer to them is nothing more than a variation of the traditional attitude: resign yourself to the demands of society and for the rest, dream on, young lady, dream on. Dream of being an eternal virgin or, better still, sexless in a world of European aristocrats and friendly E.T.s.

Although this is not quite so apparent in the Takarazuka theatre, the dream has a darker side too. Girls' comics show a strong preoccupation with evil, horror and death. This is no doubt partly due to the universal horrors of puberty, during which physical changes can be traumatic. Identification with monsters in girls' stories is understandable at an age when many see themselves as ogres in the mirror every morning.

Typically, though, evil is no more absolute in these comics than it is in ancient Japanese mythology. Even the blackest characters can be redeemed by demonstrations of remorse and sincerity. In one comic, entitled 'The Glass Castle', set in a timeless London, Marisa, who has the 'character of an angel', is bullied, tortured and cheated in the most brutal manner by her evil stepsister, Isadora, who even murders their father, a benign but distant figure in the best Japanese patriarchal tradition. But she does repent in the end, confessing how lonely she felt and how miserably inferior to her angelic sister.

This is the magic formula, for she is instantly forgiven. Like a true Japanese heroine, angelic Marisa even decides to sacrifice herself, taking the blame for her sister's murder. 'This world is as breakable and impermanent as glass,' says the balloon above Marisa's head, as she is taken to prison where she soon perishes.

Isadora could be seen as Marisa's adult alter ego. Marisa lives in the all-forgiving world of childhood, the 'dimly white dream-world'. Apart from murdering her father, Isadora more or less behaves in the way that adult society expects. Family, marriage, and social status are always uppermost in her mind, but, as she laments in the end, 'one small lie leads to worse and worse crimes'. It is inevitable that Marisa, or childhood if you like, is sacrificed. Time cannot stand still, there is no turning back.

This pessimism is deeply rooted in Japanese culture. In Western Europe and especially in the USA people, ideally, if not always actually, choose their own destinies in an imperfect world which we have to improve ourselves. Thus many youthful fantasies, of girls and boys, are about saving the world from the devil. The world is not innately bad, it is only sinful human beings who make it so. This, at least, is the Christian, or more precisely, the Protestant view, in the shadow of which many Occidentals are raised, whatever their creed. And as a large number of Hollywood heroes have shown us, the possibilities for individuals to change the world are infinite. That, after all, is why Mr Smith went to Washington and Mr Deeds to town.

Also, up to a point, there is more tolerance in the West of nonconformist behaviour. In Japan, as the proverb says, 'a nail that sticks out, must be hammered in'. The pressure to conform outwardly to fixed rules of conduct is far more relentless than it is in Western countries. Most Japanese are mortally afraid of seeming odd or strange, or in any way different from their neighbour. 'Ordinary' (*heibon*) is cited by the majority of Japanese as the most desirable thing to be.

This is not the same as the Christian idea of being good. Conscience, that disturbing angel with whom so many literary characters in the Occident wrestle, carried to its Protestant extremes means that one's only confidant is God. It is to Him and not just to society that one is ultimately responsible. Conscience, in the Christian sense, transcends society. Japanese etiquette does not.

Conscience, individual integrity, being true to oneself, or whatever one wishes to call it, appears to count for less than the expectations of the social environment one happens to live in. When things go wrong, it is rarely the responsibility of individuals. A person might take responsibility and even commit suicide, but this too is a question of doing the right thing; for the one who takes his own life is not necessarily the one who did anything wrong. Good Marisa dies for bad Isadora.

Thus, in fiction at least, people are always the victims of fate, never its master. It is society, often described as dirty or polluted (*yogoreteiru*), which makes people bad, not the other way round. Society forces one to act, to behave as expected, which may not be the way one feels at all. Though being 'true to oneself' is not a Japanese maxim, and behaving as expected is certainly the proper way, there is still a nagging conflict here: for the more one is forced to act, the further one drifts away from the pure state of childhood. Thus the emphasis in so many Japanese stories, including those on the Takarazuka stage, is on the ending of youth, on the destruction of it, rather than its flowering. The alternative is to remain an eternal youth or virgin, neither man nor woman, which is the same as not growing up at all.

Although girls' comics in the West are full of impossibly beautiful young men with long eyelashes and stars in their eyes, they are still unmistakably men; they drive around the Riviera in sports cars and get the lucky girl in the end. In Japan, as we have seen, they are more ambivalent, and sometimes get each other. The word for these androgynous young heroes is *bishonen*, beautiful youths.

Covers of girls' comics – and sometimes boys' comics too – often feature *bishonen*. Takarazuka heart-throbs are often *bishonen*. And teenage television *talentos* in their frilly shirts and dimply smiles are *bishonen*. A famous artist called Takabatake Kasho, currently back in vogue, drew nothing but *bishonen* and his work can still be seen in popular comic-books. A typical Kasho picture is of a *bishonen* in a short kimono or sailor-suit being instructed by an older boy in horse riding or fencing. Another popular motif is the *bishonen* in distress, bullied by older boys, for instance, or caught in a frightful storm at sea. He is invariably rescued by an older mentor who puts his protective arm around the boy's willowy waist. When the pretty youth is pictured alone, he is playing a flute like Adonis, or staring dreamily at the moon, or taking a bath, or lying down in the grass, a book of poetry in his sensitive hands.

The atmosphere in these pictures seems unmistakably homoerotic; and so, of course, it is. One girls' comic, called *June*, is quite explicit, showing decadent English aristocrats in velvet dinner jackets seducing exquisite *bishonen* under the crystal chandelier. This magazine is rather exceptional in that it represents the extreme fringe of girls' tastes, but it is suffused with the same heady combination of high romance and fascinating evil that characterizes those girls' comics which do not feature naked boys having sex with decadent old men.

One example will, I think, suffice to make the point. Rather cryptically entitled *Ribbon on the Clock* this story is about a *bishonen* who loses his mother when he is only twelve years old and lives off prostitutes at the age of fourteen. He goes on to marry a rich countess, but then decides that men are more in his line and becomes a gay gigolo.

It is hard to say what goes through the young minds of readers of this comic (readers who are not overtly homosexual, that is). Letters from the readers do not tell us much either, though one girl gives us a hint by writing that 'this fantasy world sends pleasant shivers up my spine'. Obsessed as the Japanese are with appearances irrespective of the real meanings behind them, we

can perhaps assume that many of these youthful dreamers are
much more innocent than the contents of their dreams would
suggest. As innocent, at any rate, as the crowds of schoolboys
buying souvenir chains, fishnet tank-tops and other paraphernalia
of New York's gay underworld during the first Tokyo
screening of the film 'Cruising'. They thought it was *kakko ii*, a
Japanese expression almost untranslatable in English. The
Italians have a word for it: *bella figura*, to cut a dash.

Possibly many young girls – and to a lesser extent young
boys – feeling that their natural inclinations are being slowly
crushed by an adult world that forces them to be calculating and
conformist, find an outlet in homosexual fantasies, too remote
from their own lives to be threatening: a faraway romantic ideal
like 'the Paris of our dreams'. *Bishonen*, homosexual or not, are
treated in a similar way to vampires and creatures from outer
space. Outcasts all, they are the pure, eternally young victims of
adult corruption.

To be sure, homoerotic fantasies, in more or less disguised
forms, are common among adolescents everywhere. Certainly it
is much less of a taboo in Japan than in the West. Homosexuality
has never been treated as a criminal deviation or a sickness. It is a
part of life, little discussed, and perfectly permissible if the rules
of social propriety – getting married, for instance – are observed.

Homosexuality as an ideal form of love goes back further than
girls' comics or the Takarazuka theatre. For many centuries
homosexuality was not just tolerated, but was actually encouraged
as a purer form of love. As in Sparta and Prussia, to name

the two most obvious examples, this was part of the warrior tradition: gay lovers make good soldiers, or so it was hoped. At the height of samurai power during the Kamakura period (1185–1333) women were despised as inferior creatures, 'holes to be borrowed' for producing children. Only manly love was considered worthy of a true warrior.

By the beginning of the Edo period, at the start of the seventeenth century, the wars were over, the battles fought. The two-and-a-half centuries of Tokugawa rule were a time of frustrating peace during which the samurai had hardly any recourse to use their weapons at all, except to cut an uppity peasant or merchant down to size. The ideal Way of the Warrior, however, stayed long after it had served its purpose. It was further refined as a form of dandyism. This includes the ideal of manly love and the cult of the bishonen. Its manifestations were rather like the belated chivalry of European knights in the middle-ages, which also became fashionable when knights had little else to do but organize jousts and pine after unattainable ladies.

Nothing was thought to be purer than the torment of unfulfilled love. In the words of one of the last troubadours:

> And now I see with its own fulfilment
> that love dying which once wounded sweetly.[12]

Knabenliebe among the samurai is possibly the closest thing the Japanese ever had to this Western ideal of romantic love. The *Hagakure*, an influential eighteenth-century treatise on samurai ethics, teaches that 'once love [for a boy] has been confessed, it shrinks in stature. True love attains its highest and noblest form when one carries its secret into the grave'.[13] In an essay on this text Mishima Yukio wrote that 'the *bishonen* embodies the ideal image – he lives an ideal of undeclared love'.[14] This is quite different from the sexual passions ending in romantic suicides in Chikamatsu's plays, or the maternal sentiments of golden-hearted prostitutes.

To be sure, homosexual chivalry, like the love of knights for their ladies, was based on sacrifice, or more precisely, it being Japan, death. Because loyalty could no longer be proved on the battlefield, the ideal of sacrificial suicide took its place. The difference with Chikamatsu's love suicides is that there death was often the only way out of a socially impossible match. While between males it was more a sign of pure loyalty and honour – or so it was presented.

There are many tales of *bishonen* following their older mentors in death by slitting their bellies in various ways, one of which was to make an excruciatingly painful incision in the shape of the friend's name. This kind of self-torture was in fact probably quite rare, but the many stories about it attest to the power of the ideal.

The ideal is still alive in various more or less disguised forms. Movie heroes in gangster films such as Takakure Ken and Takahashi Hideki, for example (their golden age was the late 1960s and early 1970s), came close to fitting the *bishonen* ideal: very young, very handsome, very pure of heart, devoted to their mothers – Ken-san in particular would always talk about his mother – frightfully sincere, endearingly naive and full of what the Japanese call *stoisizumu* (stoicism), meaning that they rejected female love.

Instead, they had each other. They would almost invariably perish together in a splendidly suicidal last stand against an impossible majority of enemies. Often this orgasmic finale is the only time one sees them looking happy. One such film, starring Takahashi Hideki, lasts about 90 minutes but during 80 of them the hero looks miserable, pining and straining and plunged in the depths of some vague despair. His instinctive sincerity and naive purity are constantly repressed and trampled on by the bad, bad world. But in the end salvation comes: he is allowed to die.

Joined by his best friend, another melancholy desperado, he sets off to face certain death at the hands of the superior forces of the enemy. The title-song swells on the soundtrack and the two heroes swap jokes, indulging in happy horse-play like school-boys on the way to a fair. Laughing they slip off their kimonos to reveal fierce tattoos. They rush into the enemy headquarters and after about five minutes of brave and savage butchery they are both felled in the mud, half-naked and covered in blood. They link arms and croak out their last sweet nothings; they are happy at last.

The point of this is that the tradition in Japan of homosexual chivalry helps to explain the homoerotic overtones which are evident in popular romance even now. Certainly, the cult of the beautiful youth is not limited to young girls and homosexuals in Japan. The *bishonen* ideal is as much a part of Japanese aesthetics as the geisha and the female impersonator, and in a way all three are linked.

The writer Nosaka Akiyuki once said that a true *bishonen* has to have something sinister about him. The vision of pure youth, because of its fragility perhaps, reminds one of impermanence, thus of death. It is no coincidence that the film 'Death in Venice', after Mann's novel, continues to be a huge success in Japan.

On the Kabuki stage the *bishonen* is played by an *onnagata*, just as Peter Pan is traditionally acted by a woman. This is Mishima's description of a traditional female impersonator in a short story:

> Masuyama sensed . . . something like a dark spring welling forth from this figure on the stage, this figure so imbued with softness, fragility, grace, delicacy and feminine charms . . . He thought that a strange, evil presence, the final residue of the actor's fascination, a seductive evil that leads men astray and makes them drown in an instant of beauty, was the true nature of the dark spring he had detected.[15]

In one of his most famous novels, *Kinjiki* (*Forbidden Colours*),[16] Mishima created the archetypal evil *bishonen*, his male version of Tanizaki's Naomi. Yuichi is the perfect male work of art. He is taught by an old misogynistic novelist how to feign emotions, to pretend to love women — 'an impersonation is the supreme act of creation' — in order to destroy them. His beauty is both natural and totally artificial, like that of an *onnagata*. But it cannot last long and this is precisely the point.

Inagaki Taruho, scholar and connoisseur of Knabenliebe, wrote that 'female beauty matures with time. But the life of a young boy is just one day in summer, the day before the blossoms come out. The next time you see him, he's just an old leaf. As soon as he becomes a young man, smelling of genitals it's all over.'[17]

In *The Great Mirror of Manly Love* (1687) Saikaku wrote: 'If only young boys could stay the way they are, it would be truly wonderful. Enshu, the great rake, used to say that young boys and potted trees should never grow.' The bonsai, the artificially dwarfed tree, tortured and twisted in its infancy to prevent it from growing up, is an aesthetic symbol sometimes used to describe the Japanese themselves. Be that as it may, it is certainly connected to the dream of stopping youth for ever in its fleeting moment of purity. But unlike Americans who try to hang on to the illusion of youth as long as is medically possible, Japanese on the whole resign themselves more gracefully to its fleeting nature. In fact, youth is beautiful precisely because it *is* so short-lived. The cult of cherry blossoms, which only last about a week in Japan, is the same as the worship of the *bishonen*, and the two are often compared.

Taken one small step further it is the cult of death. According to the *Hagakure* the 'ultimate meaning of the cult of young boys is death'. And one of Saikaku's homoerotic tales begins: 'The fairest plants and trees meet their death because of the marvel of their flowers. And it is the same with humanity; many men perish because they are too beautiful.' In the same story the young hero, dressed in a white silk kimono embroidered with autumn flowers, says to himself: 'Beauty in this world cannot endure for long. I am glad to die while I am young and beautiful and before my countenance fades like a flower.' He then proceeds to rip his stomach open with a dagger. Whatever one may think of Mishima's rather laboured looks, similar thoughts were certainly in his mind when he undertook his extraordinary suicide.

The sacrifice of kamikaze pilots in the prime of their youth spoke to the popular imagination for the same reason. Still celebrated in comics and films, they are always compared to cherry blossoms. Indeed the explosive coffins they crashed into American battleships were called cherry blossoms (Ōka).[19] The songs and poems they left behind are full of blossom images, such as this haiku written by a 22-year-old kamikaze pilot just before his final departure:

> If only we might fall
> Like cherry blossoms in the spring
> So pure and radiant.[20]

Death is the only pure and thus fitting end to the perfection of youth. *Bishonen* heroes in history, legends and modern pop culture almost always die. One contemporary example, again from a girls' comic, is Angeles. He is a very Japanese hero despite his blond locks and the fact that he is only half-human (the human half being his father, a Japanese 'descended from the gods', and his vampire half coming from his mother, a German and thus responsible for his 'impure blood').

The only one to understand the purity and beauty of Angeles is a young girl who 'loves Heine, Byron, Shakespeare and love'. Her mother is evil and the story ends with a terrible battle with the mother and the police on one side and the girl and Angeles on the other. The vampire/*bishonen* dies in the girl's arms, watching his castle burn in a surrealistic blaze: 'That castle was our youth', are his last, anguished words.

The most famous *bishonen* in Japanese history is arguably Japan's most popular hero, immortalized in numerous plays, films, books, comics and television dramas. Quite recently he was played on television by the feyest of *talentos*, Sawada Kenji. He was born in the twelfth century and his name was Minamoto no Yoshitsune. Like many *bishonen* Yoshitsune was raised by an older man, in his case a fatherly monk in a Buddhist temple near Kyoto – monks, one would believe, had a special fondness for taking good care of *bishonen*.

Despite his fey good looks, in the legend at least, Yoshitsune became a skilled and enthusiastic sword-fighter. One of the most famous legends of his early years is his first encounter with Benkei, the giant warrior monk. It is said to have taken place on the Gojo bridge not very far from where the main Kyoto railway station is now.

Benkei needed funds for his temple and to this end he promised to rob a thousand passers-by of their swords. He got as far as 999 with relative ease when he saw a slender, effeminate youth approaching, playing a melancholy tune on his flute. At first the giant monk refused to fight this girlish boy who was looking up at him through his long, curled eyelashes. But he needed the money badly and drew his sword. As if by some miracle, however, he was completely outclassed. With a few elegant flicks of his slender wrist Yoshitsune managed to knock down the giant with his painted fan.

This is a typical detail in *bishonen* legends, for there is always some sinister power hidden under the beautiful exterior, almost something supernatural. Young boys or simpering *onnagata* smashing an overwhelming opposition of sword-wielding fighters by waving their pretty fans or ornamental daggers like fairy wands is one of *the* clichés of Kabuki drama.

Japanese audiences are fascinated by the idea of spirit overcoming force, and skill overcoming brawn. Not for nothing is judo a Japanese invention. Little Davids are forever meeting brutish Goliaths in boys' comics, perhaps because many Japanese like to see themselves as spiritual Davids in a world of boorish giants. Many were convinced that the show of pure spirit of kamikaze fighters would shock the enemy into defeat. And people were literally crying in the streets when the giant Dutchman Anton Geesink beat a smaller Japanese at judo during the Tokyo Olympic Games: an old, especially cherished illusion was shattered.

Benkei was so impressed by his *bishonen* adversary that he swore to serve him for the rest of his life as a retainer. This also fits a common pattern: every Don Quixote needs a Sancho Panza and behind every winsome *bishonen* stands a strongman. The Kabuki play *Suzugamori*, for instance, opens with a fight in the execution ground between the bishonen Shirai Gompachi and a gang of rough palanquin-bearers. His easy, flick-of-the-wrist victory so impresses Banzuin Chobei, the legendary protector of the slum-dwellers of Edo, that this encounter is, as they say, the beginning of a beautiful friendship.[21]

At first Yoshitsune and Benkei enjoyed some notable successes, culminating in the victory over the Taira clan at the battle of Dannoura in 1185. But this also marked the beginning of their downfall. Yoshitsune's youthful high spirits and recklessness, which made him so popular ever after, evoked the disapproval of his scheming, cautious brother Yoritomo, who wanted him dead.

Yoshitsune, followed by Benkei and the rest of his faithful retinue was forced to retreat and this was really the part of his life about which people still get excited. The battle at Dannoura is for history books but his downfall is the stuff for legends. It was also, typically, the most passive part of his life. In the No version of the legend Yoshitsune is played by a child actor, and on the Kabuki stage by an *onnagata*. All the heroics are henceforth performed by his retainers, most of all Benkei.

One episode in particular is still celebrated on the stage.[22] In order to pass through the road-blocks set up by Yoritomo, Benkei is disguised as a monk and Yoshitsune as his humble porter. At one point they draw the suspicion of the officer in charge, who makes Benkei recite the subscription list that monks would normally carry with them. Of course Benkei has no such thing, but he wildly improvises a history of Todai temple, filled with arcane theological references.

This splendid piece of bluffing works, and the party starts to move off. But then, suddenly, somebody recognizes Yoshitsune, who has been lagging behind. Benkei, realizing that all is lost, takes one final, extreme measure: screaming abuse, he starts to beat the porter (his own master), scolding him for causing this delay. Seen in the context of his time, this was almost as painful as a devout Catholic priest trampling on an image of Christ. This demonstration of desperate loyalty so moves Yoritomo's officer that he lets them go. Pity for the underdog (*hōganbiiki*) gets the better of him.

But the end inevitably comes, albeit a little later. Yoshitsune is surrounded by the enemy at Ōsho in the north-east. Even Benkei's ferocious fighting cannot keep them off for ever. In one version of the story Benkei stands nailed to the door, transfixed by enemy arrows. But his figure is so awesome that nobody dares approach him, until his corpse falls over by itself. In another version he rips his stomach open and tosses his entrails into the faces of the attackers as a gesture of utter contempt.

After this Yoshitsune calmly disembowels himself, 'plunging his sword into his body below the left breast, thrusting it in so far that the blade almost emerged through his back'.[23] His wife, and his seven-day-old daughter are then killed by a faithful retainer called Kanefusa.

The beauty of the tale is that the passive hero falls like a cherry blossom in full bloom, although, if we are to believe a curious legend, he later reappears in a kind of resurrection as no-one less than Ghengis Khan. As Ivan Morris pointed out, 'he increasingly came to fit into an archetypal pattern of the mythical hero whose destruction guarantees the survival and stability of society'.[24] This is a prerequisite of most youthful Japanese heroes.

Yoshitsune reminds one of Adonis, that other flute-playing *bishonen* killed in the prime of his youth. Both are scapegoats, young and pure of heart, dying and coming alive again in an endless cycle of life and death; symbols of the crops as well as of human birth and mortality. According to one theory the cult of

Adonis was actually a death cult;[25] the same could be said of Yoshitsune.

In their tendency not to distinguish between fact and fiction — in historiography, that is — it is typical of the Japanese to have projected this universal myth on to a historical figure. It is equally typical that a man, who, according to a contemporary witness, was a 'small, pale youth with crooked teeth and bulging eyes', would in legend become an incomparable beauty. Anyone dying such a poignant death just had to be as perfect as a cherry blossom.

8

The Hard School

The road to manhood is a hard one. This hardness is dramatized in most cultures by an initiation of some sort, usually involving a test or quest; anything from killing a lion to finding the Holy Grail. In Europe this reached its aesthetic pinnacle with the exploits of legendary medieval knights such as Parsifal.

In Japan the loss of childhood purity is as traumatic as it is anywhere else, and the test of manhood, not to mention the infinite variety of Grails, is an endless source of myth and drama. As in most places, the main requirements for passing the tests are blind perseverance and a victory of mind over body. Both are considered to be particularly great virtues by the Japanese who like to claim a unique spirituality as their cultural heritage.

The nearest thing the Japanese have to the European knight-errant is the type of roaming samurai polishing his swordsmanship and soul by beautifully executed murder. One such seeker recently became world famous: Miyamoto Musashi, artist, killer and mystic. Not only are Musashi's exploits rendered in many versions on television, in comic-books and films, but he has become something of a cult figure in the U.S., where it is said that businessmen read his martial pontifications (*The Book of the Five Rings*) in order to penetrate inscrutable Oriental business practices.

About the real Musashi we know little, except that he was born around 1584. The rest is legend. There are many, sometimes wildly conflicting, versions of his life, a Musashi to suit all tastes, as it were. It will suffice to describe here a kind of composite

Musashi as he appears in contemporary films and comic-books. As such he still remains the archetypal young hero seeking to overcome the hurdles on his way to manhood.

Like many Japanese tough guys, Musashi lost both his parents at an early age. And like Yoshitsune, he displayed a talent for murder very soon after: when he was thirteen, to be exact. At that tender age he managed to beat a warrior to death with a stick. He further earned his spurs as a typical Japanese hero by fighting on the losing side in the battle of Sekigahara in 1600 when Ieyasu succeeded Hideyoshi as shogun. The rest of his life was spent mostly on the road as a free-spirited drifter, with a penchant for sleeping in caves and peasant huts.

He can not have been very prepossessing in the flesh, for, most uncharacteristically for a Japanese, he refused to take a bath lest he be caught without his sword. Equally unusual was the fact that he never married. In fact – and this is not so unusual with Japanese heroes – he was something of a misogynist, for ever fighting off the advances of women who threatened to pollute the purity of his quest. In one famous scene, repeated in every version of his life, he conquers his natural desire for an attractive woman by standing stark naked under an ice-cold waterfall.

In a way he was a nihilist, or *nihirisuto*. In this he was like many macho heroes in Japan. Entirely without social ties, he lived for himself alone. But to be a true *nihirisuto* one must be a cynical adult. And Musashi spent most of his life as an ageless adolescent seeking the Way. His story is the story of an education. Yes, he broke all the rules of polite society, but only to attain his single-minded goal: enlightenment through the Way of the Sword.

The Way of the Sword involved much killing, to be sure. But it was all in a good cause, for it was more than simply an efficient method of murder; it was, above all, a spiritual way of murder. Musashi and many heroes following in his footsteps were exponents of what the Japanese call *seishinshugi*, meaning the victory of spirit over material things. It helps if this spirit is Japanese. The term is not really used for foreigners who, one can only assume, lack such a thing. Another expression often used in this context is *konjo*, also meaning spirit, but more in the sense of overcoming hardship. *Gutsu* (guts) is also common. A well known Japanese boxer even appropriated it as his name: 'Gutsu'

Ishimatsu. (The name Ishimatsu, incidentally, was taken from a historical figure called Mori no Ishimatsu, an outlaw blessed with a great deal of *gutsu*.)

The stories, films and comics about heroic seekers, starting with Musashi, are called *konjo mono*, spirit things. *Seishinshugi* or *konjo* often involves a Zen-like suppression of reason and personal feelings, a blind devotion to direct action and an infinite capacity for hardship and pain. The education of Musashi is in fact a form of Zen training. Unfortunately the suppression of one's own — no doubt illusory — feelings means a total disregard for other people's feelings too, resulting in a kind of supreme selfishness. It must be said, however, that most of Musashi's victims were fellow seekers.

The most famous of these was a young boy called Sasaki Kojiro. In one comic-book version Kojiro is depicted as a typical *bishonen*, who spends as much time challenging Musashi to duels as he does snuggling up to him in bed.[1] In a film version of this story Kojiro is played by Takakura Ken, sporting a splendid pony-tail, and Musashi is played by a specialist (in 1955 when the film was made) in pure, young heroes, Nakamura Kinnosuke.[2]

We are shown how Musashi gradually learns the mystique of murder, or how to be spiritual while hacking the other man down. Kojiro's weakness is that he does not understand all this. He is too eager, too cocky, too . . . unspiritual. 'All that counts is the strength of the sword', he claims. His master, watching Musashi, replies: 'It is not the sword that must be polished but the soul.'

When Musashi goes off, alone, to the island where their final duel is to take place, he is held back by his faithful female admirer, who follows him wherever he goes. He brushes her off as if she were a troublesome fly: 'The sword knows no pity,' he growls, 'the Way of the Warrior is hard.'

The battle on Ganryu island is swift. Musashi cracks his opponent's skull with one swoop of the long sword that he had cut out of an oar on his way to the island. On the way back home he stares at his hands, covered in blood, and thinks of all the people he has killed. In a moment of disgust he throws his sword overboard. From then on he will fight duels only with a wooden sword. He has seen the light at last. The end of his quest is in sight: the more one wins, the more futile it all seems – or, as a samurai master in a Kurosawa film put it: 'The most skilful sword never leaves its sheath.'[3]

Images of Musashi vary a great deal. In the last scene of one film we see him running towards us from a mountain of corpses, jumping with joy at his murderous skills, shouting: 'Lock, Mummy, I've won!' Although this may be a penetrating insight into the pathology of the adolescent mind and arguably the closest to the real truth of the matter, it is far from typical.

The usual Musashi is an introspective brooder, a kind of samurai Hamlet, agonizing about his life. The cause of his mental anguish is, I think, also the key to understanding his timeless popularity. His selfish brutality can be ascribed perhaps to the especially brutal times he lived through – the sixteenth century was a period of constant war. And the philosophical musing that sells so many books in the USA serves to justify his often bizarre violence.

But the real issue is Musashi's dilemma, the Gordian knot of his quest, so to speak, which is still valid in modern Japan: how to reconcile self-effacement and Zen with self-aggrandisement and the sword.[3] If one takes away Zen and the sword, neither of which plays much of a role in modern Japanese life, one is still left with a paradox every Japanese adolescent has to face: how to be an achiever, which is what is expected, particularly by one's family, and a self-effacing conformist at the same time? Or, to put it in another way, how to be a winner in a society that discourages individual assertion?

One cannot fight without getting blood on one's hands. One cannot be a winner in this world without being tainted by it; without losing one's purity. What then is the answer? Blind, unthinking action based on pure instinct, like a finely tuned animal? Or fighting with a wooden sword, perhaps? Or dropping out of society altogether? The nature of Japanese society makes this dilemma especially dramatic, but every adolescent in the world has to face it. Hamlet and Musashi simply express themselves in different ways.

Let us look at another, more recent example of a struggling adolescent: Sugata Sanshiro, the hero of Kurosawa Akira's very first film – and of his second, made a year later, too. This film is in many ways the prototype of all his later films, for like 'Ikiru',

'High and Low', 'Red Beard' and most other Kurosawa pictures, it is about a spiritual transformation, about the Test.

The story of Sugata Sanshiro closely resembles Miyamoto Musashi, for it too revolves around the spiritual side of a martial art; judo this time. And again we see the initiation of a boy into manhood. Like Musashi, Sugata is naturally gifted and soon after joining his master who, like Musashi's, lives in a temple – his business, after all, concerns the spirit – he becomes an invincible fighter. But the master is not satisfied. Sugata might know all the tricks, but not the true Way; or, as he puts it in typically vague terms: 'the Way of loyalty and love. It is the ultimate truth and only through it can a man face death.' In the manner of a Zen *koan* (a deliberately absurd question attempting to bypass logic) the master orders his pupil to die. 'Die!'

Without blinking Sugata jumps into the pond behind the temple, where he spends the entire night staring at the moon, hanging on to a wooden post for dear life. It is his initiation. At dawn his spiritual crisis comes to an end: he has seen the ultimate truth in the beauty of nature. Wildly excited he jumps out of the pond to tell his master the good news.

He is now on his way to becoming a man. But how to remain pure in a man's world? This dilemma soon comes to the test. The father of the girl he loves challenges him to a fight. His first reaction is to opt out. Then he decides to accept but to lose on purpose. Both solutions are perfectly decent, but are they pure? Are they not examples of just the kind of deceitfulness that pollutes the adult world? The spiritual human being must be innocent, says the master; and to be innocent means rejecting the calculating decency of society. To remain pure he has no choice but to choose direct action and he proceeds to throw his opponent like a sack of potatoes.

This kind of character-building is quite different from the old-fashioned British way. A gentleman is a good loser, affecting a studied nonchalance to what is after all only a game, old boy. To the likes of Musashi and Sanshiro being a good loser is not only unnecessary, it is utterly contemptible, for it shows a lack of purity.

The Japanese ideal raises another question: assuming that 'loyalty and love' include compassion for others, how can this be reconciled to the Zen idea of direct, unthinking action? The answer is perhaps that it does not include compassion, at least not the Christian ideal of principled, indiscriminate compassion. One is compassionate when one feels compassionate not when out of principle one ought to feel compassionate, for this would seem to be emotionally dishonest. (Reality, one often feels, is less ideal; compassion in Japan, as in most countries, is often directly related to what one can get in return.)

A recent, highly controversial example of this way of thinking is the Japanese attitude to refugees, particularly from South-East Asia. The government has been consistently reluctant, to put it mildly, to help the refugees. And the almost total indifference of the majority of Japanese leaves this policy entirely unchallenged. Only after tremendous pressure, mostly from Western nations, has a handful of 'boat people' been admitted with rather bad grace to Japan. Both the government and the press – not normally pro-government – have complained about this unwelcome pressure and they are probably quite genuine in their lack of understanding of what all the fuss is about. The distress of foreigners, and despised Asians at that, is simply too far removed from daily Japanese reality for people to feel any real compassion.

I do not wish to suggest that the Japanese people are mean or merciless. On the contrary, when it directly concerns someone near and dear, they show great compassion. But, unlike many Europeans, most Japanese lack the taste for revelling in shows of compassion for those with whom they do not feel in any way involved. In Japan this is called honest. Others might call it a lack of empathy. Both are true.

In the case of Sugata Sanshiro and fellow hard men, love and loyalty mean the same thing. It is the love one feels for the Master or the leader. It is expressed in obedience and sacrifice. Thus it is highly personal and anti-individualistic at the same time.

The suppression of rational thought, as propagated by Zen heroes, tends to make people more than usually self-centred. The rational mind considered to be impure by the likes of Musashi and Sugata, is thought in the West to act as a censor of impulsive emotions, which might be unreliable, and thus dangerous. Although the final purpose of a certain kind of much-admired nihilism in Japan is to do away with emotions altogether, the Japanese are far from that goal. Perhaps more than most people, the Japanese, on the whole, are ruled by their emotions. When a

Westerner tries to argue his case, he will say, often in desperation: 'But, don't you see what I mean?' His Japanese counterpart, only just able to keep his anger in check behind a rapidly collapsing wall of etiquette, will say: 'But, don't you see what I feel?' One appeals to a common sense of logic, the other to his own heart.

Not everybody is equally inclined to submit to the spiritual tests of manhood. In Japan, as everywhere else, there is a Papageno to every Tamino. In fact the sensuous Papagenos who cannot be bothered with the spiritual rigours of *seishinshugi* are probably the vast majority in Japan. There is an interesting distinction in the Japanese language between the two types: the *koha*, the hard school, and the *nanpa*, the soft school. Musashi and Sanshiro are of course very much part of the *koha*.

Typical characteristics of the *koha* are *stoicizumu* (stoicism), meaning a fondness for hardship and a horror of sex, and purity coupled with a fierce temper. The *koha* hero has to prove his manhood over and over again in fights. The *nanpa* is of course the direct opposite of all this: its members lack spirit, hate fights and like girls. Unlike the *koha* heroes, the soft school is rarely celebrated in popular culture. The ideal school is the hard school, which is imbued with an odd kind of nationalism.

There is, for example, a boys' comic called *I Am a Kamikaze*, featuring a young, very *koha* hero named Yamato Shinko. Yamato is also the classical name for Japan (after the original Kingdom), often used jingoistically, as in *Yamato no tamashii*, the spirit of Yamato.

Young Yamato has all the right requisites for his heroic role. To start with he is diminutive: spirit makes up for size – Japanese spirit versus foreign brawn. He also has large, flashing eyes under his bushy eyebrows, glittering with youthful integrity. He is utterly without humour – a joking *koha* hero is as rare as a laughing samurai. He is short-tempered, of course, and stoic to a fault, pure in his emotions and single-minded in his cause . . . in short, he is the perfect image of the romantic suicide pilot.

Actually, our hero himself is not. His father was. But to his chagrin and disgrace, he crashed his plane without getting killed. So, to make up for his shame, he wants to make a perfect man out of his son. The comic strip is about Yamato's education, just as

the stories of Musashi and Sugata Sanshiro are about theirs.

It is unusual for one's father to be one's master as well. But Yamato's father is adept at the same bullying techniques for which spiritual masters are known. He hits his son on the head with bamboo swords, he ties him to a pier during a howling storm, he throws him off a speeding truck, in short, anything short of pushing bamboo splinters under his nails. Yamato, being a spiritual lad, is duly grateful for this parental guidance.

The main test of his strength is not staving off his father's attacks, but those of an older boy called Wada, who seems perfect in every way: handsome, big, clever and strong. His spirit leaves something to be desired, however, for he cheats at school and he tends to hide behind the criminal back of his father, the local gangster boss. Unfortunately he is stronger than Yamato, who loses every fight. But, far from being a 'good loser', he remembers his father's lesson: 'Once a Japanese man decides to do something, he carries it out to the bitter end, at all costs.' This reminds one of a popular song about kamikaze fighters:

What a wonderful child!
He fought until the very end
With the pride instilled by his mother,
Infused with the Japanese blood of three thousand years
('The Kamikaze's Mother')

Yamato Shinko does manage to beat the bigger man in the end with his bamboo sword. The place of the final battle is . . . Ganryu island, the very spot where Miyamoto Musashi killed Sasaki Kojiro. Yamato does not kill his opponent, though. Instead, beating him against all physical odds, he shows him the Way to true manhood.

'Your example of perseverance has purified my heart', the reformed bully says gratefully, as he lies next to his victor on the beach, hand touching manly hand. Just then the sun rises from the sea, the red rays beaming gloriously as in the Imperial Navy flag: the spirit of Yamato is victorious again, the shame of the surviving kamikaze wiped out.

One of the most extraordinary manifestations of *koha* worship is not a legend or comic story, but actually takes place, once a year, in an old baseball stadium in Osaka. Every August since

1915 (apart from an interruption during the war, when baseball was deemed foreign and frivolous) the entire Japanese nation becomes excited about high-school boys trying to win a baseball tournament.

There they stand, the fifteen-year-old *koha* heroes, in straight rows, heads identically shaven, unsmiling faces staring straight ahead, flags held proudly aloft, and songs solemnly sung. Television commentators muse about the 'purity of youth' and 'sincerity of spirit'. It is all eerily reminiscent of those similar rows of wolf-faced German youths, described by their leader as 'lean and slim as greyhounds, lithe as leather and hard as Krupp steel'.

These shaven baseball youths are the objects of a cult in Japan that has little to do with sport; it is the cult of youthful purity. Long articles appear in the press about the austerity of their training, and ominous tales are told of entire teams disqualified because one person got drunk or fooled around with a girl. Famous critics and writers, even in such left-leaning periodicals as the *Asahi Journal*, out-do each other in literary hyperbole describing the 'essence' of this national event. To cite just one example out of many, the film director Shinoda Masahiro called the high-school heroes 'Japanese gods' and the baseball park a 'holy ground' where the game is propelled by 'divine power'.[4]

It does not make much difference if it is judo, swordsmanship or baseball: it is the process that counts, the spiritual education. One of the great propagandists of this yearly feast was a journalist of the *Asahi Shimbun*, a leading Japanese newspaper. Though sometimes referred to as 'the Voice of God', his actual name was Tobita Suishu. This is what he wrote about his beloved event just after the war: 'If high-school baseball should become just a game, it would lose its essential meaning (*hongi*). High-school baseball should always remain an education of the heart; the ground a classroom of purity, a gymnasium of morality. Without this spirit, it will lose its eternal value.'[5]

No wonder an obituary of this master mentioned that he taught Japanese youth 'not only how to throw and hit a baseball, but also the beautiful and noble spirit of Japan'.[6] And no wonder that the present chairman of the Highschool Baseball Association let it be known that it is 'official policy' not to let foreign reporters into the ground. Presumably they would sully the holy purity of the event.

The spiritual purity of *koha* adolescents can lead to far odder things than baseball, however. Let us turn once more to the world of make-believe: a film made in 1966 by Suzuki Seijun, called 'Elegy to Fighting' ('Kenka Eregee'). The hero of this still very popular movie is typically *koha*: a close-cropped, humourless, sexually frustrated schoolboy called Kirokku. Growing up in the turbulent 1930s, Kirokku has two passions: violent fighting and a very pure girlfriend. The two passions are intimately related for his love is more than just a platonic obsession. It is the worship of an idol, so inhumanly pure that it cannot be physically expressed. Every time she comes near him, he stiffens like a terrified soldier on parade. 'Michiko, oh Michiko,' he writes in his diary, 'I can't relax with a girl, so I fight instead.' Whenever there is a gang fight against another school, Kirokku leads the way, jumping on his enemy from trees like a mad bushman, smashing people's skulls with bamboo swords, or running wild in the class-room, clearing the way with his primitive version of karate chops.

Yet he is not simply a bully, for his emotions are always pure, his actions dictated by his heart. And, true *koha* type that he is, he is not afraid of pain himself. In one scene, after being rude to a brutish military instructor, he is made to walk barefoot over a path strewn with nails. The hero does not flinch.

The film is a witty and straightforward account of his fighting schoolboy career until the last scene, which is rather ambivalent. It dawns on the boy that there are bigger fights than the schoolyard squabbles which he finds increasingly pointless – like Musashi, Sanshiro and all the rest of his comrades in arms, he no longer finds just winning enough; there has to be a spiritual awakening to give it all meaning.

One day he walks into a coffee-shop near his school. In the corner he sees a stranger reading a newspaper. He does not know why, but the man is like a magnet, mesmerising Kirokku by his presence. The man is none other than Kita Ikki, the radical nationalist and theorist behind the militarist coup of 1936, during which several cabinet ministers were assassinated. Kita himself was to be executed.

In the next shot, Machiko, the hero's idol, comes to say goodbye before entering a convent (they are from a southern part of Japan, where a number of Catholics still live). On her way back she is caught by a heavy snowstorm. Picking her way on a narrow road, she is roughly pushed out of the way by a column of marching soldiers on their way to spread the Japanese Spirit in China. The cross she wore round her neck is trampled on by their heavy, stamping boots. Then, suddenly, we hear an announcement at the local railway station: it is 26 February, 1936, the day of the militarist uprising.

The juxtaposition of these events is confusing, for it is unclear what the director really means to say. Is he implying that the pure violence of the adolescent is robbed of its purity once it is put to use by a corrupt society (the marching soldiers, the coup)? Perhaps, but if so, it is not suggested anywhere that the cult of the *koha* is in any way connected with that peculiar form of Japanese militarism which led to the attempted coup in 1936.

Perhaps the presence of Kita Ikki suggests that the incident itself is an example of youthful purity. Although, as we shall see later, that is indeed a widely held belief in Japan, it is unlikely that Suzuki subscribes to it. Perhaps the clue lies in something Suzuki himself once said: 'I hate constructive themes. Images that stick in the mind are pictures of destruction.'[7] Thus the film is literally an elegy to fighting, to the innocent violence of youth. It is a nostalgic yearning for that period in life when one can be self-assertive without being punished too severely, that time of grace before the hammer of conformity knocks the nail back in. The hero is still innocent, because his feelings are sincere.

The purpose or effect of this sincerity is secondary to the emotion itself. As the father says when he watches his son, Yamato Shinko, fight like a madman: 'I bet it's for some childish cause, but at least he's throwing himself into it with all his heart.' Thinking back to his own kamikaze days, he turns to the reader and says: 'Yes, the boy's certainly got my blood in his veins.'

The pure schoolboy using his fists or his bamboo *kendo* sword to settle his scores evokes such nostalgia precisely because the Japanese, perhaps more than most people, realize that as an adult in the corrupt world, he will no longer be able to behave in this way. And besides, however hard, stoical, manly and macho he may be, there is always one person who is finally stronger; the only one to beat the fanatic ex-kamikaze comic-book martinet at his own *kendo*-bashing contest is that sweetest, meekest, softest of creatures . . . his own wife, the mother of Yamato.

9

The Loyal Retainers

Honour, obligation and sacrifice form the basis of the most popular play ever written in the Japanese language: 'Chushingura' or 'The Tale of the Forty-Seven Ronin.' But before we enter into the details of this extraordinary drama, it is necessary to reflect a little upon the meaning of social obligations in Japanese life.

To begin with, every Japanese is born in debt: first of all to his ancestors for keeping the family going, next to his parents for bringing him into the world. Until the end of the Second World War he would have been in debt to the emperor, as the supreme father, too, but this burden has been lifted now. This kind of debt by birthright is called *on*.[1]

There is another kind of *on* which one passively collects, as it were, as one goes along. *On* is owed to teachers, helpful relatives, the baseball coach, the landlord, professors, matchmakers and go-betweens, company directors, in short anybody who does one a good turn in the course of one's life. Life in Japan is to a large extent ruled by these mutual debts and obligations. And people can be quite ruthless about them, as one can easily find out to one's cost. It is quite possible, for instance, for a person to receive a phone call from an old acquaintance reminding him of a favour done for him years ago, followed by a request for a favour in return. He might have quite forgotten about that favour, and the request might come at a very inconvenient moment, but, if he wants to survive in Japanese society, it is essential for him to comply.

Not only do favours have to be returned, but they must be returned in kind. This is called *giri*: a sense of honour; a sense of duty; a debt of gratitude. Too large a favour would put the other person in debt and too meagre a return would not be enough, and would even possibly be taken as an insult. The potential for one-upmanship here can be imagined and indeed many Japanese have turned it into a fine art, outfoxing each other in a never-ending competition for the most advantageous debts. Politicians have to be past-masters to be effective. The national passion for presenting gifts is of course part of this game and foreigners over on business, being deluged with expensive watches, jewels and other luxurious knick-knacks do well to remember that it is easier to give than to receive, for it puts the obligation firmly on the recipient.

It is not always easy to distinguish this custom from real bribery, particularly when cash changes hands. It is a common practice, for instance, for mothers to pay substantial fees to teachers in return for a helping hand in securing a place for their children in prestigious schools. This is just one example of semi-institutionalized bribery. There are many, many more, from paying landladies to rent an apartment, to offering cash to politicians to arrange an aeroplane deal.

Society is also ruled by the duties and obligations of hierarchy. This is not strictly a matter of favours; it comes closer to the debt one owes one's parents. Japanese groups are structured very much like families, with the senior members playing the part of parents over the juniors who are the children. It is expected, however, that childlike submissiveness by the 'children' is rewarded by parental indulgence from the top. This can make life at the top as strenuous as at the bowing and scraping bottom; more so, perhaps, because the responsibility for anything that may happen, even if it is entirely beyond his control, rests on the broad shoulders of the parent. Children, after all, have no responsibilities.

This is why real power is often difficult to locate in Japanese organizations; it is diffused as much as possible so that nobody has to take complete responsibility for anything, and thus risk losing face. The nominal head, whether a company director or the emperor himself, is usually a powerless symbol, a kind of talisman, an ikon on the wall, a vacuum like the empty chamber in the holiest part of a Shinto shrine. Ultimate responsibility lies in that empty space; in other words, with nobody.

None the less, although real power is slippery, the hierarchy itself is not. And because people define themselves in terms of the hierarchy and the group any attack on the system is an attack on themselves. In this sense one owes *giri* to oneself, or rather to one's position in the hierarchy, which often comes down to the same thing. A personal loss of face means the entire group loses face. This clearly will not do, so people go out of their way to avoid it. It means, among other things, that individual incompetence is often tolerated to an astonishing extent. Others will discreetly cover up for the offender.[2]

This network of social obligations, duties and debts, largely Confucian in origin but thoroughly Japanized in time, is far more complex than this bare outline suggests. Relationships on different levels, depending on rank and age, are all subject to different rules, which in turn much depend on time and place. There is an endless amount of nuances and subtleties in the social code, not all of which can be rationally explained. Although the code was devised to avoid the unexpected – the scourge of Japanese life – the Japanese are not simply etiquette-crazed robots either. In the end much comes down to what the Japanese call *kan*, feeling. When a confused foreigner asks a Japanese how he knows exactly the right tone to adopt to a certain person, the Japanese will cock his head to one side, hiss through his teeth, stress that foreigners could never understand, and then mention the word *kan*.

In a way he is right. For to acquire this sensitivity it is almost a necessity to be brought up as a Japanese, to have one's brains plugged into the social computer bank, as it were. The code is internalized in the same way that Christian morality is internalized in most Westerners. But when a Japanese is unplugged, by going abroad for instance, the computer can go berserk, for unlike Christian morality the Japanese code is not thought to be universal – it applies only to Japanese.

The problem with obligations is that they can conflict. What happens, for example, if a favour owed to a friend clashes with the debts towards one's parents, or one's employer? And what happens to the obligations of politicians belonging to a faction led by a man so deeply involved in a bribery scandal that he has to be removed from the party in order to save it? This is exactly what happened in the case of ex-prime minister Tanaka. The answer is that while the leader, Mr Tanaka, has to be officially removed, his faction bearing his name remains as strong as ever. (So, at the time of writing, does Mr Tanaka himself, but behind a safe screen.)

The worst case is when obligations go against one's feelings of humanity, *ninjo*. Or, more precisely, when the conflict between different obligations results in inhumanity. Then the computer can even go haywire in Japan itself. Kabuki plays are full of characters obliged to kill their own children to save their lords or sell their wives to brothels to repay their debts. This conflict between *giri* and *ninjo*, duty and humanity, is one of the basic themes of Japanese drama. This was true of the traditional theatre of the Edo period; it is, by and large, still true today, on television, in books, comics and films. It is a problem the Japanese still wrestle with, both actually and vicariously in the imagination.

And this, finally, brings us to that archetypal *giri-ninjo* play, its bible, so to speak: 'The Tale of the Forty-Seven Ronin'.[3] Almost every writer on Japan, from Ruth Benedict to Arthur Koestler, has used this play as a model and, perhaps a little perversely, I shall follow in their illustrious footsteps. One just cannot avoid 'Chushingura'. For rarely, if ever, has one story captured the imagination of an entire nation to this degree; certainly no single story has caught as many aspects, as succinctly, of Japanese life, as this one.

Like many Japanese legends, it is based on historical fact, but has gone through as many different versions and interpretations as Shakespeare's plays. These, in brief, are the facts: On 14 March 1701, a country baron called Asano Naganori, whilst preparing an official reception for an imperial envoy from Kyoto, attempted to assassinate another nobleman, senior in rank, called Kira Yoshinaka. He only managed to wound the older man, but this was still such a serious breach of etiquette that the shogun ordered Asano to commit suicide in the ritual manner by slitting his belly. His lands were confiscated and his retainers set adrift as ronin, literally 'wave men', masterless samurai without a job.

All they could do now was plot their revenge. Kira knew this and had them closely watched. Nevertheless after much patience, deprivation and cunning they managed to break into his mansion on one unusually snowy night in the winter of 1703, and killed him. Their mission finally accomplished, they were arrested without further fuss and after some serious deliberation it was decided that they too, like their master, could disembowel themselves.

This was an act of great clemency, for *seppuku*, better known in the West as *hara-kiri*, belly-slitting, was an honourable warrior's death and not the punishment of common assassins, which is, of course, what they really were. Apparently the shogun was swayed by reasoning such as this by the Confucianist scholar Ogyu Sorai:

> For the forty-six samurai to have avenged their master on this occasion shows that they have followed the path of keeping themselves free of taint, their deed is righteous . . . if the forty-six samurai are pronounced guilty and condemned to commit *seppuku*, in keeping with the traditions of the samurai . . . the loyalty of the men will not have been disparaged.[4]

The loyal retainers, after dying their gory deaths, intestines spilling out of their gaping stomach wounds, became instant folk heroes. And they have remained so ever since. People still make pilgrimages to their graves, crying a ritual tear when contemplating the melancholy beauty of the forty-seven cherry trees planted in their memory.

Already in 1706, only three years after the event, they were immortalized in a puppet play by Chikamatsu. Kira became Ko no Moronao and Asano, Enya Hangan. After that a new play came out almost every year, but the finest and most famous was 'Chushingura', written in 1748 by three men, the most important of whom was Takeda Izumo. This play is still performed every New Year in the puppet as well as the Kabuki theatre. It has also been filmed countless times and, like the play, is usually screened around New Year, the most 'Japanese' of feasts. And it is still part of every Japanese schoolboy's mythology through comics, books and television serials.

Why did Asano, or Hangan as he shall henceforth be called, try to kill Moronao? For him to have even contemplated such a thing in the strict society of eighteenth-century samurai, one can only assume that the provocation was unbearable. It was, after all, as if a fairly minor Nazi dignitary, a Gauleiter, say, had tried to kill Himmler. Moronao must have been a very nasty man indeed. This is certainly the view of the many playwrights who all depict him as an arch-villain, with the face of a lecherous sadist and the gravelly voice of the devil incarnate.

But why did Hangan do it? Nobody knows. There is no reason on record anywhere.[5] As to Moronao (Kira), there is some historical evidence that he was a most benevolent gentleman, greatly loved by the people he ruled. This much is actually known about the incident: Hangan was in charge of receiving an imperial envoy. This kind of ceremonial occasion was of great importance to warriors who probably had little else but protocol to occupy their time. Moronao was to be Hangan's mentor, being an experienced man in this type of procedure. In return, to pay off his debt, Hangan was obliged to give him a present of some kind and the common assumption — it is only an assumption — is that he did not give enough. Consequently Moronao treated him with disrespect, which then provoked Hangan, out of *giri* to himself, to retaliate violently.

There are many other versions of the story, however, all of which reflect the attitudes of the audiences at which they were aimed. This offers a unique insight into the way of thinking of various sections of Japanese society. For example, the eighteenth-century audience of the Osaka puppet theatre, for whom Takeda Izumo wrote 'Chushingura', consisted mostly of merchants with a taste for erotic intrigues. Thus in the theatre version the repulsive Moronao smacks his lecherous lips every time Hangan's young wife is around and makes several attempts to seduce her. She rejects him politely but resolutely. And out of sheer spite Moronao then taunts and bullies Hangan beyond the point of endurance, comparing him to a carp stuck in a well, ignorant of the world outside.

This is of course a classic *giri* conflict. What can Hangan do? *Giri* to his own honour and his personal inclinations tell him to defend the honour of his wife, but *giri* to his seniors in rank and ultimately the shogun himself, dictates the utmost restraint. It is one of those 'damned if you do, damned if you don't' situations that make stage-samurai squirm to the delight of plebeian theatre audiences.

In another version, often used by story-tellers who were especially popular with carpenters, roof-builders, mat-makers and other urban craftsmen, Moronao deliberately humiliates Hangan by teaching him the wrong protocol, causing him to lose face in front of the imperial mission. By appearing in the wrong clothes and preparing the wrong food, he is like a courtier arriving in fancy dress at a formal palace reception. Story-tellers have a field-day describing his blushes, his embarrassed stammering and his effusive apologies to the offended envoy.

In reality, this is highly unlikely to have happened, for in such a breach of etiquette Moronao would have seemed as culpable as Hangan. He was supposed to be the teacher, after all. But never mind that. It is typical of the gamesmanship that goes on in any organization, especially one that is based on a strong sense of hierarchy and a long apprenticeship, such as, for instance, any Japanese artisan trade.

As in old-fashioned English public schools, losing face this way is a part of the initiation. The seniors establish their authority by exposing the ignorance of the newcomer. In Japan where the relationships between seniors and juniors or masters and apprentices are especially severe, this type of situation would strike a very responsive chord.

I myself have worked as a lowly assistant to a photographer in Tokyo, whom, in the traditional artisan style, we had to call Master. Neither the Master, nor his other assistants would tell me what to do, let alone how to do it. One had to 'learn with the body', as they called it. One acquires the *kata* (the proper form) by sharpening one's 'instinct', by making mistakes and being humiliated. 'But you never told me . . . ' is never an excuse in Japan.

This is sometimes hailed by Japanese and foreigners alike as a wonderfully spiritual way of doing things: like Zen training – do not think, but learn to act 'instinctively'; hit the target with your eyes closed. This is all very well in its way, but it is also open to the kind of abuses Hangan had to suffer in the story-teller's version. Many Japanese, especially those at the bottom of the ladder, or those who have not forgotten the experience, know this. That alone would make Hangan a popular hero.

The ensuing revenge by the loyal retainers, led by Oboshi Yuranosuke (Kuranosuke in real life) has been interpreted in as many different ways. The wartime version stresses blind loyalty to the leader. The forty-seven braves are like soldiers of the Imperial Army valiantly offering their lives for the greater glory of emperor and motherland.

Later dramatizations project a completely different picture. The national broadcasting company, NHK, did two different adaptations for television, in 1964 and again in 1975. Here we see the loyal retainers putting up a heroic last stand against the oppressive Tokugawa government. They are fighters for '*demokurashi*' *avant la lettre*, resisting the feudal system.

In another modern version, a film entitled 'Salaryman Chushingura', the action is transplanted to a modern trading company full of agitated salarymen sweating in their suits. Here, naturally, the emphasis is on corruption and office politics, showing the evil Moronao as a fat-cat on the take. Lastly, but not to be despised, is an animated version featuring dogs. It is called 'Wan Wan Chushingura' or 'Woof Woof Chushingura' in English.

The one common factor in all versions is *giri*: everybody acts out of duty, paying off his or her debts. The retainers are obliged to kill Moronao out of *giri* to their leader. They have to finish what he left undone, for otherwise his spirit could never rest in peace. We have already noted how dangerous Japanese spirits can be when they have an axe to grind.

But Moronao would have been their enemy even if Hangan had not died; an insult to the leader is an insult to them all. I remember being present at a party of a well-known avant-garde theatre group in Tokyo. All went well until a drunken actor – not a member of the group – said something mildly disparaging to the director. Without a moment's hesitation all the male actors of the group pounced on him. He had to be carried out on a stretcher.

The point is that the leader need not necessarily be right; it is the ikon on the wall, the regimental flag that is attacked, not a mere mortal. Just as Moronao may well have been a kindly man, there is evidence that the real Hangan was a dangerous hot-head. One of his most popular retainers Horibe Yasubei, admitted as much, stating in a letter that his lord had acted rashly and was clearly at fault.[6] But, he said, once a samurai starts a quarrel it must be fought to the bitter end.

The *giri* of the loyal retainers is not based on logic, or reason, or on who is right or wrong, but on something quite different, called *iji o haru*, which could be translated as 'persisting in one's position' or 'showing the strength of one's sincerity'. This is why it does not matter one iota what the real reason was for Hangan's attack on Moronao: as long as the retainers remain faithful to their lord's cause. Everyone can read into the story what he wants to, even the retainers themselves. This is the principle of Japanese leadership: keep the goal as vague as possible, so that it can suit all purposes. Ideology can be changed from one day to another – as it was in Japan when the war was lost – and the leaders can still claim *giri* from people of the most diverse private persuasions.

Hangan and his faithful retainers were *makoto*. The usual translation of this is 'sincere', but that is not exactly what it means. Sincerity in English means being honest, frank, open, meaning what one says. *Makoto* is more like 'purity of heart', believing in the rightness of one's cause, irrespective of logic and reason. No matter if the position one has adopted is wrong or untenable: it is the purity of motive that counts.

The critic Sato Tadao has explained this in terms of early childhood experience: 'When a child does something it thinks is good, it becomes deeply disturbed if an adult, for whatever reason, considers it to be bad. The child then learns how to assert its emotional position by misbehaving. It can't explain this rationally. All it knows is that if it does not assert itself in this way, it ceases to exist as a human being true to its own heart.'[7] The effectiveness of this kind of behaviour can be considerable among a people not used to explaining themselves rationally.

Ivan Morris has pointed out that Japanese heroes are almost always fighters for a lost cause.[8] The more untenable the cause, the purer the motives are seen to be. With nothing to gain and everything to lose, sincerity can be the only possible motive. To a large extent the actions of the forty-seven loyal 'wave men' were dictated by circumstances. They were educated, but unemployed and cut off from society. They felt powerless and superfluous. Perhaps because of this, they felt ready to die. Nevertheless their cause was – is – seen to be noble. The same thing could be said about such modern 'wave men' (or women) as the 'Red Army' terrorists in Japan. They too have been admired in certain fashionable quarters, not so much for their ideology as for their moral fortitude in a corrupt society.

In fact they have lost most of their support by now and most Japanese would profess to despise them. Why should this be? After all, do they not fit quite neatly into Ivan Morris's definition of the failed Japanese hero? Perhaps the following incident, or rather the reaction to it, will explain.

In 1972 five members of the 'Red Army' tortured to death eleven comrades, including the husband of one of the leaders, for their alleged lack of loyalty to the group. They then seized a mountain lodge, taking the proprietress hostage. This was followed by a siege involving 1,500 policemen and lasting ten days of televised national hysteria, during which one of the police officers was shot dead. Finally after a long build-up the police moved in using helicopters and out came the terrorists, unkempt, unshaven and exhausted.

The following week the *Mainichi Shimbun*, one of the three largest and most prestigious Japanese daily newspapers, always careful to follow majority opinions, came out with the following editorial entitled 'Thoughts on Revolutionists'.[9] It is worth quoting exactly as it appeared in the English language edition:

Differing from other extremist groups, their creed is 'direct resort to arms'. It was believed that after exhausting their ammunition, they would either take their own lives or die fighting hand-to-hand with the riot police.

But this belief was utterly *betrayed* [the italics are mine]. When the police rushed in, the five youths . . . offered almost no resistance. At the last moment they had lost all will to fight and meekly submitted to arrest. Such an attitude brings out their 'pampered spirit!' . . .

The student radicals boasted of fighting to the finish. But no, they were not that high-spirited when the end came. Why? It all boils down to their pampered way of thinking . . . I recall a friend in my high-school days who staked his life for the cause he believed in . . . he was finally caught by the Special Thought Police in 1941. As was usually the case in those days, the result was the loss of his life . . .

The radical fanatics have no fear of being killed; they are carrying out their anti-social activities on a surety of life . . . The second point which comes to my mind is the extreme gap existing between the parents and their sons and daughters. The father of one of the extremists hanged himself to death the same day his son was arrested. He took his life in a tragic gesture of apology for his son's actions.

The feelings of the other parents, no doubt, are in common with that of his father. But the sad part of it is that the father's death cannot fill the spiritual gap existing between father and son . . .[9]

This was not written in 1703, or 1944, but in 1972. The most serious charge against the students was not that they brutally murdered eleven of their friends and a policeman or that their cause was, at best, absurd, but that they failed to die for it. They lacked sincerity, their hearts were not pure. The editor who wrote this piece could hardly be called a sympathizer with the 'Red Army's' goals. But whether he was or was not was beside the point. It was the purity of motive that counted. If only their attitude had been right, they could have been heroes.

For the same reason, people who are by no means militarists can still be sentimental about the brave suicide pilots in the Second World War: they were *makoto* and their deaths were *rippa*, splendid. And following the same reasoning, admirers of the forty-seven ronin, then as now, certainly need not subscribe to the samurai ethic. But they died for their cause. (Significantly the estate of Moronao's unfortunate grandson was confiscated, as he had failed to fight to his death in defence of his grandfather.)

In the Edo period there used to be a very useful custom – for the authorities, that is – whereby one could petition the government to look into an alleged injustice: crippling taxes resulting in widespread famine in the countryside, for instance. The snag was that the case would only be investigated if the petitioner was ready to die. Thus the government killed two difficult birds with one stone: the sincerity of the request was proved beyond doubt and the authorities were rid of a potential troublemaker.

Modern Japanese hero-worship still bears the traces of this. People admire rebels and fanatical non-conformists (the more fanatical the better). But in the end, these heroes must destroy themselves, like the incompatible lovers of Chikamatsu. Rebels may make waves when jumping headlong into the water, but by drowning they have to make sure that the surface returns to its unrippled self again. Japanese audiences, in short, love to see their heroes die. The certainty that non-conformity will ultimately be punished, that the stubborn nail will be knocked back in, is in a way reassuring. It lends a fixed contour to the lives of people who are terrified of the amorphous. It enables them to see the precise limits of their existence.

To illustrate this further, let us turn to a film based on another historical incident, somewhat similar to the tale of the forty-seven ronin. It is called 'Disturbance' ('Doran'), made in 1979 and based on the '26 February Incident' (*ni-ni-rokku jikken*), already mentioned.

Briefly told, the real incident went like this. Japan was slowly recovering from a severe economic depression in the 1930s which had been especially hard on the rural population.[10] Much of the popular blame fell on 'greedy industrialists' and 'effete, corrupt politicians'. Anti-government feelings ran especially high among young, often frustrated army officers, many of whom were recruited from the depressed rural areas. A number of them were in favour of ridding the country once and for all of parliamentary democracy, such as it was, and establishing military rule, basking in the glorious light of the infinitely benevolent emperor.

On the night of 26 February 1936, a thick blanket of snow covered Tokyo, just as on that fateful night when the forty-seven braves assassinated Moronao. More than 1,400 men from the Army's First Division moved stealthily out of their barracks and in the following few hours a former Prime Minister, a General, a Minister of Finance and several other dignitaries were stabbed or shot to death in their beds. It was a brutal act of terrorism. And the army authorities, realizing that things had gone too far, for the time being anyway, squashed the rebellion. The leaders were duly executed. But the parliamentary system did not recover from the shock until General MacArthur put it back on its shaky feet again nine years later.

One leader of these right-wing fanatics in the film is played by the most popular hero of the 1960s, the pure, righteous, stoic, handsome Takakura Ken himself. Had this Japanese Robert Redford made a volte-face and turned into a cinematic baddy all of a sudden? Not a bit of it. The publicity slogan of the film was: 'When men were still men and women still women.' And the programme notes informed us that 'although times change, one thing never will: the Japanese spirit (*Nihonjin no kokoro*)'.

Like the loyal retainers, the militarists are heroes. The assassinations are shown as heroic and romantic deeds of young idealists – honourable examples of purity and *giri*. Though the film suggests that they were primarily motivated by the sorry plight of the rural population, in fact their professed ideology was far more abstract, echoing the nationalist propaganda of pre-war education.

At the trial they were mostly concerned with the purity of their motives.[11] They repeated vague slogans about their adoration of the emperor and their burning patriotism. And how the access to the throne was monopolized by evil men who had to be destroyed so that the emperor in his eternal wisdom could see the truth of their ways. They were particularly anxious that he would 'understand their feelings'. In short, the whole exercise was a typical example of *iji o haru*, a violent demonstration of sincerity. And in so far as people in 1979 were still prepared to admire them for it, they were remarkably successful.

An important element in their heroism (the same is true of the forty-seven braves) is the directness, the unthinkingness of their actions. There is a certain type of hero who appeals greatly to the popular imagination. He is the opposite of the stereotyped image people generally have of the average Japanese – which is perhaps partly why he is a hero. One is often told, usually by Japanese themselves, that losing one's temper is tantamount to losing face. This may be so, but this type of hero is nothing if not quick-tempered. Hangan is of course the prime example: his first reaction is to use his sword.

There is another character in 'Chushingura' called Honzo, the retainer of a samurai, Wakanosuke. His behaviour is in direct contrast to that of Hangan's loyalists. His lord is the first to be insulted by the evil Moronao. And Wakanosuke, like Hangan, immediately wants to retaliate. Honzo calms him down and without telling him, bribes Moronao to stop bullying his master. In other words, he is a prudent politician, a diplomat keeping his lord out of trouble. This same Honzo further distinguishes himself by pulling Hangan back when he tries to kill Moronao, thereby preventing the murder in the hope that Hangan will thus be spared the ultimate punishment. All this may seem entirely honourable to us, but it had the effect of making him the forty-seven ronins' most hated man, besides Moronao himself.

Honzo's kind of prudence is anathema to the true Japanese hero. He only manages to redeem himself near the end of the play, by deliberately provoking his own death at the hands of one of the loyal retainers. All is then finally forgiven as he chokes out his last words: 'I held [Hangan] back because I thought he wouldn't have to commit *seppuku* if his enemy did not die. My calculations went too far. It was the worst mistake of my life . . .'[12]

The contrast between the hot-headed rebels who murdered cabinet ministers in 1936 and the officers who opposed them follows the same pattern: the rebels belonged to the so-called *Tendoha*, the 'Imperial Way Faction', and the more prudent staff officers were part of the *Toseiha*, the 'New Control Faction'. Members of the latter group belonged to the old military establishment and many of them favoured diplomacy and politics rather than direct action; while the officers who staged the coup, who, one must add, often felt left out of army politics,[13] behaved exactly according to Sato Tadao's description of the young child screaming to be heard.

Direct action, as opposed to calculating diplomacy, was also the difference between the heroic Yoshitsune and his supposedly evil brother Yoritomo: in fact Yoritomo was one of the ablest politicians in Japanese history,[14] achieving far more than his impetuous brother, but that was precisely his crime – politics are by definition polluted by the calculating ways of society.

Makoto, writes Singer in *Mirror, Sword and Jewel: A Study in Japanese Characteristics*, 'spells readiness to discard everything that might hinder a man from acting wholeheartedly on the pure and unpredictable impulses that spring from the secret centre of his being.' This way of thinking is a synthesis of Shintoist purity, Zen and the philosophy of Wang Yang Ming, the sixteenth-century founder of the Idealist School of Confucianism, which advocates 'taking the leap from knowledge into action'. This school of thought was much in vogue during the Edo period and it served as an inspiration for many suicidal fanatics, including Mishima Yukio.[15]

This emphasis on blind, emotional action points to one of the most significant paradoxes underlying Japanese culture: namely that a highly conformist people obsessed with etiquette and social propriety should ideally be swayed by their innermost emotions. But then it may not be so paradoxical after all, for it is precisely this tendency that makes restraint and good manners such a necessity.

It does put *giri* and other social obligations in an interesting light. For while *giri* is ostensibly part of a social system to keep the wilder and more unpredictable emotions in check, it can just as easily be employed as an excuse to give them free rein. After all, any amount of fanaticism can be excused in the name of *giri*, particularly as rationality is not only not a necessity, but not even really desirable.

It is, however, private inclination restrained to bursting point that provides the real tension in Japanese drama. The consummate Japanese hero, admired even more than the honest hot-heads, never breaks out wildly immediately. Of course he is not calculating like Honzo, for he would dearly love to act at once, but somehow he manages for a while to keep the lid on his emotions. Heroes, especially on the Kabuki stage, are a little like hissing and puffing pressure cookers, and it is at the final breaking point, when they simply cannot take it any more, that the audience applauds. It is the period of enduring the unendurable that makes the final act of revenge so cathartic.

Gaman, meaning perseverance, endurance or sufferance, is as much a virtue as *makoto*. Thus the real heroes of 'Chushingura' are the retainers, especially their leader Oboshi Yuranosuke. In one of the highlights of the play he pretends to be a dissolute and drunken reveller in a Kyoto brothel and his sword is 'rusty as a red sardine'. He even eats raw fish on the anniversary of his master's death, an act of blasphemy and extreme disrespect.[16] And all this when he is in fact thinking constantly of revenge. One is also reminded of Benkei, disguised as a monk, beating his master, Yoshitsune, at the road-block. That, like Yuranosuke ignoring his Lord's anniversary, is a show of true *gaman*.

The way in which the impatient ronin have to be patient, the humiliations they have to endure, in short the *gaman* they have to bear before their final act of violence is the true substance of the play. It is their suffering that moves the audience more than anything else: the twitching mouths, the squinting eyes, the stifled growls show the barely contained hysteria. The initial assassination attempt by Hangan (though not his suicide, which is a big scene) is a mere interlude, while the final revenge is little more than a coda.

In a similar way, one of the most extraordinary and violent books about the 1936 incident, *Patriotism* (*Yukoku*) by Mishima Yukio,[17] does not even describe the incident itself. It is about the *gaman* of a man who did not take part. His closest friends did, and he is compelled by duty as an officer to take action against them. This Lieutenant Takeyama Shinji cannot bring himself to do: he is caught in an awkward *giri–ninjo* bind: duty versus personal feelings. He certainly cannot let them be executed, while staying alive himself. And so the only proper thing to do is to die a traditional warrior's death by cutting his stomach open. The inner conflict of the Lieutenant can only be resolved by personal sacrifice. The rest of the story is a graphic description of the preparation and execution of his ceremonial death, followed by the suicide of his faithful wife.

Death in this rather histrionic tale is directly linked to sex, as it was in Mishima's own life.[18] Just before his suicide, the handsome young Lieutenant, looking 'majestic in military uniform' with his 'dark and wide-gazing eyes [conveying] the clear integrity of youth' makes love to his wife for the last time. But just before that, lying on his mattress waiting for her, he muses about the meaning of it all:

Was it death he was now waiting for? Or a wild ecstasy of the senses? The two seemed to overlap, almost as if the object of his bodily desire was death itself. But, however that might be, it was certain that never before had the Lieutenant tasted such total freedom.[19]

The combination of sex and death is hardly typically Japanese. Moreover, this passage could be read more as an example of the author's rather idiosyncratic psychodrama than as an analysis of Japanese thought. And yet, whatever one might think of the man and his works, Mishima did have a way, albeit a very theatrical one, of putting his finger on aspects of his culture which many of his countrymen prefer to ignore.

It could be said, in fact, that sex and death are the only purely individual acts allowed in a rigidly collective society. We have argued that sex was a kind of quest for freedom during the Edo period – though at the cost of slavery for many young women – and how it is still used as a form of subversion. Death also has a significance that it lacks in the West: it is a release from the dictatorship of the group, while at the same time preserving it. (The same goes for many communist countries, with their high suicide rates, but their governments have not yet been clever enough to institutionalize voluntary death as a virtue.) Death, in other words, may be the ultimate freedom and the pinnacle of purity, but it is also the final and most important debt to pay.

10

Yakuza and Nihilist

The death cult is at its height in the modern gangster film, which is in many respects a continuation of the Chushingura mentality. But here too, one must be careful to keep myth and reality apart. The *yakuza* (gangsters) in the cinema are creatures of the popular imagination, just as the samurai of the Kabuki theatre were, and they bear little resemblance to real members of Japan's highly organized criminal fraternity. This is not always apparent, because real mobsters in Japan are among the greatest fans of this cinematic genre, often imitating the style of movie *yakuza*, proving Oscar Wilde's point about nature mimicking art. (I should also add that one of the main producers of *yakuza* films is the son[1] of a powerful gang-land boss – killed recently by a rival gang – which might have added even further to the romantic image of the criminal underworld.)

Like so much in modern Japan, the cult of the gangster has its roots in the Edo period. The word *yakuza* refers to the lowest numbers in a popular card game. It was the name for gamblers, outlaws, thieves and other petty criminals who drifted around the larger cities and seaports in those days. They did not belong to any specific class, not even the *eta*, the religiously polluted outcasts who lived off animal slaughter and leatherwork (Buddhism forbids the taking of animal life). Some of them were no doubt samurai who had fallen on bad times.

At the same time the Tokugawa government controlled the huge population in the cities by appointing neighbourhood chiefs, rather like village headmen. These men had to command enough respect to be able to keep order. Very often they were firemen or builders, the typical macho occupations of their day. The former in particular had a reputation for derring-do and fierce independence. In the popular imagination these local macho men, called *kyokyaku*, became rather larger than life. Like Robin Hood they had the image of fighting the rich and powerful to help the poor and weak. Banzuin Chobei, the man who helped the *bishonen* Shirai Gompachi in his distress, is a typical example of a kyokyaku glamorized on the Kabuki stage.

During the nineteenth century society became increasingly unstable and corrupt and many of these macho chiefs became involved in gambling and crime until they were virtually indistinguishable from ordinary *yakuza*. But the Robin Hood reputation remained and thus grew the myth of the noble gangster, the *yakuza* with the strict code of honour, vaguely based on the Way of the Samurai. The fantastic exploits of such local heroes as Kunisada Chuji and Shimizu no Jirocho became popular subjects for plays, story-tellers and later the cinema.

The modern film *yakuza* has another predecessor: the super samurai, who is equally caught up in the nobility of his cause. Though the two types have much in common, there are basic differences too. Paradoxically, the samurai heroes are in some ways less traditional, less essentially Japanese than the *yakuza*. They owe much to American Westerns and even to those swashbuckling Errol Flynn vehicles which were highly influential in the early Japanese cinema.

Like the noble drifters of the Wild West, many super samurai move from town to town helping the locals out of trouble, 'punishing evil and rewarding the good'. Their morality is strongly Confucian and deeply rooted in the hierarchical structure of Edo society. A good example of the genre is a series called 'The Bored Bannerman of the Shogun' ('Hatamoto Taikutsu Otoko'). The hero is so bored that he throws a stone up in the air and sets off in the direction where it lands. He always travels incognito, so nobody can guess his high rank.

Like John Wayne or Gary Cooper, he always finds some kind of nasty business to clear up. In one film he runs into a gang of Chinese smugglers conniving with corrupt Japanese dignitaries. He overpowers the gang, tells one of the female prisoners to jump into the sea 'to join her loved one for eternity', and finally scares the corrupt officials half to death by revealing his true identity. This showing of the colours is a climactic moment. As soon as the metamorphosis of the lonely drifter into the shogun's retainer takes place, the villains fall on their knees, hammering their heads on the grounds, frothing at the mouth, making terrified, whimpering sounds.

The audience is satisfied in two ways: the noble samurai is a larger than life father-figure, descending straight from Heaven, like a *deus ex machina*, to deliver the common folk from the villains. But at the same time, he is one of them, until the last revealing moment. We rarely see him in surroundings appropriate to his station in life; he is always disguised as an ordinary townsman, displaying all the habits of that class.[2]

These samurai heroes serve an important function. They are reassuring because they demonstrate the basic benevolence of the social order. After having shown that they can be ordinary people, they re-establish the natural hierarchy. They appeal to a deep strain of conservatism in the Japanese people who would rather go through purgatory than upset the social order.

Though the super samurai has by now all but disappeared from the cinema, he can still be seen nightly on television, often several times in different guises. Very popular, for instance, is Toyama Kinshiro, the judge sporting a plebeian tattoo on his shoulders. Or Mito Komon, a kindly nobleman with a white beard, who always ends each episode with a hearty laugh, after revealing his true identity like a benign trickster.

The idealized samurai, whether as a fatherly superman or a suicidal scapegoat, has been an anachronism for centuries. But, as Ivan Morris has pointed out, most Japanese heroes are anachronistic. As with all forms of hero worship, the reason must be sought with the worshippers. Not only do most people fear social disorder, but there has always existed a strong belief that the past was somehow better and purer than the present (the same was true in traditional China). People seem to be forever gazing back nostalgically at paradise lost: a paradise in which 'men were men and women were women', and in which values were clear and simple. Heroes are by definition reactionary, fighting with their backs against the walls of history.

This stereotype goes back to the earliest Japanese heroes: to Totoribe no Yorozu, for example. His claim to fame was his willingness to die for a lost cause. This, as we have seen before, is not unusual. Neither is the fact that he slit his throat with a dagger after losing the battle against the Soga clan in A.D. 587. The Soga warriors, who consequently became the archetypal villains of early Japanese history, were in the context of their times 'progressives'. It was they who introduced Buddhism, that foreign creed, as the official religion of the Japanese court. Yorozu was a retainer of the Monobe clan; they were the 'reactionaries' in charge of policing dissent and presiding over Shinto ceremonies, thus obviously hostile to novelties such as Buddhism. They were, in short, fighting for a world that was fast slipping away. The very hopelessness of their fight made it seem more noble, because it was more sincere.

A similar situation existed in the middle of the nineteenth century when the anti-Tokugawa factions fought to topple a corrupt and severely weakened government, hoping to reinstate the emperor as the head of a 'modern' state. Many popular heroes who are still celebrated in films, novels and comics were not on the rebel side, however, but, on the contrary, were fighting for the Tokugawa Shogun, the ultimate loser. Some were out-and-out reactionaries, such as Kondo Isamu, who was a member of the highly repressive state police, just as the Monobes had been more than a thousand years before.

Once the new government was established in 1868 its only member to become a really popular hero was Saigo Takamori, who is celebrated for fighting the very government he helped to create. The reason? He loathed the new 'Western' ways of the commercial and political establishment.

This brings us finally to the *yakuza*: they, in the myth at least, are clearly fighting a rearguard action against the corrupt modern age. At no time in Japanese history has the advance of modernity been as swift and perhaps as devastating as it was after the Second World War, particular in the booming 1960s. The samurai had by that time receded too far back into the past to be credible any more, at least to young people who went to the cinema. In the cinema, though not on television, the *yakuza* took over the super samurai role as defenders of the faith, becoming the noble outlaws of modern Japan.

Like popular genre films everywhere, *yakuza* movies are bound to strict patterns. Given the ceremonial nature of so many things Japanese, they are even more ritualistic than similar fare in the West. The important thing about these films is not the story itself, which is basically always the same, but the style, the etiquette even. The life of the noble film *yakuza* – to a certain extent based on reality – is as much governed by elaborate rules of conduct as that of a seventeenth-century samurai. And the *yakuza* film, like Kabuki plays, is a vehicle for actors to display their skills in dramatizing these rules.

I do not use the word ritualistic lightly, for that is really what *yakuza* films are: rituals in a tightly knit world based on a mythical and idealized past. The ritual is also intimately connected with death.[3] In spirit the *yakuza* film is closer to the Spanish bullfight than the American gangster movie, from which it has borrowed certain, mostly sartorial, trappings. The bullfight is a ceremony in which the death of the brave bull functions as a kind of purification. The *yakuza* hero whose death is as inevitable as the bull's, serves much the same purpose.

In a typical *yakuza* film the sequence of events is more or less as follows. In the very first shot we are shown a glimpse of Japanese paradise where tradition still rules supreme: a religious festival, for example, in an old quarter of Tokyo. We hear the piercing sounds of festival flutes and the irregular beat of drums, almost drowned by the rhythmic shouts of young men carrying the neighbourhood shrine on their shoulders. Everyone is dressed traditionally, of course, in happi-coats, now so popular with tourists, or kimonos.

Then, suddenly, a large foreign car – usually of American make – disturbs the scene, loudly honking its horn and dispersing the happy *matsuri* throng. In the car we see a fat man in a loud Western suit, smoking a big cigar. We immediately realize that he is the villain in the piece. The theme has been established: paradise invaded by the modern world.[4]

There are variations on this, but the meaning is always the same. One well-known film starts with the burning of all the ceremonical attributes of an old gang about to break up: the old world has come to an end. This is followed by a succession of shots of big steel and glass buildings, smoking factories and oil refineries: the bad new world is about to begin.

In the next scene the gang of good, noble *yakuza*, all

immaculate in happi-coats bearing the gang's insignia, is helping
the good local people in some worthy, traditional activity: setting
up a street market, for instance, or organizing a festival. And
once again peace is shattered by the bad men, dressed in flashy
foreign suits, aloha shirts and sun-glasses. They kick over the
stalls and rough up a few cowering tradesmen. One of the good
men intervenes and beats up the bullies. Being natural cowards,
they run away, but not before shouting something like: 'We
won't forget this!'

The camera cuts to the fat man again, smoking his cigar and
talking to another fat man in a foreign suit, also puffing a cigar:
the bad gang boss and a corrupt politician. They are discussing
the construction of a big office block. Money passes hands. The
office block is to be built on the site of the street market upon
which the good tradesmen depend for their living. 'Leave it to
me,' growls the bad boss, with a hideous leer, 'I'll take care of
them.'

What we are witnessing is clear: they are the archetypal
Japanese villains since the Monobes fought the Sogas: the
scheming entrepreneur and the conniving politician, both
influenced by wicked foreign ways, both, in a way, 'progressives'. One hardly needs to point out that they are also
caricatures of the architects of the modern Japanese Economic
Miracle. To push the point about the old combination of
foreignness and evil home even further, they are not just
cigar-smoking fat men, they are very often Chinese or Korean
cigar-smoking fat men. (In films set in the immediate post-war
period, Japanese-Americans, rich and arrogant, are popular
villains too.)

Then we are taken back to the virtuous, loyal and pure
Japanese men in their happi-coats. They are listening to their
benevolent boss, the *oyabun*, literally 'father-figure', a sickly old
man, shaking and trembling from some crippling disease, and
always dressed in the simplest of kimonos. The contrast with the
bad *oyabun* could not be greater. The ideal Japanese leader, let us
remember, is more like a symbol than a strong boss; he is the
banner, or, as one unusually perceptive *yakuza* said, 'the portable
shrine on the shoulders of the *kobun* (child-figures)'.[5] His function
is like God: he is always on our side. For this reason he must
remain vague, passive and preferably old and weak – an idol to

protect rather than a Führer. In short, he is like a typical Japanese emperor.

At the same time he has to display an almost maternal indulgence to keep his 'children' happy. His will is never clear-cut but always open to many interpretations. If the young officers in the 1936 uprising had been told that the emperor disapproved of their actions (which he apparently did), they would merely have answered that he was being prevented from seeing the true Way by evil advisers, and their emotional demonstrations would have become more violent still. This indulgence demanded of Japanese leaders in return for loyalty from the children perhaps also helps to explain the frequent lack of control of Japanese Generals over their officers during the Second World War.

The bad *oyabun* is just the opposite: he is strong, vigorous and healthy, a real leader ruling with an iron fist. He is actually much closer to the romantic bootlegging heroes of American gangster films in the Bogart and Cagney era, who were exaggerated versions of capitalist go-getters.

The good *oyabun*, then, admonishes his children to be patient, not to rock the boat, to hold their feelings in check. They may be gangsters, but they are noble gangsters who do not start gang wars at the slightest provocation of mere thugs. This is hard to swallow for the younger *yakuza* who at this point go through their eye-popping, mouth-twitching, nostril-flaring routine, like bulls impatient to enter the arena. But *gaman* (forbearance), for the time being, wins the day.

The provocation becomes worse, however: more stalls are kicked over, some are even burnt down. In a sub-plot somebody's girlfriend, often a golden-hearted prostitute connected to the good gang, is killed. One of the good *yakuza* brothers is beaten up. It is only with the greatest difficulty that the dignified old *oyabun* can restrain his children now.

Then something happens to push them over the brink, that brings them to the end of their *gaman*. Just as he is enjoying a quiet stroll in the evening with his little grandson, the good *oyabun* himself is shot in the back. This is typical, for villains carry guns, something strictly for cowards and foreigners. True Japanese heroes fight with their swords.

Now we go to the deathbed scene. The old *oyabun*, tucked into his blankets, whispers his last words, usually a last appeal for restraint, to the sobbing children surrounding his bed. This is the moment late-night aficionados of the genre have been waiting for. A fan shouts 'Cry, damn it!' at the screen, and, sure enough, the sobbing of the loyal gangsters becomes louder and louder until they sound like professional wailers at a primitive wake.

Hysteria finally takes over: the *kobun* prepare to attack the enemy in one mad rush. But then the real hero of the story steps in: 'How can you behave like this in front of our *oyabun*?' he says. 'You stay, I'm going alone.' 'No, no, let us come with you!' plead the *kobun*, eyes bulging. 'Don't you understand!' cries the hero. And being Japanese gangsters, they rather reluctantly do understand. Order must prevail and this means that honour can only be saved by one scapegoat.

The hero removes his happi-coat with the gang insignia, symbolically breaking with the group. He becomes an individual acting alone. He is helped into his best kimono by his wife who, understandably, finds it rather hard to bear. But she too understands why her husband has to die. *Kimochi ga tsujita*, the feeling is understood.

He sets off to meet the enemy. His last journey, though often solitary, is much like the michiyuki, the lovers' suicide trip on the Kabuki stage: it is accompanied by the melancholy title-song on the soundtrack:

> When you decide to do it, you must carry it out to the end
> If we discard our sense of *giri*
> Life is just a dark pit
> Do not hesitate or stop
> Rain falls softly in the night.[6]

This may not seem like a very belligerent or even macho song. But then it is not meant to be. Neither were the songs by kamikaze pilots before they set off on their last sortie. The point of the scapegoat warrior is not that he kills others, but that he faces certain death himself. It is the sad poignancy of this moment that moves the audience. Late-night fans might shout 'Yare!', 'Go to it!', but this is like Spanish encouragement to the bull, backing up the sacrificial victim, before he purifies us with his death.

Purification through death is a universal phenomenon: Christianity is based on it. But the Shinto cult, upon which Japanese purification ceremonies are based, has strong taboos about death and also about any form of bleeding. Both are forms of pollution. The Edo-period scholar Hirata Atsutane wrote in *The Jewelled Sword* (*Tamadasuki*) that even in the case of 'nose bleeds, one should purify oneself by performing ablutions and make a pilgrimage to a shrine'.

Yamamoto Jocho, author of the *Hagakure*, and an ex-priest obsessed with death, was aware of the contradiction. How can one be purified by something as polluted as death? He resolved the conflict in a very Japanese way – by simply ignoring it.

'I believe in the effectiveness of praying to the gods for military success . . . If the gods are the sort to ignore my prayers simply because I have been defiled by blood, I am convinced there is nothing I can do about it, so I go ahead with my worship regardless of pollution.'[7]

Mishima suggested that 'samurai could not always be faithful to such ancient Shinto precepts. It is rather a convincing argument that they replaced with death the water that purifies all these defilements.'[8] In other words, death, if chosen with pure motives, purifies itself.

I am not convinced of this. Rather it seems a case of aesthetics acting as a purifier. Death in the *Hagakure*, and indeed in Mishima's own life and works, is a work of art, an artificial act, albeit with rather extreme consequences. In this way the ritual robs the taboo of its danger. Mishima once wrote that 'men must be the colour of cherry blossoms, even in death. Before committing ritual suicide, it was customary to apply rouge to the cheeks in order not to lose life colour after death.'[9] This seems to me an apt summing up of that odd mixture of effeminate dandyism and macho posturing that is such an important feature of death in the samurai cult, the Kabuki theatre and *yakuza* films.

The final climactic battle of the lonely hero against an army of bad men is the spectacular and bloody catharsis to complete the ritual. We see the hero, sometimes with a friend, reveal his tattoo before slashing his way through the ranks of villains who desperately pump more and more bullets into his naked torso.

But the spirit, in the best Japanese tradition, is stronger than the flesh, and the hero keeps going oblivious to the shots fired at point blank range. He keeps on slashing until he finally cuts down the bad _oyabun_, hitherto hidden behind a protective wall of kobun. Blood squirts, streams and splashes all over the screen in true Grand Guignol manner.

Finally, mission accomplished, the hero staggers to his inevitable demise, his tattoo covered in blood. The dying man who has been the silent type all through the film usually deems this the appropriate moment for a long speech about his deepest feelings. At this supreme emotional climax he is usually held in the tender arms of his best friend, it being, as we have noted before, very much a man's world.

Emotional statements are an important part of dying in Japanese drama, Kabuki or _yakuza_. As usual this tradition arrived at its present form during the Edo period when it was rather dangerous for a person to speak his or her mind openly. It was – and still is – also considered a trifle vulgar. Feelings are to be felt, not talked about; opinions may be held, but not voiced. Strong opinions can upset social harmony and thus, one is told, silent communication of feelings is an outstanding feature of Japanese social intercourse.

Earnest Japanese anxious to explain their culture to the ignorant foreigner still like to harp on this. It is as if every Japanese is equipped with a non-verbal emotional transmitter which functions only with other Japanese.

Only imminent death seems to release previously unsuspected wells of loquaciousness. The common explanation is that certain death frees one at last to say what one really thinks or feels. Thus famous last words are always last speeches in Japanese drama, for the great soliloquies are always left to the very end.

Various types of _yakuza_ heroes represent different qualities the Japanese particularly admire. Because most _yakuza_ films are the product of the same company (Toei) these stereotypes are often played by the same actors. The young Turk, pure, stoical and itching for a fight is acted by Takakura Ken. The good _oyabun_ is usually played by such rickety matinée idols of yesteryear as Arashi Kanjuro. The violent type, whose purity and honesty always lead him into trouble is played by Wakayama Tomisaburo. But one actor in particular seems to combine all the elements that make a perfect *yakuza* hero; he is the most archetypal, most traditional, most essentially Japanese of them all: Tsuruta Koji. He is to the Japanese what 'Duke' Wayne was to Americans, even though the two men could not be more different.

The one thing they have in common is that both men are like angels of a lost paradise, making a brave last stand for values that can only exist in a mythical past. Tsuruta Koji has the melancholy, haunted look of a man who has seen it all but still, somehow, manages to keep going, like an ageing courtesan or a seasoned gambler who sticks to the old rules in a bad new world where everyone plays dirty. He is the essence of what the Japanese call *iki* – the raffish elegance of hard-won experience.

His heyday as a *yakuza* star is now over, but he still appears on television as a singer of noble gangster songs or sentimental wartime ballads, sometimes dressed in full naval uniform. Fan magazines and record-jacket notes never cease to inform us that Tsuruta was on the list to be a kamikaze pilot. But this chance of glory was cruelly cut short by Japan's final defeat and like the rest of his countrymen Tsuruta Koji was forced to suffer the insufferable.

Suffering is very much part of his image. Mishima wrote about him that 'he makes the beauty of *gaman* shine brightly'.[10] Indeed, Tsuruta is all *gaman*. The main thing he suffers from is being an anachronism. A typical beginning of a Tsuruta film shows him coming out of jail after several years, dressed in a kimono. He finds the world a changed place: his old friends wear suits now and work for construction companies taking kick-backs and bribing politicians. He is of course appalled and appeals to his friends' sense of *yakuza* honour and humanity. 'Ah, you're talking about *giri* and *ninjo* now, are you,' they sneer, 'well, those days are over. Besides they were just tricks to make us go to war.' 'Whatever they are,' answers Tsuruta, 'they suit me. Without *giri* there's nothing left.'

Tricks to make us go to war. By having the villain equate splendid old-fashioned values with militarism the makers of the film drop a subtle hint that the wartime Japanese were somehow more noble than we are today. Ah ha, one thinks, right-wing propaganda. Certainly nobody could accuse producers of *yakuza* films of being leftists, but in fact, Right and Left are virtually meaningless in Japan as far as these matters are concerned. The yearning for the pure and noble past is not a sign of renascent fascism or 'feudalism' so much as a popular reaction to the cultural confusion of modern times. *Yakuza* heroes, especially during the turbulent 1960s, were as popular with radical students as with nostalgic old soldiers of the Empire. Images of Takakura Ken were brandished by students behind the barricades of Tokyo University in 1969. There is a connection between this kind of radical romanticism and nationalism, to which I shall return.

Tsuruta almost always dies at the end of his films. Usually he is shot in the back by cowards in suits, sometimes symbolically set against a background of brand-new oil refineries or smoke-belching factories with blood-red skies like images out of some modernistic Hell. His death is as inevitable as the suicide of the forty-seven ronin. There is no place for the reactionary hero in the modern world, whether he is Yorozu in the sixth century or Tsuruta in 1967. He is like a spirit of the past conjured up like those living ghosts in No plays. His function – this is certainly true of spirits in No – is to remind us of the fleeting sadness of the world of man and once the ceremony is over he has to disappear.

Tsuruta also suffers because his adherence to the code of honour often conflicts with his private feelings: the age-old battle between *giri* and *ninjo*, in other words, but with a slight twist. The yakuza code of honour, expressed in such terms as *jingi* (righteousness) or *ninkyo* (nobility), is not the same as justice in the West. Unlike Gary Cooper or John Wayne, or Mr Smith going to Washington, Tsuruta never thinks of anything as abstract as justice. Justice, in London or Hollywood, is a universal concept. It is symbolized by a blindfolded goddess weighing the scales, almost ruthless in her fairness. To the Japanese way of thinking this seems too cold, almost too impartial, because it fails to take the many, often irrational complexities of human relations into account. Justice for its own sake is meaningless to the Japanese hero. His code of honour exists only in the context of his own personal relationships, usually, in the case of *yakuza*, confined to the gang. Nobility in Japanese heroes is highly parochial.

There is a stock scene to be seen in countless Japanese gangster films: a *yakuza*, escaping from the law perhaps, or the vengeance of a rival gang, seeks temporary refuge with another gang. He becomes a *kyakubun*, a 'guest member'. But before he is accepted he has to go through an elaborate introduction ceremony executed in an awkward crouching position, bending the front knee and stretching the right hand, palm up, towards the other person. This ritual whereby the guest intones his name and personal history in stilted traditional language, as if reciting a liturgy, can take minutes of screen time. This is typical of the ceremonial atmosphere of the mythical *yakuza* world.

In return for his shelter, the guest is obliged by *giri* to his hosts to do whatever they ask him. He can be ordered, for instance, to murder a rival *oyabun*, who may be a perfectly honourable and innocent man. Justice would of course forbid him to undertake such a mission, but *jingi* does not. He must do it. If the guest is an honourable man, he will say to his adversary: 'I have nothing against you personally, sir. You seem to be a man of honour, but alas *giri* to my hosts obliges me to take your life.' 'I thank you for your polite words,' replies the victim, 'let us proceed.' They draw their swords and the murder is duly executed.

As the story goes on, however, the bad 'host' gang's behaviour gets worse and worse, until the *gaman* of the guest member reaches its limits and his feelings of decency (*ninjo*) get the better of him. But simply to go over to a rival gang would break all *yakuza* rules. He probably would not even be accepted. This means that he must turn on his hosts, but always at the cost of his own life. By cutting himself loose he acts as an individual and, as we have seen before, the price for that is death. This is why the friend who joins the hero on his last death march is very often just such a former guest member of a bad gang. Nevertheless, even this last dramatic deed is not prompted by justice so much as by his personal feelings.

Tsuruta Koji is faced with a similar kind of predicament in one of the best films he ever acted in, entitled 'Presidential Gambling'. This time the bad gang is his own. Though the next in line to be boss is Tsuruta himself, the post is taken over by an evil man who acts as the regent for a young and ineffectual *oyabun*. Tsuruta's best friend, played by the specialist in hot-headed heroes, Wakayama Tomisaburo, popularly known as Wakatomi, rebels against this unfair state of affairs. Tsuruta, of course, simply shows his usual *gaman*. The code must be preserved until the very end, even though he himself may be the victim.

Eventually Wakatomi's violent rebelliousness becomes such a threat to the group order, that Tsuruta is forced to break the *saké* cup that sealed their original brotherhood. With the heavy symbolism typical of the genre, this scene is shot in a cemetery, dark and wet in the pouring rain. Finally, out of *giri* to the young *oyabun*, who is attacked by the impetuous Wakatomi, he is compelled to do the unthinkable: kill his own best friend, whose rebellion was started for Tsuruta's own sake in the first place.

With tears in his eyes, Tsuruta plunges his sword deep into his friend's heart. Covered in blood he rushes down the stairs and meets Wakatomi's little son (there is nothing like a child to produce the three handkerchiefs). His face is a battlefield of ravaged *giri-ninjo* emotions as he takes the boy in his bloody arms. Then, and only then does *ninjo* overcome the last vestiges of *gaman*. The code of honour has to give way and Tsuruta goes after the villain, who is still officially his senior in the gang, with his sword drawn. The bad man, little toothbrush moustache twitching, pipes: 'Are you trying to attack me? Where is your sense of honour?' 'Sense of honour?', says Tsuruta, 'I have no such thing, just think of me as a common murderer.' And he stabs the evil schemer to death.

It is this sense of shame (*haji*) that further endears Tsuruta Koji to his fans. *Hazukashii* (I am ashamed; embarrassed) and *sumimasen* (I am sorry) must be amongst the most commonly used words in the Japanese vocabulary. Though it is perhaps too simplistic to call Japan a shame culture, as Ruth Benedict has done, shame is certainly a frequent emotion in a people to whom appearances and social face mean so much. But Tsuruta's shame goes deeper: he is always conscious of individual feelings being oppressed by the very code he stands and falls by. Thus even doing what is socially right can be a shameful thing – killing your own friend, for example.

Tsuruta is ashamed of his very existence. 'I'm just a worthless gangster', is one of his favourite phrases. This humility, so different from the swaggering bravado of the super samurai, makes it easier for the audience to identify with the hero. It also adds yet another twist to the *giri–ninjo* conflict. In 'Showa Kyokyakuden'[11] Tsuruta saves two boys from being killed by a bad group of gangsters. They beg him to exchange *saké* cups with them as a token of *yakuza* brotherhood. Tsuruta refuses, not wanting them to 'belong to the same dregs of society' as he does.

One of the boys follows him anyway as his faithful disciple. But Tsuruta still refuses to make him a *yakuza*. When Tsuruta has to go into hiding after killing one of the villains, this disciple is caught and tortured half to death. Tsuruta rushes to the hospital where the boy is dying. The boy's sister begs Tsuruta to make him a *yakuza* brother, so that he can die happily. The disciple looks up at his master with tears in his eyes, begging him for this last favour.

What can the hero do? The boy's loyalty ought to be rewarded, but by making him a *yakuza* he will die as an outcast. 'I want him to die with an unpolluted body,' says Tsuruta, 'not as a *yakuza* like me.' He refuses to grant the boy's wish. This may seem a little cold-hearted. But to the Japanese audience it is not. By insisting on the purity of his disciple's death, he shows the highest humanity, as well as his own humility. This is pure *ninjo*. The *giri* part is taken care of after the boy dies.

Tsuruta goes off to meet the enemy alone. And he dies too, of course, in the arms of his *oyabun*, a kindly old man equally ashamed of being a *yakuza*. His greatest wish is for his daughter to marry a *katagi*, a 'straight person'. (Actually she is in love with Tsuruta and vice versa, but out of *giri* to his boss, he chooses *gaman*, much to her annoyance; all these feelings remain unspoken, of course.) And so Tsuruta dies, crying 'Oyabun! Oyabun!' while his *yakuza* brothers cry softly, 'let us be men, let us die like men'.

The final twist of Tsuruta's *giri–ninjo* complications has to do with his love-life. Unlike many younger heroes, Tsuruta is something of a womanizer and his emotional entanglements lead to the cruellest bind of all: what to choose? His woman or the group, love or the code of honour? He is both Papageno and Tamino, a most unfortunate condition.

The dilemma is already painfully clear at the beginning of that *yakuza* classic 'Jinsei Gekijo' ('Theatre of Life'). Tsuruta goes into hiding with his girlfriend, making him useless to his gang. Consequently he is torn between *giri* to his brothers and love for his girl. Out of sheer guilt – 'I have to live like a man' – he dons his best kimono one day and assassinates the rival gang boss.

While he is in prison for this deed, still pining for his woman, she falls in love with Takakura Ken, a former member of Tsuruta's gang, who has no idea that she is his 'brother's' woman. It all comes out when Tsuruta is finally released. Ken-san goes on his knees, begging Tsuruta's forgiveness. The girl is torn between the two. Tsuruta, though furious, tells him to go off and take the woman. His *gaman* and nobility achieve their finest hour.

Now Ken-san is in a bind. What should he do? Be loyal to the *yakuza* code which would never allow him to live with the woman of a brother? Or should he follow his true feelings? He resolves the conflict in the only possible manner: he goes on a lonely suicide mission to the old rival gang. Tsuruta arrives just in time to hold him in his arms as he dies: 'Finally you've become a man', he says, and Ken-san dies happily.

Tsuruta, in his turn, knows what to do and as he walks to his certain death, the ballad on the soundtrack swelling, his woman tries to stop him. 'Get out of the way, woman!' he shouts. 'Don't you see he finally became a man!'

'But I love you!'

'I love you too.'

And he pushes her out of his way. *Giri* must prevail in the world of men, for as the song says: 'Without *giri* the world is dark.' And thus Tsuruta Koji goes on suffering the insufferable, ensuring his popularity by doing so.

Let us pause here to reflect on the connection between the mythical *yakuza* world and the real one in which most Japanese live. For just as old Hollywood films bore some resemblance to the world for which they were made, *yakuza* films reflect certain important aspects of Japanese life. In many ways the *yakuza* world with its *giri*, its emotional conflicts, and its social suffering, is a stylized microcosm of Japanese society, just as the Kabuki theatre was during the Edo period.

Loyalty to the gang, conflicting with one's personal feelings; having to choose between the woman one loves and obligation to one's seniors: these tensions between the individual and his group are still very real. Despite the much vaunted façade of harmony (*wa*) and consensus, the Japanese are individuals who can, and obviously sometimes do suffer from the grip of collectivity, much though they may need the security of it, just as

Tsuruta does. What the *yakuza* hero represents, more than the swashbuckling samurai, is the loneliness of the Japanese crowd.

'Salarymen' are often obliged to sacrifice their private lives for the company. They are frequently compelled to see more of their colleagues – often the only people they see – than their families, whether they want to or not. Human relations on the shop floor are bound by similar restraints of hierarchy and loyalty to those of the cinema *yakuza*. I was even told by a foreman in a motor-cycle plant that he watches *yakuza* films to learn how to cope with his job.

An individual in Japan is always part of something larger (the few exceptions are considered to be bizarre loners). The same is true of many occidentals, but they do not identify their 'selves' with the companies for which they work to the same extent as Japanese. They have a 'private life', which is usually respected. The Japanese do not, or certainly not as much. In fact one only really exists in the context of one's group. Relationships in these groups are not necessarily based on friendship. Japanese groups, whether they are motor-cycle companies, theatre troupes or *yakuza* gangs, are more like extended families, with the exception that as soon as one leaves the fold, one ceases to be a member.

For example, a well known avant-garde theatre group recently published a lavish book about its history. There was one peculiar omission: the leading star of the group who had been the major attraction for the last ten years was not mentioned even once. The reason: he had decided to leave the troupe just before the book was written, so he simply did not exist any more. An interesting detail in this story is that the book was edited by one of the country's leading drama critics. He defended the omission by claiming *giri* to the group's director.

Audiences identify with the *yakuza* hero because he is essentially a loner. His identity is dependent on his group, which is why he clings to its symbols. Every conversation, every form of human contact in a *yakuza* film is another ceremony, another exercise in etiquette to keep the group together. Apart from the occasional outburst of hysteria and the climactic decision to die, every expression of private feelings is stifled by ritual. *Yakuza* brothers are more like actors going through a series of stylized motions than individual adults behaving as friends. The private human being behind the ritual façade is at all times miserably alone. This is perhaps the human condition of all of us. But without wishing to take the parallel too far, it is, I think, especially true of the human condition in Japan; enough, at any rate, to make Tsuruta Koji and his brothers truly Japanese heroes.

It is a psychological truism that suppressed aggression turns inward. Instead of self-assertive heroes, Japan has many masochistic ones: the more heroes suffer, the more heroic they seem. Macho in Japan is often masochism turned into a fine art. In the case of gangsters this is quite literally so: most of them – in films all of them – sport full body tattoos, painfully carved into their skins from the neck to the knees – and sometimes even to the ankles.[12] One can imagine their capacity, indeed their gluttony, for pain.

In one particularly memorable scene a young hero is ordered by his *oyabun* to work in a street market as a bookseller. To be a merchant is difficult for someone of his temperament and each time he is provoked by a local gang of bullies, he hits back, quite effectively. But this will not do: he is a merchant now and has to learn to take punishment to peddle his wares. (Violence used to be strictly forbidden for merchants in traditional society, for that was the privilege of the samurai class; now the *yakuza* seem to have taken this traditional role over from the warriors.)

The intemperate young hero is slapped in the face by a senior man in the market place. Chastened by this he learns his lesson. The next time the bullies attack him in the usual Japanese way, all against one, he allows them to beat him up: he is kicked in the groin, punched in the face and knocked half-unconscious. But he is happy, as are the other merchants who gather round him: he has shown his spirit. He has literally been beaten into his proper place in society. And acceptance of one's social fate is what separates the men from the boys in Japan. This would be hard to imagine in Hollywood, where social mobility and individual assertiveness ('there is nothing you cannot do if you try' was the message when Mickey Rooney and Judy Garland put on yet another Broadway show) are traditional ideals.

The all-American hero can never accept the world for what it is; it can always be better; that is what he originally came to America for, after all. The Japanese has no old world, let alone a new one, or even a neighbouring one to compare with his own. Besides, centuries of Buddhist resignation and Tokugawa rule have beaten any illusions of fundamental change out of him long ago. Even the modern Japanese, who often feels a sneaking admiration, tinged perhaps with envy, for American optimism, still finds this attitude childish, and even a trifle barbaric.

Social tragedy, which is in effect what Japanese drama, Kabuki and *yakuza*, is about, naturally revolves around a closed world from which there is no escape. In the words of the poet Watanabe Takenobu, 'it is the fate of the *yakuza* hero to live and die in a closed space'.[13] During the Edo period Japanese society was of course literally sealed off from the outside world. This is no longer true, but the mentality has lingered on; the outside world still seems hardly real for many Japanese and for most it is still inconceivable to tear themselves away from their familiar nests. This means putting up with the restrictions of what in many ways is still a closed society.

As popular entertainment clearly shows, this is reassuring as well as tragic. It is reassuring because, as Donald Richie, the film critic, put it, 'it so clearly defines one's choice. This seems especially comforting on the stage, or the screen, because this simplification can suggest that there is nothing more than this to life . . . '[14] It is tragic because any attempt to break loose inevitably – in drama, if not always in life – leads to disaster. To quote a character in a *yakuza* film: 'There are only two roads for a *yakuza*, prison and death'.[15]

For the average citizen real life is not quite this drastic, but too much individualistic behaviour can result in serious ostracism and, even worse, expulsion from the group. The worst punishment for any individual in a traditional Japanese village was just that: *mura hachibu*, to be sent to Coventry, to be treated as a non-person. To be socially ignored in the tightly knit village community that modern Japan still in many ways resembles is perhaps a fate worse than death – it is, in fact, something like living death.

Being a ceremonial art, as well as a tragic one, the *yakuza* film depends very much on its symbolism. Without an understanding of its often highly arcane symbols, rituals, manners, the iconography of the tattoos, and the meaning of gestures, it remains inscrutable, rather like Japan itself. All ceremonies are inseparably connected to a specific time and place. Torn from its environment ceremony becomes meaningless. Balinese ritual performed on a stage in London or New York may be a satisfying spectacle, but it loses its significance: it is mere folklore.

In Japan, as elsewhere, common symbols are part of the glue that keeps groups together. The more secret and complex the symbolism, the easier it is to keep outsiders out and insiders in. The penchant of traditional Japanese masters for passing down whatever they have to teach (anything from flower-arranging to classical cuisine) in the form of old mystical secrets, is part of this, as is the old idea that it takes an impossibly long time to perfect the rudiments of one's art. Although these methods impress a large number of people, Japanese as well as foreign, much of the mystique is simply a device to make people conform to the hierarchy of the group. They also serve, as the great No actor Zeami wrote in 1400,[16] to protect the family itself.

But what happens when people are lifted out of their natural habitat, to places where their symbols are not understood and thus fail to impress? One solution, often adopted, is just to pretend one has never left, to hide inside the air-conditioned tour bus, so to speak. Another is to exaggerate the symbols, as if to convince oneself of their validity even in alien territory, to turn them into a parody of themselves: the colonial Englishman wearing tweeds in the tropics or staging – for that is what it was – elaborate picnics in the African bush: 'Got to keep the standards up, you know.'

The natural habitat of the *yakuza* film is urban Japan and the time stretches roughly from the end of the last century to the late 1950s. Mythical *yakuza* do not travel well. This makes the one example of a *yakuza* film that oversteps its natural boundaries all the more interesting. Both solutions described above are in evidence and they offer a fascinating insight into the mechanics of Japanese nationalism. The film is called, appropriately, 'Drifters on the Mainland', starring Tsuruta Koji. It is set in Hong Kong.

The story, briefly, is that a white gang is fighting a Chinese gang for the control of a water reservoir built by the Japanese. Tsuruta arrives to 'show the Japanese spirit', as the narrator informs us. This 'spirit' is written all over the film. The myth of the *yakuza* becomes the myth of the Japanese. Tsuruta's fiancée, in the best Kabuki tradition, sells herself to a brothel to raise money for the Japanese gang. When he protests, she tells him to do his 'duty as a Japanese – it doesn't matter what happens to me'.

In any other *yakuza* film she would have told him to do his duty 'as a man'; as we have seen, women sacrifice themselves so that their men can be men. He himself would have thought in terms of doing his duty 'as a *yakuza*'. Now 'man' and '*yakuza*' have turned into 'Japanese': the world of them and us, men and women, *yakuza* and *katagi* (straights) has expanded to Japanese and foreigners.

A curious character in the film is a Japanese living in Hong Kong who professes to hate his country, a not infrequent condition of Japanese living abroad. To one who has escaped the narrow confines of the national womb, it can look remarkably like prison. Now this poor man is captured by the villainous white gang and tortured to death. But just before his painful exit he manages to whisper into Tsuruta's receptive ear: 'Now I can finally die as a Japanese.' His dilemma of being an individual human being as well as a Japanese abroad is resolved in death. One is reminded of Tsuruta's fellow *yakuza* outcasts crying, 'let us be like men, let us die like men'. Or even, in a way, of Chikamatsu's lovers united in double suicide. Only by death can one be granted what proved impossible in life.

Then racialism comes through clearly: the Japanese decide to link arms with the Chinese (whose opinions on the matter are never really considered) to gang up against the white man. 'The East is one', says Tsuruta solemnly as he shakes the Chinese boss's hand. One is tempted to take this as a satire or a parody even of Second World War propaganda, but no, there is no tongue in anybody's cheek, least of all Tsuruta's. Nothing could be further from the *yakuza* – or national – myth than satire. The truth is that wartime myths are by no means dead in Japanese entertainment – neither are they in ours, for that matter. It is surely no coincidence that at the time of writing the same company that produced this film has presented the public with a picture called 'The Great Japanese Empire', celebrating among other things, the attack on Pearl Harbour.

Just as the *yakuza* code, and indeed the codes of most Japanese companies, are based on vague spiritual values, membership of the Japanese race means one can lay claim to the 'unique' spirit of Yamato. This is as spurious as the 'nobility' of the *yakuza*, or the Way of the warrior, or indeed similar spiritual claims in other nations, but it is highly potent to its believers.

Being thus privileged, one naturally has the duty to protect others less blessed than oneself: the pure Japanese in Asia must act as true elder brothers to the Chinese and protect them against the evil white man. This is the myth. That this protection in reality meant terrorism does not change the myth at all; neither, after all, does the real *yakuza* menace to ordinary citizens make them any less noble in the cinema.

The *yakuza* hero and the 'Japanese' have much in common in their attitudes to the outside world. Both realize they are part of it, yet they feel cut off, misunderstood, even discriminated against. They convince themselves that they are blessed with a unique spirituality, yet they humble themselves at the same time: 'We are a small, poor country'; 'I am the dregs of society.' People identify with the ambivalence of the *yakuza* hero. He is proud, yet an outcast, part of a group, but still alone. *Yakuza* heroes are ultimately the heroic victims of this world, which is exactly the way many Japanese like to picture themselves.

Of all the *yakuza* outcasts, Takakura Ken was the hero of the radical young during the romantic 1960s. Tsuruta represents the older generation. He has seen it all, indulged in every vice: too wise to be cynical. He knows he is fighting for a lost cause, which is precisely his tragedy. Ken-san is the adolescent hero, pure, naive and angry. Women and gambling are not for him. He is imbued with the puritanism of a revolutionary. He is in fact the perfect student radical, always boiling over, and unlike Tsuruta, whose deliberate death is an act of resignation, Ken-san's last gesture is an explosion of frustrated anger – increased perhaps by his sexual abstemiousness – at the inhumanity of the modern world.

The radical young of the 1960s, having grown up in post-war 'demokurashi', never as democratic as it purported to be, felt deeply confused by the role of the individual in a collectivist society. Like their hero, they sought the answer to their problems in a violent combination of group fanaticism and individual sacrifice; or at least, the radical fringe did; most young Japanese, like young people everywhere else, took their lives for granted and were quite content to see Takakura Ken explode for them, safely confined to the cinema screen.

As everywhere in the industrial world, the end of the decade dashed many student dreams. May 1968 became a fading illusion in Paris, London, Berkeley, and Tokyo too. Hopes of violently changing the world petered out and a new era began. Significantly the era of the orthodox *yakuza* film and thus the Golden Age of Ken-san and Tsuruta ended at exactly the same time. This was partly because the formula had worked itself out. Any art as mannered as the *yakuza* film cannot be repeated *ad infinitum*, even in Japan where people have a high tolerance for repetition.

But apart from that it was the pure myth that exploded, for the time being, at least. The symbols, so dependent on time and place, became redundant. It was not the end of the *yakuza* hero, but he changed completely. He was not even played by the same actors any more. The new *yakuza*, like the ever more violent student radical fringe, is a perfect example of what happens when the Japanese hero is stripped of the codes and rituals that normally hold him in check. He becomes a *nihirisuto*.

Arguing that the Japanese individual is educated to become a member 'of a mythical body to which he sacrifices his life and thought in order to receive his true self', Kurt Singer goes on to say: 'Wherever this process is disturbed an anarchical state of mind is sure to develop, according to the same law that makes nihilism the end result of European attempts to replace reasonable freedom — as the goal of education — by a cult of the irrational.'[17]

The orthodox *yakuza* films were officially known as 'Chivalry Films' ('Ninkyo Eiga'). The new type is known as 'True Document Film' ('Jitsuroku Eiga'). Realism of the most sordid kind took over from the myth. Tsuruta Koji wanted to have nothing to do with this new development. His characteristic comment was that these were not true *yakuza* pictures.

The title of the most successful series, 'Fighting Without Nobility' ('Jingi Naki Tatakai'), is typical of the whole genre. The new heroes are not noble men agonizing over the finer points of duty and humanity, but tough brutes such as Sugawara Bunta, slouching around like Chicago hoodlums on a Kabuki stage, in dark glasses, black gloves, silk suits, and white raincoats draped around the shoulders like capes, collars well up, and the faces held in perpetually angry scowls.

The myths and symbols are smashed. In this world everybody, including the hero, plays dirty. The old ceremonies, for which Tsuruta lived and died, are almost forgotten. In one hilarious scene in 'Fighting Without Nobility' Bunta attempts to cut off his finger. This is a classic *yakuza* ritual to make up for lost face: the injured party is presented with a severed finger, neatly wrapped in a piece of white paper, by the one who did the injury. Bunta, being a gangster without nobility, has no idea how to conduct this painful ceremony properly, and when at last he manages to hack off his little finger with a kitchen knife, it gets lost in the ensuing scuffle. The entire gang of silk-suited scowlers then goes on hands and knees to retrieve Bunta's finger.

This would have been inconceivable in the solemn *yakuza* films of the previous decade. One would think it were a farce, if it were not for the following scenes in which people get their eyes stabbed with hot skewers, their stomachs slit with scissors and their backs slashed with knives. Bunta and others of his kind are like raging animals shut up too long in a cage. They do not talk, they grunt. One senses a pathological state of frustration constantly on the brink of violent hysteria. In one extraordinary scene in a film called 'The Ando Gang', celebrating the blood-thirsty adventures of Ando Noboru, a real *yakuza* turned poker-faced film gangster, we see Bunta alone in a garish neon-lit bar. After downing half a bottle of whisky in one noisy gulp, he smashes the bottle on the table and drags the jagged edges across his own face.

It is the kind of violence that builds up in heavily repressed people, suddenly let loose without any restraints, like soldiers in a war going on a rampage. But although there is hardly any method to the madness in these films, there is a perverse kind of beauty in the way violence is choreographed. One especially memorable murder in 'Fighting Without Nobility' takes place in a toy shop, with the victim's blood mingling prettily with the gaudy colours of tinkling toys and festival decorations. The contrast between violent death and garish kitsch, turning the scene into burlesque, in an important element in Japanese aesthetics of this kind.

What strikes one is the complete gratuitousness of the violence. Just as there is little or no attempt in Japanese film comedies (called 'nonsense films' — *nansensu mono* — in the olden days) to connect the jokes in any coherent order, there is no logic behind the violence in these pictures. Acts of violence are strung together more or less at random like those old-time jokes or sex scenes in a porn film.

But this is precisely the point: there is no logical reason for the hideous cruelty indulged in by the Bunta-type hero, for he is a *nihirisuto*. The cycle of obligations and loyalties that chain the ordinary mortal simply do not exist for him. The true nihirisuto just smashes his way through the tight web of Japanese society. He is heroic in his utter badness.

Nihirizumu is as much part of the Japanese heroic tradition as the suicidal retainer or the noble scapegoat. It is most likely influenced by that most *nihirisuto* of creeds, Zen Buddhism. *Nihirizumu* is the result of the victory over the ego, over the discursive mind. The ego-less mind is a mind without emotions, without pity. The ideal Zen hero can easily be turned into an unthinking murder-machine, whose pure spontaneity takes him to a twisted kind of Buddha-hood.

The *nihirisuto* does what nobody else can do; he is a super-individualist in a society that suppresses individualism. Deep in his heart no doubt many a meek 'salaryman' or, before him, the Edo townsman, would like to be a sword-waving killer or a Bunta with a gun, just as the macho tradition in the West invites people to identify with John Wayne or Charles Bronson.

In the West, however, a hero must ultimately be on the side of virtue. Even anti-heroes never turn out to be as bad as they look. Jean Gabin as Pepe le Moko, king of the casbah, is rather a good fellow underneath the tough exterior. James Cagney 'turns yellow' in front of the electric chair in 'Angels With Dirty Faces', to stop the neighbourhood boys from worshipping his memory. Such a deed would be unthinkable for a Japanese villain. Bad heroes in Japan need not have any goodness in them; they are as they present themselves.

Susanoo, the Sun Goddess's brother, was a true *nihirisuto*, breaking all the taboos. He was violent, pathologically anti-social and, like many *nihirisuto* heroes, finally condemned to a life of drifting as an outcast, although he was redeemed in his old age.

And yet he is a popular deity. Badness is accepted as part of the human condition and Susanoo is a very human god. Because of this one feels that Japanese heroes are judged aesthetically rather than ethically. The bad man can be a hero as long as his behaviour, however murderous, has a certain kind of style; as long as he is *kakko ii* – *bella figura*.

In a way the *nihirisuto* is like the super samurai, except that he is not a god on earth defending the weak against the bullies, but more an angel of vengeance striking at random. Some of the most celebrated *nihirisutos* are samurai. Most of them lived, in fantasy and fact, in that most '*nihiru*' of times, the *bakumatsu*, the chaotic tail-end of the Edo period.

The middle of the nineteenth century was a time of constant fighting, spying, police terrorism, radical fanaticism and endless intrigues. The foreign powers were pushing Japan to open her doors. The military government was collapsing under its own weight. Class barriers were breaking down and anti-Tokugawa samurai, mostly from the south, were grabbing for power.

Little in this confusion made much sense to the population at large, for it was difficult to know just who was fighting whom – often the contenders themselves hardly knew, for loyalty was a fickle thing and allegiances were switched at the flash of a sword.

One of the most typical *nihirisuto* heroes of the *bakumatsu* is the protagonist of a story, filmed many times, entitled 'The Great Buddha Pass' ('Daibosatsu Toge'): Tsukue Ryunosuke, a roaming sword-fighter whose only purpose in life is to kill people with one clean swoop of his well tended weapon. He is not on the side of anybody or anything; and he is not choosy about his victims, as long as he can practise his murderous skills.

Fairness is irrelevant. Many of his victims, elderly pilgrims and the like, are entirely defenceless. This does not detract from his heroic stature; it just adds to the *nihirizumu*. What is important is that he has style. One of the most interesting film versions of the story was directed in 1957 by Uchida Tomu, a specialist in blood and gore; but blood and gore presented with great panache. The grotesque violence of the roaming killer is shown as a piece of wonderful kitsch: the screen goes blood red as heads are lopped off and bodies are sliced in half. The hero is the epitome of badness, lips curled in an evil leer, growling, 'let's see if my sword still cuts', fondly caressing his blade. But he is also an artist and as such he is admired.

Violence in these films is a combination of stylization and detailed realism, like late-Edo Kabuki. One can hear the bones crunching when a victim is being jumped upon – this example is actually from a children's film; one can also hear the squelching sound of a sword entering a slit stomach; one can see an eye being dislodged or a face being consumed by flames.

Violence is committed as a form of art for art's sake. Bloodshed is aestheticized in a way hard to imagine in the West. Sam Peckinpah's films come to mind, but he is enough of an exception to be controversial. I am not suggesting for a moment that aesthetic violence is uniquely Japanese, but in the West violence, like sex, needs an excuse, however spurious. (Or it becomes pure fancy, as in fairy tales or horror stories which, in any case, depend more on shock effects than graphic depictions of real violence.) Even Peckinpah could not justify cruelty in his films on purely aesthetic grounds, although he has been accused of being immoral. Under his macho exterior lurks an American puritan showing the violence that man is capable of in order to denounce it. He is hypocritical in so far as he (and his audience) obviously revels in the violence he publicly condemns. But then this kind of hypocrisy is very much part of our cultural heritage.

Japanese aesthetes of cruelty do not feel the need to justify themselves in this way. Their aestheticism has nothing to do with morality, for they take the Wildean view that beauty is amoral, just as heroes, and indeed the gods themselves are amoral. Moreover, the pure gratuitousness of their cruelty shows, once again, the melancholy arbitrariness of fate. This does not mean that Japanese audiences are cruel or sadistic. They are perhaps more tolerant of extreme violence than is common elsewhere: ultra-violent television programmes for children seem to bear this out. The reason is that there are no absolute moral rules against it; unlike the Marquis de Sade, Japanese *nihirisutos* have no Christian morality to rebel against.

In Japan violence is like sex: not a sin as such, but subject to social restraint. The only release from these restraints is *asobi*, play; the tougher the restraints, the more grotesque the play. Violent entertainment is a way of letting off steam as in a brothel, or even a religious festival. It is surely no coincidence that the gruesome paintings by such typical *bakumatsu* artists as Ekin (1813–76) should be used as temple decorations, to be viewed on festival days. His favourite subjects were the cruellest, bloodiest scenes of the Kabuki theatre, such as the *bishonen* Gompachi hacking his attackers to death or the noble retainer Matsuo watching his own child being murdered. Like Uchida Tomu's films and the Kabuki theatre of his own time, Ekin's paintings served as a release of aggressive energy suppressed by a disciplined and safe society.

The Japanese concept of dramatic entertainment comes very close to Artaud's theory on the theatre of cruelty: 'The audience can believe in the theatre as a dream; not as a copy of reality . . . They let themselves go in the magical freedom of their dreams. This freedom is recognized by the audience when it is coloured by fear and cruelty.'[18]

As long as it is aesthetically pleasing. The Kabuki actor Bando Mitsugoro once said that 'Kabuki is the art of presenting cruelty as a thing of beauty, as cruelty that doesn't feel like cruelty'.[19] Beauty, in other words, purifies it, and presumably, by doing so, purifies us too.

There is an element of farce in all this. It is at first a little disconcerting to see people giggling in theatres and cinemas just as somebody is being cruelly tortured. Undoubtedly this is partly a natural reaction to break the nervous tension. It is also an aspect of what the Japanese like to call their 'festival spirit', *matsuri no seishin*. Indeed, the ultra-violent films, featuring nihirisuto heroes, are often advertised as 'blood festivals' (*chi no matsuri*), which is exactly what they are. Often these 'blood festivals' are farcical. The tradition goes back to the grotesque trickery in nineteenth-century Kabuki plays which was a form of slapstick, with artificial legs snapping and heads rolling, red and grue-some, across the stage. The cruelty, like sex in traditional pornography – called 'comic art' in the olden days – is simply too grotesque, too stylized, too extreme to seem real. Naturally people laugh, exorcizing the menace of real violence.

Sato Tadao, referring to the work of a famous aesthete of cinematic violence, Suzuki Seijun, used the Buddhist term *mujo*,[20] the transience of life, to describe this theatre of cruelty. Suzuki, whose films, quite consciously, have come to resemble the Kabuki theatre more and more, deliberately mixes farce with violence. In one classic film entitled 'The Tokyo Drifter' ('Tokyo Nagaremono'), the nihirisuto hero is played by a popular teenage idol of the time (1966), dressed in an immaculate white suit. The final massacre takes place in a kitsch night-club, painted in glittering white to contrast prettily with the splashes of red blood. With every killing – shades of Uchida Tomu here – the strobe lights change from white to yellow, to purple, to bright, horror-show red.

Suzuki himself relates his *nihirizumu* to his wartime experience. As he remembers it, life was not only cheap when he was sent with his friends to die for the emperor, but also totally absurd. Nothing made sense and the sight of death even seemed comical at times: 'When they sunk your ship, you had to be saved by other ships. I shall never forget the sight of those men climbing up the ropes, swaying from side to side, hitting their heads all over the place. By the time they got on board they were black and blue . . . Some of them died, of course and they had to be buried at sea. Two sailors would take the corpses on either side and the trumpets would go tatata and then they'd throw the corpse overboard: tatata, another corpse, tatata, another one . . . (laughs).'[21]

It could be a scene from one of his films. He could not but become a *nihirisuto*, for whom humour and aesthetics are the only antidotes to the cruel fleetingness of life. The tragic sense of mujo can only be relieved by laughter. The pollution of violent death can only be purified by beauty.

11

Making Fun of Father

It is axiomatic that every full-blooded Japanese hero loves his mother. But what about his father? Is he as much loved, or at least respected? Given the strong sense of family in Japan, one would have thought so. None the less, much in popular culture seems to suggest otherwise.

About ten years ago a comic-book series called 'Stupid Dad' ('Dame Oyaji') appeared. It was meant for children, but as usual in Japan, it was very popular with adults. The contents of this comic are remarkable for their virulent sadism of which the victim, as the title implies, is always Dad. Dad is a sad little man with glasses and buck teeth, a little like a 'Jap' caricature in Second World War American propaganda films, dwarfish and ugly like a stunted fish.

After spending his days bowing and scraping at a nightmarish office, Dad is tormented by his wife, a vicious, screaming harridan, nicknamed 'the devil woman'. His son, a bald little horror and his daughter, a whining sadist, both happily assist their mother in acts of unspeakable brutality. In one typical episode the father is chained to a post like a dog. When he speaks, he is kicked in the head by his wife, who screams, 'If you want something, go woof woof!' 'Yes', he answers, cowering in the corner. This earns him another kick from his little son, screeching with glee.

He is then made to go shopping, running on all fours, with a basket in his mouth. 'Woof woof' he goes and the local grocer feeds him peanuts. The grocer then sticks a pair of ears on him and a tail of wire, ordering him to be a pig. 'Oink oink' goes stupid Dad when he returns home. This change of identity merits another kick in the face from the devil woman. 'If you want to be a pig so much, we'll roast you in the oven.' In the last picture of this episode we see Dad, his body a mass of horrible burns and bleeding wounds, cowering under the big feet of his wife, who is standing on him like a successful game hunter, while his son dances around him like a mad cannibal.

And so the sad saga of stupid Dad goes on and on in a never-ending round of cruelty. He is thrown into a trap full of thistles; he is roasted alive in a crematorium; he is frozen in ice-cold baths when he is ill. In one episode his wife, out of sheer spite, serves him his only joy in life, his little pet bird, for dinner. I repeat, this is a comic meant for children.

This may seem somewhat puzzling in a country which is often called semi-feudal, rightly or wrongly, and where a strict sense of hierarchy coupled to a strong military tradition would suggest a certain respect for the patriarch. But even a cursory glance at popular culture will show that this comic, though perhaps a little extreme, is by no means exceptional. The father, especially since recent notions of 'demokurashi' have further eroded his already shaky position, is very often a figure of fun.

When he is not ludicrous, he is sad; the lonely old man in the corner, drinking away his misery. He is certainly almost never a hero. The family hero, when there is one at all, is still the blessed mother. The strong patriarch as the rock on which the family rests, as one sees in American Westerns, for example, is almost wholly absent from Japanese entertainment.

Although it would surely be wrong to suggest that every Japanese father is a ridiculous weakling or a lonely boozer, the myth is not entirely divorced from reality. Many men are in the life-long grip of their mothers. The power of these mothers can be considerable, as are the hardships suffered by their daughters-in-law. This is one of the main themes of modern television drama – as well as the Kabuki theatre – avidly watched by millions of sympathetic housewives.

The mother-in-law, considering the depth of emotion invested in her son, often has reason to be jealous of the wife, who tends to take over the mother's role. The husband's dependence is the mother's power.

This is not immediately apparent to the outsider. Foreigners who see how meek Japanese housewives are bossed around by loud-mouthed husbands incapable, or at least unwilling to do anything for themselves, often draw the conclusion that men are very much in command in Japan. They note how in the case of elderly couples, raised in less emancipated times, the wives walk a few paces behind their husbands, often burdened with all the luggage too, while the men tell them to hurry up.

I remember the shock of foreign guests at a dinner party, when the Japanese husband carelessly dropped and smashed a plate full of food and, without getting up, ordered his wife to clean up and look sharp about it.

Given the skill of the performers, it is no wonder that this charade fools the average outsider. In many cases the meek, housewifely exterior is a public façade for a tough mother very much in control, while Dad's growling boorishness hides a helpless man clinging to his masculine privilege. The slave and the sergeant-major are public roles which have little to do with the real strength of individuals. The wife shows respect for her husband in public, because it is expected of her, but it is a respect for his role, rather than for the man himself. What happens in private is quite a different matter.

One is reminded of a comic-book called *Kinjiro of the Hard School* (*Koha Kinjiro*) in which the stoic young hero finally, after many struggles and protestations, is ensnared by the charms of (oh horror of the hard school) a woman. To show that he has not lost any of his masculine purity, he orders her to walk several paces behind him as a sign of respect. 'Yessir!' she shouts and then turns to the reader with a conspiratorial wink, saying: 'Isn't he just the cutest thing in the world?'

The gap between real intentions and public posture is clear to every Japanese. It is an accepted feature of civilized life. It is also the main source of Japanese jokes which, like humour everywhere, are based on precisely that gap between social pretension and reality. And in no case is the gap quite as wide as with the father who is really a child.

There are many examples of this. A typical television commercial for, say, processed cheese, will start with an image of father silently scowling: the disgruntled sergeant-major. In comes mother with the cheese. 'What's that?' growls dad, screwing up his face in distaste. 'Try it and see', says mother. This he does with rather bad grace, and the effect is astonishing: suddenly disgruntled Dad is like a demented little boy, hooting and screeching with his children, as if the product contained a drug inducing hebephrenia. We move to a close-up of mother who has done it again. Turning to the camera, she smiles indulgently, thinking how adorable they all are.

Everywhere men are ruled to a certain extent by their public roles, feeling that they have to live up or down to them, as the case may be. It is because the public roles are so theatrical in Japan that the gap between public and private seems so obvious. The higher the public role, the funnier the pretensions are. This is why the Japanese are good at social satire, which, besides a universal type of scatology, is their main, if not only, comic tradition.

Japanese comedy thrives on deflating public pretension, on bringing things back to human proportions. The great comic figures of Edo-period fiction are pretentious pedants, corrupt, pompous officials, arrogant warriors or wealthy fools, exposed by their very human weaknesses. A typical and not very elegant comic poem of the period goes: 'I am at a loss about the lavatory, says the warrior in armour.'[1] The idea of an earnest warrior having to dispense with all his social trappings for such a simple human function must have seemed extremely comical to the Edo townsman. And indeed the blustering warrior and the stupid lord (*baka tono*) are still stock comic characters in Japanese vaudeville, to be seen nightly on television.

The pompous father trying to uphold his public image in the home is clearly part of this tradition. Many comedies are about cutting father down to size. A good example is the so-called 'Company Director Series' ('Shacho shirees'), made during the 1960s, but still endlessly revived on television and in local fleapits. The format, as usual in these series, is similar in every film. The company director, always played by an actor called Morishige Hisaya, is invariably a pompous fool. But he is none the less the *shacho* (director) and has to be treated accordingly: having his shoulders massaged by obsequious subordinates; ordering people to do this and that and making long, unwanted speeches at public occasions. The joke lies, of course, in the contrast between his public and his private persona. He bosses his employees like a general, but he is putty in the hands of his daughters, who needle him mercilessly, blackmailing him into buying them expensive presents and generally doing what they want. He will not allow his secretary to marry the girl he loves, but he has several mistresses himself. The mistresses, moreover, are more like faithful mothers in whose presence he becomes a petulant little whiner, making them cut his toe-nails and clean out his ears.

Despite all his huffing and puffing he always turns out to be a good man in the end, which only adds to the joke. In one film he almost drives a woman to her deathbed because he will not let her marry one of his underlings. She recovers, but he is tricked into thinking that she has not, which makes him feel so guilty that he relents. He looks absurdly foolish, standing there in the hospital room wearing his kimono and carrying his cane, his basic decency unwillingly revealed by an elaborate hoax.

Traditionally the father's role was perhaps taken more seriously than it is now. Father was a model for the son to live up to; a distant figure of authority often bearing little relation to the actual person wielding it. For many children he might have remained a shadowy figure because the education in the home was handled almost entirely by the women. For the male child, to quote an American social scientist, 'the mother became a symbol of lifelong dedication and sacrifice, the father, an image of unapproachable authority'.[2]

In traditional society one's role was more or less predetermined. The son of a carpenter usually became a carpenter too, the same was true of an actor, a samurai or a priest. In these terms, 'to become like your father' made sense. Obviously the higher the father's social status – within his class – the more sense it made, particularly if he was the head of the whole family.

It is probably true to say, however, that the patriarch's authority was strongest amongst the samurai. Even in traditional Japan the father's authority was certainly not absolute in poor households where mere economic survival could depend as much, if not more, on the mother.

After the Meiji restoration in 1868 the official role of the father became even stronger. This was partly a result of the 'samuraization'[3] of Japanese society: the spread amongst all classes of samurai values. Under the civil code adopted by the

Meiji government in 1898 the father was given full control over all family property, the right to determine the family members' place of residence, and the right to approve or disapprove marriages and divorces.[4]

There is an interesting parallel here with the position of the emperor, who, for the first time in many centuries, came out of his powerless closet. Japanese emperors had hitherto literally been shadowy ikons, well hidden from the public view, divine but bereft of real power. Now, suddenly, there he was: sitting on his horse, dressed in full uniform and sporting a bristly military moustache, ever inch the stern Meiji patriarch. How powerful he really was is open to dispute, but certainly obedience to the father at home and to the emperor as the father of us all, came down to the same thing; one was the logical extension of the other.

Paradoxically at the same time social changes were making the actual grip of the father on the family progressively more tenuous. In a rapidly industrializing society it no longer followed that one did what one's father did. More and more one's future was decided by examinations rather than hereditary factors. As a steady stream of sons left their villages to study in the big cities, the old class system began to break down. The father was no longer necessarily an image to look up to, but was sometimes an unwelcome reminder of a rustic background. Moreover, he often expected to be taken care of in his old age by his citified sons.

With industrialization came the age of the 'salaryman'. Much has been written about his role in contemporary Japanese society. Suffice it to say here that the modern Japanese company has inherited many of the hierarchical characteristics of traditional society, rural and urban, samurai and merchant, while at the same time further severing the family from the place of work.

This separation is an important aspect of industrial societies all over the world, but the implications in Japan are slightly different, because the family system itself is different. In the West, as well as in China, the family is based on blood-relationships. A Chinese in San Francisco feels obliged to offer hospitality to a person from Bangkok if kinship can be proved. Europeans generally do not go that far. All the same, to be related means being of the same kin. Adoptions occur, of course, but they are the exception rather than the rule.

In the traditional Japanese concept of family the dividing line between kin and non-kin is less sharply drawn. Family in Japan is partly based on place, as well as blood, especially the place of work. It is significant that the earliest meanings of *oya* (parent) and *ko* (child) were leader of a work group and a member.[5] We have already seen how *yakuza* gangs are structured like families with father-figures (*oyabun*) and 'children' (*kobun*). To strengthen their relationships gangsters conduct rituals whereby they mix each other's blood. They feel as much part of a family as many mafia members do, though, unlike the mafia, this is not based on kinship.

Traditionally a daughter-in-law living under the same roof would be considered a closer relative than a real daughter married into another family. It is still quite common for a son-in-law to be adopted to carry on his wife's family line. Sometimes long-standing employees were considered part of the family under the old system. In fact, one can see many traces of this in modern companies. This is constantly stressed by management: the Yamaha family, the Toyota family. How the average worker really feels about this is open to question, but the ideal, at least, is there.

In traditional society, which still lingers on among artisans, the father played a double role: the master carpenter, the *oyakata*, was both a father-figure to his employees and to his own children. As such he was – and still is – a highly respected figure, especially if he was head of the larger family, a position of great responsibility. It is certainly a pointer that among father-figures of fun in modern entertainment one rarely comes across a ridiculous carpenter or builder. The ludicrous father is almost invariably a 'salaryman'. There are examples of pathetic, drunken craftsmen unable to survive in the modern world, but they are to be pitied, never laughed at.

The nuclear family based only on kinship, the *kazoku*, is a modern (post-1868) concept borrowed from the Western world.[6] The modern, salaryman father is not called *oya* or *oyaji*, but 'papa', an English loanword which retains little of the old respect. A mixture of tradition and modern fashion puts the salaryman papa in an awkward position torn between two families: the company, being the common roof under which he works, and his *kazoku*, the wife and children. The nuclear family is being pushed as an ideal by advertisers trying to boost consumerism with such modish slogans as 'mai homu' (my home) 'mai kaa' (my car) and 'mai famiree' (my family). The English word 'my' is favoured by advertisers and consumers alike, because somehow the Japanese equivalent would sound too possessive, too egotistical, stressing as it does, the private over the collective.

But still, the average salaryman spends most of his time with his company family. This is perhaps more a matter of peer pressure than choice, though one cannot be sure – the look of utter boredom on many a papa's face as he drags along with his family on Sunday afternoons in his 'leisure wear' suggests something less than delight. Nevertheless the pressure is intense – even sometimes from his own wife. There is the often quoted case of the non-conformist husband returning straight home after work, instead of going out drinking with his colleagues, which is the done thing. His wife soon put a stop to that, because, she said, the neighbours were gossiping. 'Have you noticed how he returns early every day . . . Maybe he's not doing well at work . . . There must be something wrong with him . . . ' There is no doubt about it, the 'mai homu papa' is ridiculed rather than respected.

The typical salaryman as described and depicted in comics and films is weak, irresponsible and interested only in sex – always unsuccessfully – and money. The archetype was played by a comedian called Ueki Hitoshi, hero of the so-called 'Irresponsible Series' ('Musekinin Shirees'). He is the salaryman who wins no respect and pretends not to care. All he wants are his creature comforts. The series was made in the early 1960s, just as the Economic Miracle started to heat up. The theme song goes:

Suisui Sudarara
The chairman and the section chief like to play with girls
Shame lasts for an hour, but money a whole life
Who wants to be serious, responsibility I've never known.

Salarymen in comic-books are invariably pathetic. When they are not busy licking their boss's boots, they are peeping under the secretaries' skirts. The most enthusiastic readers of these comics, by artists such as Sato Sampei and Shoji Sadao, are salarymen.

Stripped of responsibility and thus of respect, the father can no longer be a model. This is one of the underlying themes in the films of Kurosawa Akira, an artist who keenly feels the loss of samurai values in modern society.

It has been pointed out, rightly I think, that the relationships in Kurosawa's films between older and younger men are all variations of the father–son relationship.[7] One thinks of the experienced police officer and the young rookie in 'Stray Dogs', the doctor and the gangster in 'Drunken Angel', and the judo teacher and the young boy in 'Sugata Sanshiro'. In Kurosawa's view spiritual guidance is part of imparting a skill; in fact, true enlightenment can only come through work. His ideal father-figures are all spiritual guides in the way that traditional fathers sometimes were and modern fathers can no longer be. In the only two films in which the 'father' is not a man with a particular skill to impart, but a real 'papa', the sons will not listen. The father in 'Living' ('Ikiru'), a petty bureaucrat dying of cancer, is totally ignored by his beloved son; the father in 'Record of a Living Being', obsessed with the danger of nuclear war, is treated like a maniac.

Not only does the modern papa, especially if he is a salaryman, have little to teach his sons (and if he has, he is ignored), but the gap between private and public status can make it hard for him to assert any authority at all. One of the funniest and most melancholy comedies in Japanese cinematic history is Ozu Yasujiro's 'I Was Born, But . . .' It was made in 1932, but it still rings as true as ever. In a typical salaryman suburb of Tokyo a group of little boys argue about whose father is most important. The brothers Keizo and Ryoichi are convinced their father is more important than little Taro's, who is actually his boss. They win the argument conclusively because they are bigger and stronger than Taro.

One day they are invited to a party at Taro's house. Taro's father then proudly shows his newest home film, a tremendous symbol of status in those days. To gales of laughter from all the guests Keizo and Ryoichi's father suddenly appears on the screen, jumping and clowning and pulling faces, acting the fool to please his boss. The boys are deeply shocked. The man they were taught to look up to, the most important father in the neighbourhood, is suddenly reduced to this pathetic, obsequious fool dancing for his supper.

Why is their father not stronger than Taro's? What is the point of going to school if they are to end up bowing and scraping to the boy they can easily beat in the playground? The father tries to explain that he has to pay the bills, that they all have to eat, after all. What can one do about it? That is the way the world is.

The boys then go on hunger strike. Better not to eat, than to bow. Papa, at his wits end, pathetically whines to his wife that he does not want them to be 'wretched salarymen like me'. The humiliation of the father in this film is not that he does anything wrong, as, for instance, the father in De Sica's 'Bicycle Thieves' who has to steal to eat. On the contrary, he makes a fool of himself by doing what is in the circumstances right. He behaves entirely as expected. To survive in the salaryman world he must obey his boss, especially in Japan where such hierarchical relationships are far more important than personal merit. Like the bicycle thief, he too is a victim of society; both men are robbed of their dignity. The difference is that the bicycle thief never lost the respect of his son, and De Sica obviously thought society was at fault and consequently had to change. Ozu did not think in terms of right or wrong. For him, as for many of his countrymen, Japanese society was the human condition: sad, yes, comical, maybe, but what can one ultimately do about it . . . ?

There are of course examples of dramatic fathers trying to assert their authority in the manner of the Meiji patriarch, but this is almost invariably resented by his family. Frequently his wife will join the children in ganging up against him. The most famous example in the post-war Japanese cinema must be Kinoshita Keisuke's 'Broken Drum', made in 1949. The father is Tsuda Gumpei, a self-made man in the construction business, the usual occupation of a post-war *nouveau riche*. He is a strict *pater familias* demanding absolute obedience from his family: he orders his daughter to marry the son of a business backer; he will not allow his elder son to start his own business and he forbids his younger son to become a musician.

Kinoshita cleverly shows how the family atmosphere around the perfect mother is immediately poisoned by a resentful gloom as soon as father appears on the scene. But times have changed, these being democratic days, and the elder son decides to disobey his father. He leaves home, followed by his mother (who could not possibly live without her son), and the rest of the family, including the daughter who breaks off her forced engagement.

As a result the father loses his financial backing and his business fails. Tsuda Gumpei, the autocratic martinet, suddenly finds himself all alone, a sad old man deserted by those he ruled. But even the most pompous, unfeeling, authoritarian father is not all bad and a show of sincere repentance soon brings the family together again. Now that father is shown to be a pathetic loser, all ends well.

'Broken Drum' was made at a time when enthusiasm for the new 'demokurashi' was at its peak. Kinoshita suggests that the fall of father Tsuda is a peculiarly modern phenomenon; that there is no room for Meiji authoritarianism in modern 'individualistic' Japan. In the sense that the façade of patriarchal authority, which enjoyed a strong revival during the fascist period, has fallen down, this is probably true. After all, the old martinets *had* lost the war and the shame of this was hard to wipe out.

The psychiatrist Kawai Hayao described such a case in real life:

> The father of the delinquent young boy had been a courageous soldier in the Imperial Army . . . At first the child was doing quite well, but when he reached the age of rebellion, he became uncontrollable. The father then gave him everything he wanted. The 'strong father' who had faced the enemy without flinching couldn't handle his own son. As a member of a large group he was strong, but as an individual he proved to be weak.[8]

I doubt if this is only a question of post-war 'demokurashi'. The positive eagerness with which the family in 'The Broken Drum' rallies round the father when he is down suggests perhaps that it is there that they really want him: as an idol to protect, worship even, but not as an authoritarian boss. The ideal Japanese father-figure never was a dictator, not in the home and not in the state. Power in the hands of one person is resented.

Where Ozu's fathers are pathetic in his early, pre-war films, such as 'I Was Born, But . . .', the older fathers, always played by a great character actor called Ryu Chishu, in his later work are sad and lonely. Ryu Chishu in films such as 'Late Spring' is taken care of by his daughter, who, in many ways, is more like a mother.

It seems the ideal father, as in *yakuza* films, is always old, yielding and remote. The ideal father-figure, in short, is perhaps better off dead. The highest respect the father ever gets in Japanese entertainment is as a spirit in the family altar or a gang boss on his death bed. One of the most common scenes in television soap-operas is of the son, often with his mother, on his knees in front of the family shrine, praying to the fatherly spirit for inspiration. For only in death can he reach the right degree of purity to serve as a shining example.

12

Souls on the Road

A large number of popular heroes are drifters, outsiders with no fixed abode, forever going on to the next place. Susanoo, the unruly Wind God, spent much of his life as a lonely exile. Yoshitsune, who started life as a loner, ended it as a fugitive in the unhospitable regions of northern Japan. The ronin, who make up the majority of samurai heroes, were 'wave men', wandering around more or less at random. 'The Bored Bannerman of the Shogun', following the direction of a casually tossed stone, is of course the classic example of a drifting hero. Not to mention Takakura Ken roaming around on his horse. Or Kobayashi Akira, hero of the 'Bird of Passage' ('Wataritori') series, travelling in Western gear with a guitar slung across his back, like an Oriental cowboy.

Even the most popular foreign heroes in Japan are drifters. Charlie Chaplin's tramp is still an institution in Japan, more than any other comic character, native or foreign. (His status was so high that assassinating him was seriously considered at one point during the war; surely, it was thought, that would make the Americans give up the fight.) The most often revived Western in Japan is 'Shane'. Besides having all the right ingredients for a grade A Japanese tear-jerker, including a cute little boy, it has Alan Ladd as the lonely drifter forced to ride off into the sunset after a heart-rending goodbye. (Takakura Ken himself played the Alan Ladd part in a Japanese copy of 'Shane' only a few years ago.)

Possibly this taste for travelling is rooted in the theatrical tradition. As was the case in most countries, the earliest Japanese actors were drifters, despised for being outsiders and idolized for acting out people's fantasies. Travelling and acting take one away, however temporarily or vicariously, from one's cosy, but often restricted social environment. Exotic locales are the stock in trade of the story-teller.

Many early story-tellers and dancers travelled around ostensibly to spread the Buddhist faith. Even today entertainers move around the country to perform at temples and shrines on festival days. Travelling and religion are of course intimately connected.

One of the earliest forms of travel in Japan, as in many countries, was the pilgrimage. Travel is a well-used religious metaphor for life itself. And it is still deemed to be beneficial for the soul to make a grand tour of famous temples once in one's lifetime. To prove one has been there, the temples, for a fee – nothing is for nothing in Japan – issue special stamps, so that one can die in peace and ascend to Heaven with a full stamp-book.

It is hoped that somehow the holiness of sacred spots will rub off on the visitor. Which is why people presumably bring gifts and tokens to those who stayed at home: some of it might rub off on them too. Nowadays it appears that foreign culture has taken the place of religion, with trips to Paris and London offering the same rewards to the soul as the temples did in the past. Louis Vuitton bags and Burberry raincoats have taken the place of temple tokens.

What concerns us here, however, is not the modern tourist but the fate of the lonely drifter, the heroic vagabond. Actually the most popular vagabond of contemporary Japan is, at first sight, hardly heroic. He is a tubby, middle-aged man dressed like a pre-war market salesman: a loud, chequered suit, a woollen waistband, an undershirt, wooden sandals and a shabby hat. His full name is Kuruma Torajiro, but he is popularly known as Tora-san. Tora-san is arguably the most beloved character in the history of the Japanese cinema. He is not much liked by 'interi' film buffs, but keeps drawing a huge popular audience. People who never go to the cinema will go and see the latest Tora-san movie. In a series that goes on for ever in endless variations of the same story, Tora-san is single-handedly keeping a film company alive. There have been more than thirty sequels since 1969 when the first Tora-san film, 'It's Hard To Be a Man', appeared.

Staffed by the same company of actors, except for the traditional guest star, and the same director, Yamada Yoji (who also made the copy of 'Shane'), a new film comes out twice a year to coincide with the two most important Japanese holidays: New Year and the Buddhist festival of the dead, O-Bon, in August. Both dates are regarded with religious reverence and Tora-san is there, each time, in a new incarnation, like an ancient festival god. He is an ikon of popular Japanese culture like no other.

Tora-san is as Japanese as, say, Bourvil was French or Arthur Lowe as Captain Mainwaring English. Too clumsy to be heroes in the conventional sense, they share an essential goodness which is as reassuring as it is unreal. They are national clowns making fun of what their audience think is most typical of themselves. Though no Englishman was ever quite like Captain Mainwaring, he did represent something with which the British like to identify.

Typically, being French, Bourvil was neither upper-class, nor proletarian, but a *bon bourgeois*. And so, in his British way, was Mainwaring. The Japanese hero, however, is firmly working-class. With his golden heart, his quick temper, his easy sentimentality, his zest for life, his slyness, his failures and his fast verbal humour, he is the mythical Everyman of urban Japan. Like Mainwaring, he is also a complete anachronism.

Everything about Tora-san, his clothes, his language, his outlook on life, suggests the long lost world of artisans and small merchants, large families and tightly knit neighbourhood communities where the policeman knows the beancurd-maker and values are fast and firm. His is the pre-war world of the *shomingeki*, the sentimental dramas of teeming working-class life, or, going back even further, to the Edo period, the world of the *rakugo* story-tellers, verbal comedians whose art it was to make people laugh at themselves.

The actor playing Tora-san, Atsumi Kiyoshi, was actually still part of this world. He began his career as a traditional vaudeville comedian in just the sort of places where story-tellers still thrived, patronized by a now almost vanished artisan class. His perfectly timed mannerisms were shaped and honed by their discerning laughter.

The original idea of the creators of Tora-san was to make him a tough *yakuza* but, softened no doubt with time, he ended up as an amiable tramp, wandering about selling trinkets at country fairs. He has a base, however, to which he returns between trips. It is an idealized home, as anachronistic as the man himself (there is not even a television set in the room, a complete anomaly in modern Japan): a small, folksy Japanese restaurant in a dusty row of wooden houses bordering on an old temple. It is the Japanese equivalent of the old English village where the vicar comes to tea and the sun always shines for cricket.

Tora-san's family are his uncle and aunt, his sister Sakura, her husband and their little boy. The only other characters in this artificial paradise are the kindly priest at the local temple, and the next-door neighbour, a blustering but kind-hearted character given to making tactless remarks. This cosy little group, always worrying about Tora-san's latest escapades, is meant to represent all the traditional virtues of the Japanese 'common man's' life. They are hard-working, warm, without a hint of evil and malice, pure in their hearts, and blessed with those unique Japanese antennae, always sensitive to each other's feelings which never need to be spoken.

The key word here is *yasashii* (gentle, meek, kindly), that term so often used by Japanese to describe their mothers, as well as themselves as a nation. The British are proud of their breeding, the French of their culture and the Japanese of being *yasashii*. The director of the Tora-san films often explains in interviews that his aim is to show the '*yasashii* quality of the Japanese people'. One of the central myths of Tora-san's world is that everybody is kind, meek and gentle.

To be fair, even the one foreigner ever to appear in a Tora-san film, an unlikely character selling medicine at Japanese fairs, had only goodness in his heart. This foreigner, incidentally, was as mythical as Tora-san himself, embodying all the Japanese clichés about foreigners. For a start he was American (all foreigners, at least all white foreigners, are American); he was forever bumping his head (because foreigners are so large); he was bluntly outspoken (because foreigners always are); and he had an inordinately long nose (because all foreigners have). Still, he was *yasashii*, though sadly lacking those Japanese emotional antennae. As Tora-san himself said in the film: 'They [foreigners] can't understand unspoken feelings, unlike us Japanese.'

Tora-san's home is above all a self-enclosed little world, friendly but impossible for outsiders to penetrate. There is no room for strangers here, so even the restaurant seems permanently bereft of customers. It is a comfortable womb-like world, small, warm, and once one has left there is no return. It is perhaps significant that the second-favourite word, after *yasashii*, to describe the Japanese themselves is the Japanese-English term 'wet', as opposed to foreigners who are 'dorai' (dry). What is meant is the contrast between warm, human feelings and cold reason.

Tora-san's mythical home is like a childhood memory of something that never really existed, except (who knows?) in the warm, wet womb. Many Japanese become quite sentimental about their childhood home, their *furusato*, literally 'the old village'. A large number of drinking songs are elegiac memories of that lost world:

> The evening sun is red
> Myself I feel so sad
> Hot tears stain my cheeks
> Goodbye to our village at the bottom of the lake
> Cradle of our childhood dreams[1]

This type of nostalgia is especially strong among urban cinema audiences, many of whom live a long way away from their furusato. Shochiku, the production company behind the Tora-san series, is well aware of this. According to the head of the publicity department, 'advertising is mainly aimed at shop-assistants, manual workers and students leading lonely lives away from home'.[2]

As in most if not all industrial nations there has been a steady migration of people from the country to the large cities. A young farmer wrote about this, stating that:

Children from farm families who have left the village to become useful toilers for the city think of the village only as a place that supplies them with nostalgic memories. But could it be that nostalgic memory is simply a sign of vacuity? . . . the consequence of their inability to become urbanites even though they live in the big city?[3]

Animosity towards the spread of pollution – in every sense – caused by big cities has played, and continues to play, a large part in Japanese politics: from pre-war 'agriculturalist nationalism' to the protests against the new airport in Narita. There is also the underlying theme of many popular films. The 'Bird of Passage' series, starring Kobayashi Akira, the Oriental cowboy, for example. Like many Japanese drifters he is a typical small-town boy, fighting for small-town values.

As the critic Hatano Tetsuro has noted:

Whenever anything resembling his small-town home is threatened with destruction the fighting begins. His principal driving force is nostalgia for the values of the countryside. Evil is the artificial environment of the flashy cabaret or gambling hall. When he disappears in the final scene of every film during a traditional Shinto festival, he becomes the archetypal drifter who has lost his village home.[4]

The location of Tora-san's home is cleverly chosen. Although it is in a suburb of Tokyo, it could just as well be a street in any village or town which was not bombed flat during the war. It is neither city nor country – or rather, it is both. The point is that it evokes the kind of nostalgia described above. Tora-san's home can only exist in the never-never land of dreams.

And dreaming is what Tora-san's drifting is all about. Something lost or impossibly far away is always more desirable to the romantic mind than the prosaic here and now. The home, at least in the imagination, is something to be longed for rather than lived in. Nostalgia for home, finally, comes down to nostalgia for mother.

Many poems in the *Manyoshu*, a compilation of seventh-century verse, express this sentiment beautifully:

Oh, for a sight once more of my dear mother now –
When the ships are ready
By the shore of Tsu no kuni
And I go forth.[5]

Compare this to the refrain of the theme song of Takakura Ken's gangster film series (the one in which he rides out of jail on a horse) 'Abashiri Bangaichi':

> My body drifts and wanders
> But in the dim lights of home
> I can see mother, but then she fades away.

Times have changed, sentiments have not.

Tora-san's mother is no longer alive. Instead he has his sister Sakura, who is the ideal Japanese mother-figure. All his letters, written in a quaintly formal style – another anachronism – are addressed to her. She is the only one who understands him and her worried frown becomes deeper in every film. Her husband, typically, is a totally insignificant figure, whose only function is to laugh when the others do, or look worried when his wife is. For the rest he fades into the paper doors.

Being cut off from home, from the mother in particular, is the only road to freedom, but it is also the cruellest fate imaginable for a Japanese. Thus the lonely drifter elicits a great deal of sympathy from his audience. The fact that wandering heroes are also often, though by no means always, failures, like Tora-san, makes it even easier to feel sorry for them. The vulnerable traveller, like the passive lover, is the ideal victim of the frightful fickleness of fate.

This image of fate, its unpredictability and evanescence, is an important part of travelling and also, of course, of Buddhist thought. The pathos of things, *mono no aware*, the most important characteristic of Japanese aesthetics, is an essential condition of the drifter's life. It inspired the poems of the Manyoshu, written at the time when Buddhism became the official creed. It also helps to explain Tora-san's popularity.

For he is funny, clumsy, sentimental and lazy, but above all he is lonely. All his jokes have a melancholy edge, like Chaplin's, as if he is laughing through his tears, which is exactly what the producers want the audience to do. But rather than describe his pathos, here is an example, including the stage directions. It is a scene from 'Torajiro's First Love,' made in 1971. Tora-san meets a young girl called Kimiko:

Tora-san: 'Ah, a lovely full moon tonight . . . '

Kimiko: 'I bet you think of home when you see a full moon on your travels.'

T.: 'Yes, I do.'

K.: 'It must be great, the traveller's life . . . '

T.: 'I can't complain, but it's not as easy as it may seem to you.'

K.: 'Oh, why's that?'

T.: 'Well, let me give you an example: I'm wandering all alone on a country road at night. Then suddenly I come across a farm-house with a lovely garden. I peer through the hedge and see a family having dinner in a cosy room. Then I think to myself, that's the way to live.'

K.: 'Yes, I understand. You must feel very lonely . . . '

T.: 'Yes, well, so then I go on and have a drink at some local bar before turning in on one of those wafer-thin mattresses in a cheap inn across from the station. But I can't sleep at first, listening to the whistles of late-night trains going by. In the morning I'm woken up by the clatter of wooden sandals. I forget where I am. Then I realize and think of home at Futamata, where Sakura must be just starting to prepare the soup for breakfast.'

K.: 'Oh, how wonderful . . . I feel so envious. I'd love to travel like that.'

T.: 'You would?'

K.: 'Oh yes, ever since I was a student, I've longed for that life . . . to be with someone I really love, a travelling actor maybe, and to live on the road . . . '

T.: 'Really.'

K.: 'Yes, wandering together, broke, on an empty stomach, in the rain. I wouldn't mind a bit, for we'd have so much fun . . . Ah, I'd like to go right now, leaving everything behind. What about you?'

T.: 'Mm, yes . . . ' (his voice has a note of sad resignation).

K.: 'Are you leaving again soon, Tora-san?'

T.: (looking bothered) 'Mm, . . . yes, yes . . . '

K.: 'Really? When?'

T.: 'When? . . . Well, let's say when the wind beckons me. One day I'll just be gone.'

K.: 'Oh, I feel so envious. I wish I could come with you.'

Needless to say, she does not really wish anything of the kind. Like the audience she just dreams about it. We are the insiders, he is the outsider, condemned, like the Flying Dutchman, to drift forever. He is free, yes, but for a price most of us could not possibly pay. The pathos of the situation is heightened by the fact that the girl has no idea how he really feels, while we, the audience, do.

Being a drifter, a romantic and the hero of a respectable family film series, Tora-san's love life is an unmitigated disaster. It is part of the Tora-san tradition that he falls for the guest star in every film. The pattern is always the same. 'Torajiro – The Paper Balloon' (1982), is a good example. First we see Tora-san coming home to attend a class reunion at his old school. This turns out to be rather sad, because Tora-san, the tramp in his loud suit, cracking his coarse jokes, is openly despised by his former classmates who are all respectable citizens now. Tora-san is so hurt that he gets blind drunk, giving us the first hint of what an outcast this favourite son of Nippon really is.

He then sets off to visit a friend who is terminally ill. This friend, a failed *yakuza* like our tramp, begs Tora-san to marry his young wife after he dies. Tora-san, being a good sort, promises. After the friend does indeed die, Tora-san is the first to offer the widow his help. 'You're the only one who cares for me,' she sniffs and in a scene with more sobbing than talk, it is clear that Tora has fallen in love again.

Determined to keep his promise now, he rushes back home and starts behaving in a very odd way. Daydreaming about his prospective life of marital bliss, he draws up plans to rebuild the family home. For the first time in his life he buys a shirt and tie. He has a serious conversation with the priest at the temple. He even puts in an application for a job. Nothing is stated in so many words, however, and people have to guess at the reasons for all this. Only Sakura, her sensitive antennae quivering, instinctively realizes what is going on.

Finally the great day arrives: the widow is coming! Tora-san, nervously pacing the room, prepares to pop the question. She is warmly welcomed by the family, but Tora-san can only stammer some niceties like a petrified schoolboy at his first dance. The audience is delighted by this demonstration of social embarrassment. It is considered to be good manners to show oneself to be slightly ill at ease in awkward social situations. To be too forthright and too obviously at ease is known as *choshi ga ii*, literally 'to have a smooth manner'. What is really meant is that one lacks sensitivity.

Tora-san is anything but *choshi ga ii* here. In fact he does not speak a word. This too is a sign of delicacy. Deep feelings, especially love, must remain unspoken. Coming right out and saying, 'I love you, will you marry me?' is all right for foreigners, perhaps, but not for Tora-san. While he sits there fidgeting, the widow tells the story of her life. How she used to be rather wild and how she wanted to marry so that she could settle down and have a baby. But unfortunately her husband was a *yakuza*, always on the move. At this point Sakura looks at the woman and then at Tora-san and she senses the coming disaster, as do most people in the audience who have been here before and so start grabbing their first handkerchiefs.

When it is time to go home, Sakura prods Tora-san, who is in a state of catetonia by now, to take the widow to the station. As they go along, she quite calmly and he in a terrible state, the film comes to its emotional climax, the ritual moment when, if it were a Kabuki play, people would have shouted 'We waited for this!'[6] To give you the full flavour of the situation, here is the ensuing dialogue:

> The widow: 'Did my husband ask you anything?'
> Tora-san: (trying to look non-committal) 'Huh . . . oh, no . . . not really.'
> W.: 'He told me you had promised to marry me. You didn't really mean that did you?'
> T.: 'Huh, oh, that . . . no, of course not. I was just trying to humour a sick man.'
> W.: 'Oh, thank goodness for that. For a minute I thought you really meant it.'
> T.: (Deeply distressed) 'No, of course not.'
> W.: 'Well then . . . '
> T.: 'Well, take good care of yourself . . . '
> W.: 'Yes . . . and you too.'

Tora-san is shattered. It is of course what is left unspoken that makes the scene so tragic. It is the kind of understated melodrama, if one can imagine such a thing, in which the Japanese excel. The widow realizes she cannot marry another drifter and so does Tora-san. For him to declare his love would put her in a spot, causing them both to lose face, especially as she, despite her Japanese antennae, has no idea of the depth of his feelings. So he remains silent, crying inside, as they say. Love is still the forbidden fruit for the wandering hero.

He goes back home and finds the reply to his job application. Of course it has been turned down. He laughs a bitter laugh and says: 'Well, it looks as if it's time for another trip!' The whole family is sobbing now, the violins in the soundtrack are going full blast, and the people in the audience reach for their third handkerchief. Tora-san is on his way again, on to the next place.

The film ends with a shot of the family, minus Tora-san, sitting round the table, celebrating New Year, the Japanese equivalent of Christmas; the kind of tribal feast that makes people feel happy to have been born Japanese. All is warm, wet and kindly.

And Tora-san? He is off selling trinkets somewhere, cracking jokes on the roadside. He has served his purpose for yet another film. People feel better now. Poor Tora-san, the lazy, unmarried failure: he is everything the average Japanese citizen is not. But he will always be loved for the same reason Edo townsmen loved prostitutes and actors and modern cinema audiences admire gangsters, ronin and *nihirisutos*: the tragic fate of the outsider confirms how lucky we all are to lead such restricted, respectable and in most cases, perfectly harmless lives.

13

Conclusion: A Gentle People

The Japanese, perhaps as a way of coping with the cultural rapids of modernization, have become obsessive about defining themselves: Who are We? What are We? Why are We so different from everybody else? (That they are is taken for granted by every Japanese, and most foreigners too.) Out of this national navel-staring has grown a multitude of books, films, magazines and television programmes, all dedicated to the *Nihonjinron*, literally the Theory of the Japanese. Insular though the Japanese are, foreigners are actively encouraged to take part in playing this game.

There is a certain consensus about the Japanese stereotype. As taxi-drivers, students or 'salarymen' will gladly point out to any foreigner within earshot, the Japanese are 'wet' and *yasashii*. They stick together in mutual dependency like 'wet', glutinous rice, so dear to the Japanese palate. And they are 'soft, meek, gentle and tender'. They express themselves by 'warm, human emotions', instead of 'dry, hard, rational thought'. Finally, they are also closely in tune with nature, in harmony with it, and not in opposition.

The question is how does this soft, meek stereotype (like most stereotypes it has some truth in it) tally with the extreme violence that is such a predominant feature of popular culture? To be sure, not every Japanese is obsessed with bondage fantasies, and the acceptance of sex and violence is not universal. Indeed, there are pressure groups, such as the powerful Parent-Teacher Association (PTA), who set themselves up as moral vigilantes. Nevertheless, many examples in this book, which may seem exceptionally bizarre to the Western reader, are normal features of everyday life in Japan.

Photographs of nude women trussed up in ropes appear regularly in mass circulation newspapers; torture scenes are common on television, even in children's programmes; glossy, poster-sized pictures of naked pre-pubescent girls are on display in the main shopping-streets; sado-masochistic pornography is perused quite openly by a large number of men on their way to work on the subway.

This is not to say that what is to be seen on the streets of Tokyo is any more *outré* than available merchandise in Times Square or Amsterdam; in fact it is less so, but what there is, is more openly accepted, more a part of the main-stream of life. There is no furtive huddling in dank little shops with darkened windows. People feel no need to pretend that sex and violence cater only to a sinful minority, because these fantasies are neither thought to be sinful, nor, quite evidently, are they confined to a minority. Otherwise, what would they be doing on national television and in weekly magazines?

If the Japanese are indeed a gentle, tender, soft and meek people with hardcore fantasies of death and bondage, few of these dreams appear to spill over into real life. The atmosphere in the streets with the disciplined crowds, the piped music, the plastic flowers, the tinkling bells, the pretty colours, is mawkish rather than menacing.

Does this mean, then, that vicarious cruelty does not lead to actual violence; indeed, that by providing an outlet it makes society safer, as those who are opposed to censorship in the West are wont to argue? Perhaps. But what works in Japan would not necessarily be effective elsewhere, in different circumstances. (Even if Western factory workers could be induced to sing company songs every morning, Japanese style, this would not necessarily herald an Economic Miracle.)

Modern Japan, as anyone who has ever watched a Japanese tourist group can tell, is still a group-orientated society. The desires of the individual are subordinated to the demands of his or her group. The concept of individual rights is not readily understood in Japan. *Wa* (harmony), as a recent prime minister liked to point out, is the key to the Japanese Way.

A strict sense of hierarchy effectively prevents individuals from asserting themselves and thereby unbalancing the harmony of the group. Violent confrontation between individuals is not restrained so much by a universal sense of morality (what the British like to call decency), as by a system of etiquette more rigid than anything seen in the contemporary Western world. But this system is based almost entirely on known human relationships; without a group to relate it to, it tends to break down rather quickly.

Outward harmony is preserved in many different ways. While in the West a person is supposed to have opinions, which he or she voices in public, in Japan, opinions, if held at all, are kept to oneself or carefully blended with those held by others. Political discussions are generally avoided altogether. The Japanese language is structured in such a way that it sounds as if one is constantly seeking agreement. Even a contradiction will start off with a phrase like: 'You're absolutely right, of course, but . . . ' This makes life very difficult for professional critics, and indeed they tend to write everything but criticism. If one really dislikes somebody's work, one usually refrains from writing about it at all.

So, although the Japanese can privately disagree, conflict is hidden behind a bland veil of politeness. When serious differences do come to the fore, they often lead to emotional crises ending in a complete rupture with the group. Harmony can at times be violently disturbed by bitterness and fisticuffs after simply bypassing the intermediate stage of rational debate. In short, consensus may often be a public façade, but then façade counts for a great deal in Japanese life.

Few Japanese confuse this public play-acting with reality, but everyone is agreed about its importance. 'Being True to Yourself' or 'Sticking Up for What You Stand For' are not Japanese virtues. One must play the public game, or be excluded from it, which, to most Japanese would mean living death. Pretence, in other words, is an essential condition of life. There is an expression for this in the Japanese language: *tatemae*, the façade, the public posture, the way things ought to be. Consensus is often a matter of *tatemae*. The opposite to *tatemae* is *honne*, the private feeling or opinion, which, in normal circumstances, remains hidden or suppressed. When Japanese talk about being able to communicate without using words, they really mean that they can read each other's *honne*, while keeping to the *tatemae*.

Conforming to set patterns, blending with the group, never sticking one's neck out, always wearing the company badge can be very reassuring and many, not only in Japan, seek this security. Perhaps this is more important than individual initiative or romantic love or personal originality. At least one knows the limitations of one's existence, like living in a soft-padded cell. But what does one do with those warm, human feelings the Japanese always insist they are so inordinately blessed with? What are the emotional outlets? For women, it must be admitted, there seem to be few. Romance, despite what the women's magazines promise, is not traditionally part of a Japanese marriage. It still is not of most modern marriages either. Even the most loving husband is not much good if he has to spend most of his life with his company colleagues, returning home late at night, exhausted and sometimes drunk. Women are thus left only with their children, whom they are understandably reluctant to let go.

For men there is play, which is another way of replacing reality by a fanciful façade: the artificial love of a prostitute instead of a relationship at home; revelling in blood and gore on the stage or screen rather than asserting oneself at the office. Play often functions as a ritualized breaking of taboos, which are sacrosanct in daily life. (Violence, especially any form of bloodshed, is a strong taboo in Shinto, hence, quite possibly, the incessant flow of blood in popular Japanese entertainment.)

Play is the spectacle, the carnival, the masquerade: to break away from their suffocating identities, if only for a few hours, people don masks, dress up as the opposite sex, commit acts of violence, indulge in orgies. This outlet, in some ritualized form or another, exists in every culture. Spanish bullfights, so shocking to many northern Europeans, are a good example: the taboo of death is defied by the ritual killing of the bull. Sexual taboos are broken in most religions too, usually by some form of cross-dressing.

Much of this, in northern Europe, especially since Reason dawned upon it, has lost its ritual significance. Cross-dressing, for example, is now considered to be an aberration; the festival fool now lies on the psychiatrist's couch. But in Japan, one often feels, play has not yet lost its ritual meaning.

This is not to say that Japanese rulers and their officialdom have not tried to clamp down on, or at least limit too much play. But unlike governments in the Christian West, they never had an overriding religious system to use as a proper clamp. Japanese rulers did not even have the Mandate of Heaven, which Chinese emperors needed to justify their rule. Instead they had force and a set of self-serving rules, mostly based on Confucianism, which they imposed on the populace through sumptuary laws and other, only partly successful measures.

Respect for human life, dignity, the female body and all those other matters we are taught to take so seriously in the West, are taken seriously in Japan too, but not on the level of play. For, once again, it is not the overriding principle people adhere to, but the proper rules of conduct governing human relations. One has no relationship with an actress playing a part, or a character in a comic-book, so why ever should one feel any compassion for them?

If there were a universal moral principle, everything, in fantasy and reality, would have to be judged morally. Hence in the West a cartoon in a national newspaper of a woman tied up in ropes would be considered by many to be morally offensive. In Japan even the most horrifying violence, as long as it is not real, can be judged purely aesthetically. This is even true when the violence depicted is based on a real event.

A novel which has won the highest Japanese literary prize is a case in point. The author, Kara Juro, follows an old tradition in Japanese fiction by taking a real event around which to spin a literary fantasy. The facts upon which the book, *Letters From Sagawa*, is based, are fairly straightforward: a Japanese student in Paris shot his Dutch girlfriend in the back, cut her up with an electric knife and ate parts of her body. Any attempt at documenting the truth is soon abandoned and much of the book, while retaining real names and places, is devoted to the author's personal reveries. But one is still left with the slightly uncomfortable feeling of never quite knowing what is fact and what fancy. Uncomfortable, that is, for someone raised in a tradition that regards the Truth as something sacred. Murder, in Kara's book, is neither analysed nor condemned but is aestheticized. The most famous example of a Western author doing something similar is the Marquis de Sade. Some call him a saint, others a devil, but both sides judge him on very moral grounds.

Such is not the case in Japan. Kara's book has come in for some rare criticism, but based purely on aesthetics. Morality, or the lack of it, is never an issue, neither is playing fast and loose with the truth. The author is judged on his style. A real murder, in his book, has been transformed into art, nothing more, nothing less. As such it is severed from reality and need not be morally condemned.

Encouraging people to act out their violent impulses in fantasy, while suppressing them in real life, is an effective way of preserving order. Vicarious crime is after all one of the functions of theatre. As long as the *tatemae* of hierarchy, etiquette and propriety is upheld, the frustrated company man can look at pictures of tied-up women as much as he likes.

Frustration can boil over, however, and even Japanese rules do at times break down. But much resistance must be overcome before this happens, and the resulting violence is almost always hysterical and usually confined to one's own group. Random killings are rare in Japan, but families wiped out by mothers or fathers going berserk are not.

Popular fantasies of sex and violence are usually hysterical too. They remind one of children screaming because they have no other way of expressing their needs. A scream, though, is normally a spontaneous action. Ritual screaming, naturally, is not. The bizarre excesses of Japanese popular culture are as bound by stylistic conventions as the tea ceremony, flower arranging and other aesthetic pastimes. Even play conforms to strict patterns.

One sees this clearly in that other great emotional outlet open to Japanese men: drinking. Drunken behaviour is of course as much influenced by cultural expectations as table manners or courtship rituals. Getting drunk together is the traditional after-hours way of letting off steam, letting out the *honne*, as it were. But it also conforms to its own kind of *tatemae*. What to an outside observer may seem like childish anarchy, is in fact a ritual.

Every section of a Japanese company has its regular night out to lubricate group relations. It tends to start off modestly with a few beers at a local bar. Then the group will move on to a club with hostesses, who listen to their complaints and make the men relax by strategically placed hands and reassuring sounds of complete agreement. When entirely at ease the men often regress into early childhood behaviour: shame is then suspended for a few hours. Some, mouths open wide, are chopstick-fed by the hostesses, others dance around in their underpants; several grow maudlin and throw their arms around each other's necks. It is even quite possible that one or two become aggressive and have to be restrained from hitting a colleague over the head. But suddenly, usually after the most senior member has indicated his wish to leave, it is all over. Emotions have been vented, the play is finished, the hierarchy restored and nothing remains the next morning except perhaps a headache. Even the men who insulted each other the night before are ostensibly the best of friends again. Everyone agrees to agree.

The more violent examples used in this book are like these drinking bouts: ritual explosions of *honne* played out according to the aesthetic rules of *tatemae*. They are the violent fantasies of a people forced to be gentle. What one sees on the screen, on stage or in the comic-books is usually precisely the reverse of normal behaviour. The morbid and sometimes grotesque taste that runs through Japanese culture – and has done for centuries – is a direct result of being made to conform to such a strict and limiting code of normality. The theatrical imagination, the world of the bizarre is a parallel, or rather the flip-side of reality, as fleeting and intangible as a reflection in the mirror.

Notes

Preface

1 See Roy Andrew Miller, *Japan's Modern Myth*, Tokyo, 1982.

1 Mirror of the Gods

1 These myths were first compiled in two eighth-century chronicles, the *Kojiki* (712) and the *Nihongi* (720). Both were written in Chinese and were obviously influenced by continental culture. The standard, though now somewhat archaic, translations of the *Kojiki* are by W. G. Aston, London, 1956, and by B. H. Chamberlain, London, 1932.

2 Theo Lesoualc'h, *Érotique du Japon*, Paris, 1978, p. 28.

3 *Kojiki*.

4 Ibid.

5 John C. Pelzel, 'Human Nature in the Japanese Myths', in A. M. Craig and D. M. Shively, *Personality in Japanese History*, Berkeley, 1970, p. 41.

6 Louis Frederic, *Japan, Art and Civilization*, London, 1971, p. 52.

7 Sir James George Frazer, *The Golden Bough*, London, 1922.

8 According to the psychologist Kawai Hayao this indicates how old the Japanese cult of the sacrificing mother must be. Kawai Hayao, *Boseishakai Nippon no Byori*, Tokyo, 1976, p. 28.

9 Harumi Befu, *Japan: An Anthropological Introduction*, paperback edition, Tokyo, 1981, p. 106.

10 See Georges Bataille, *L'Érotisme*, Paris, 1957.
11 Ivan Morris, *World of the Shining Prince*, London, 1964, note on p. 260.
12 Ibid.
13 See Ivan Morris, *The Life of an Amorous Woman and Other Writings*, London and New York, 1963, pp. 164–71.
14 Ivan Morris, *The Nobility of Failure*, London, 1975, p. 12.
15 Kambayashi Sumio, *Nihon Hanbunka no Dento*, Tokyo, 1976, p. 76.
16 Theo Lesoualc'h, op. cit., p. 12.
17 Ibid. On p. 30 there is a photograph of a statue of Kannon dating from the Edo period. She has hitched up her skirt, revealing her genitals. It is to be seen at the Kanshoji temple in Tatebayashi.
18 Katsu Shintaro, famous chiefly for his portrayal of Zatoichi, the blind samurai.
19 Theo Lesoualc'h, op. cit., p. 34.
20 Ivan Morris, *World of the Shining Prince*, p. 134.
21 Arthur Koestler, *The Lotus and the Robot*, London, 1960.
22 From Mishima Yukio, *Confessions of a Mask*, translated by Meredith Weatherby, N.Y., 1958.
23 Ibid.
24 Robert Redfield, the American social scientist, made a well known distinction between the 'little tradition' of rural folk-culture and the 'great tradition' of the urban intelligentsia. See *The Papers of Robert Redfield*, Chicago, 1962.
25 Sir George Sansom, *Japan, A Short Cultural History*, London, 1952, p. 131.
26 Louis Frederic, op. cit., p. 210.
27 This had a considerable effect on militant nationalism in modern Japan. See in particular Maruyama Masao, *Thought and Behaviour in Modern Japanese Politics*, expanded edition, London, 1969.
28 Mishima Yukio, foreword in Yato Tamotsu's photobook *Naked Festival*, New York and Tokyo, 1968, p. 7.
29 Ibid.
30 Audie Bock, *Japanese Film Directors*, Tokyo and New York, 1978, p. 287.

2 *The Eternal Mother*

1 Kurt Singer, *Mirror, Sword and Jewel*, London, 1973, p. 39.
2 Takie Sugiyama Lebra, *Japanese Patterns of Behaviour*, Hawaii, 1976, p. 143.
3 Doi Takeo, *The Anatomy of Dependence*, Tokyo, 1971.
4 Harumi Befu, *Japan: An Anthropological Introduction*, paperback edition, Tokyo, 1981, p. 154.
5 Quoted in Minami Hiroshi, *Nihonjin no Geijutsu to Bunka*, Tokyo, 1980.
6 From Tanizaki Junichiro, *Yosho Jidai (Days of my Youth)*, Tokyo, 1957.
7 *The Bridge of Dreams* was translated by Howard Hibbett in *Seven Japanese Tales by Junichiro Tanizaki*, New York, 1963.
8 Kurt Singer, op. cit., p. 38.
9 See Robert Lyons Danly, *In the Shade of Spring Leaves*, Yale, 1981, p. 82.
10 For an exhaustive analysis of this subject see George de Vos, *Socialization For Achievement*, London, 1973.
11 Ruth Benedict, *The Chrysanthemum and the Sword*, new paperback edition, London, 1977, p. 184.
12 Kawai Hayao, *Boseishakai Nihon no Byori*, Tokyo, 1976, p. 54.
13 Ishiko Junzo, *Nihon no Hahazo*, Tokyo, 1976.
14 Muramatsu Taiko, *Terebidorama no Joseigakku*, Tokyo, 1979, p. 185.
15 Ibid., p. 187.
16 Sato Tadao, *Nihon Eiga Shisoshi*, Tokyo, 1970, p. 18.
17 Ibid., p. 175.
18 *Bungei Shunju* (journal), September 1974, p. 103.
19 Audie Bock, *Japanese Film Directors*, Tokyo and New York, 1978, p. 40.
20 Especially the work of Kawabata Yasunari.
21 *Imamura Shohei no Eiga*, Tokyo, 1971, p. 101.
22 Interview by the author and Max Tessier published in *Le Cinéma japonais au présent*, Paris, 1979, p. 101.

3 Holy Matrimony

1 These statistics were published in *Japan, A Pocket Guide*, Foreign Press Center, Tokyo, 1982 and in *The Women of Japan*, Foreign Press Center, 1977.
2 *The Women of Japan*, p. 16.
3 Harumi Befu, *Japan: An Anthropological Introduction*, paperback edition, Tokyo, 1981, p. 48.
4 A phrase coined by Befu to denote the growing influence of samurai class values in modern Japanese society.
5 *The Women of Japan*, p. 16.
6 Harumi Befu, op. cit., p. 53.

4 Demon Woman

1 Terayama Shuji, *Inugamike no Hitobito*, Tokyo, 1976.
2 The Kabuki version, entitled *Musume Dojoji* was first staged in 1753.
3 'The Tattooer' ('Shiseishi') was translated by Howard Hibbett in *Seven Tales by Junichiro Tanizaki*, New York, 1963.
4 Mishima Yukio, *Tanizaki Junichiro*, reprinted in *Bungei Tokuhon* (a journal), a special issue on Tanizaki, Tokyo, 1977.
5 *Aguri* was translated by Howard Hibbett, op. cit.
6 Georges Bataille, *L'Érotisme*, Paris, 1957, p. 17.
7 Nomura Shogo, *Tanizaki Junichiro Denki*, Tokyo, 1972, p. 273.
8 Tanizaki Junichiro, *Renai oyobi Shikijo*, Tokyo, 1932.
9 Audie Bock, *Japanese Film Directors*, Tokyo and New York, 1978, p. 52.
10 Hara Shozo, *Nihon Koshoku Bijutsushi*, Tokyo, 1931, p. 64.
11 See Donald Keene, *World Within Walls*, New York, 1976.
12 Takechi Tetsuji, in *Eiga Geijutsu* (journal), July 1965.
13 Tanemura Suehiro in *Nihon Dokushu Shimbun* (newspaper), January 1966.
14 *Nikkatsu Romantic Pornographic Series* (publicity handout), 1978.
15 Ibid.
16 See the chapter on 'Japanese Eroduction' in Donald Richie, *Some Aspects of Popular Japanese Culture*, Tokyo, 1981.

6 *The Art of Prostitution*

1 *Kuruwa no Subete*, a special issue of *Kokubungaku* (journal), October 1980, p. 42.

2 Donald Shively, 'The Social Environment of Tokugawa Kabuki', in J. Brandon, W. Malm, D. Shively, *Studies in Kabuki*, Hawaii, 1978, p. 51.

3 *Nanshoku Okagami* (*Great Mirror of Manly Love*). There is a rather inadequate translation of this late-seventeenth-century text by E. Powys Mathers. The first private edition (1928) was entitled *Eastern Love*; it has since been reissued as *Comrade Loves of the Samurai*, paperback edition, Tokyo, 1972.

4 Donald Shively, op. cit., p. 53.

5 For a detailed account see Robert van Gulik, *Sexual Life in Ancient China*, Leiden, 1961.

6 Ivan Morris, *World of the Shining Prince*, New York and London, 1964, p. 239.

7 Ibid.

8 *Izumi Shikibu Nikki* (*Diary of Izumi Shikibu*) translated by Ivan Morris, Tokyo, 1957, pp. 408–10. Quoted in *World of the Shining Prince*.

9 Donald Shively, *The Love Suicide at Amijima*, Cambridge, 1953, p. 20.

10 *Kuruwa no Subete*, p. 42.

11 Hirosue Tamotsu, *Henkai no Akujo*, Tokyo, 1973, p. 150.

12 Donald Shively, *The Social Environment of Tokugawa Kabuki*, p. 53.

13 The social scientist Kuki Shozo considered this to be the essence of Japanese aesthetics. See his very important book, *Iki no Kozo*, Tokyo, 1936.

14 Howard Hibbett, *The Floating World in Japanese Fiction*, London, 1959, p. 27.

15 *Kuruwa no Subete*, p. 25.

16 Ihara Saikaku, *Nippon Etaigura* (*Everlasting Storehouse of Japan*), 1688.

17 Translated by Donald Keene in *Major Plays of Chikamatsu*, New York and London, 1961.

18 A famous example is the well-known suicide of the romantic

novelist Dazai Osamu, whose works are still highly popular, especially with romantic young ladies.

19 Thomas Rimer, *Towards a Modern Japanese Theatre*, Princeton, 1974, p. 12.

20 Lefcadio Hearn, *Out of the East*, first issued in 1895, but republished in London, 1927, p. 73.

21 For much of this information I am indebted to Edward Seidensticker's brilliant biography and translation of Nagai Kafu, *Kafu the Scribbler*, Stanford, 1965.

22 Kato Shuichi, *Form, Style, Tradition*, translated by John Bester, London, 1971, p. 27.

23 Edward Seidensticker, op. cit.

24 Ibid.

25 Nagai Kafu, *Fuyu no Hae* (*A Housefly in Winter*), Tokyo, 1935, expanded edition, 1945 translated by E. Seidensticker.

26 Ibid.

27 Robert Lyons Danly, *In The Shade of Spring Leaves*, Yale, 1981, p. 111.

28 Ibid. p. 103.

29 Translated by Robert Lyons Danly, op. cit.

30 Ibid.

31 Robert Lyons Danly, op. cit., p. 134.

32 Ibid.

33 Ibid.

34 Ibid.

35 This example was taken from the *Asahi Geino*, December 1981, but similar instances can be found daily in other magazines.

36 There is a rather stagey photograph of this in Takano Hiroshi's picture-book, *Waisetsu Bunka*, Tokyo, 1981.

37 Sato Jushin in *Eiga Hyoron* (magazine), December 1972.

38 It is an indication of the speed with which fads come and go in Japan that the *Nopan kissas* are already rapidly being replaced by other voyeuristic gimmicks in 1983.

7 *The Third Sex*

1 Peter Ackroyd, *Dressing Up*, London, 1979, p. 57.

2 Hara Shozo, *Nihon Koshoku Bijutsushi*, Tokyo, 1931, p. 66.

3 Quoted in Donald Shively, 'Social Environment of Tokugawa

Kabuki' in Brandon, Malm, Shively, *Studies in Kabuki*, Hawaii 1978, p. 6.

4 'Ayamegusa' ('The Words of Ayame'), translated by Charles J. Dunn and Bunzo Torigoe in *The Actors' Analects*, Tokyo, 1969.

5 Quoted in Earle Ernst's *The Kabuki Theatre*, Hawaii, 1974, p. 195.

6 Peter Ackroyd, op. cit., p. 98.

7 Ibid., p. 57.

8 See Susan Sontag's essay on 'Camp' in *Against Interpretation*, New York, 1967.

9 Kawai Hayao, *Boseishakai Nihon no Byori*, Tokyo, 1976.

10 Imaizumi Fumiko in the magazine *Eureka*, vol. 13, September 1981, p. 135.

11 Ibid.

12 Richard Barber, *The Knight and Chivalry*, New York, 1970, p. 90.

13 Mishima Yukio, *Yukio Mishima on Hagakure*, translated by Kathryn Sparling, New York, 1977, p. 22.

14 Ibid.

15 Mishima Yukio, 'Onnagata', translated by Donald Keene in *Death in Midsummer and Other Stories*, London, N.Y., 1976.

16 Mishima Yukio, *Forbidden Colours*, translated by Alfred Marks, London, 1968.

17 Inagaki Taruho, *Shonenai no Bigaku*, Tokyo, 1974, p. 18.

18 Ihara Saikaku, *Nanshoku Okagami*, translated by E. Powys Mathers and reissued in paperback as *Comrade Loves of the Samurai*, Tokyo, 1972.

19 Ivan Morris, *The Nobility of Failure*, London, 1975, p. 277.

20 Ibid., p. 276.

21 On the influence of homosexuality on the traditional theatre see Domoto Masaki, *Danshoku Engekishi*, Tokyo, 1976.

22 'Kanjincho' ('The Subscription List') was adapted from the No play 'Ataka' by Namike Gohei III and first staged in 1840.

23 'Gikeiki' ('The Chronicle of Yoshitsune'), an anonymous work dating from the fifteenth century. These excerpts were translated by Ivan Morris and quoted in *The Nobility of Failure*, op. cit.

24 Ivan Morris, op. cit., note 5.70.

25 Sir James George Frazer, *The Golden Bough*, London, 1922.

8 The Hard School

1 This particular comic version of Miyamoto Musashi is by an artist named 'Baron' Yoshimoto.
2 'Ketto Ganryujima' ('The Battle of Ganryu Island'), directed by Inagaki Hiroshi in 1955.
3 Alain Silver, *The Samurai Film*, London, 1977, p. 102.
4 *Asahi Journal*, 13 August 1982, p. 103.
5 Ibid., p. 109.
6 Ibid., p. 110.
7 Sato Tadao, *Nihon Eiga Shisoshi*, Tokyo, 1970, p. 391.

9 The Loyal Retainers

1 See Ruth Benedict's chapter 'Repaying One-Ten-Thousandth' in *The Chrysanthemum and the Sword*, paperback edition, London, 1977.
2 For a witty description of this in the business world see Frank Gibney, *Japan, the Fragile Superpower*, revised edition, New York, 1979.
3 *Chushingura* was translated by Donald Keene. There is some confusion about the exact number of ronin involved in the final revenge. There appear to have been forty-six, but one disgraced retainer redeemed himself by committing suicide, hence he became the honorary forty-seventh member of the vendetta.
4 Quoted in Donald Keene's introduction to his translation, *Chushingura*, New York, 1971, pp. 2–3.
5 Sato Tadao, *Chushingura – Iji no Keifu*, Tokyo, 1976, pp. 6–8.
6 Ibid., p. 18.
7 Ibid., p. 50.
8 See Ivan Morris, *The Nobility of Failure*, London, 1975.
9 Hatayama Hiroshi in the *Mainichi Daily News*, 2 March 1972.
10 See Maruyama Masao, *Thought and Behaviour in Modern Japanese*, expanded edition edited by Ivan Morris, London, 1969.
11 Ibid., p. 69.
12 Quoted in Donald Keene, op. cit., p. 18.

13 Sato Tadao, op. cit., p. 164. One of the incidents that sparked off the February uprising bears an uncanny resemblance to the tale of the forty-seven ronin: a young, fanatic Lieutenant stabbed an obstructive Major-General to death in the military headquarters. This served as an inspiration to his comrades, who felt compelled to finish the work.

14 Ivan Morris, op. cit., p. 104.

15 Ibid., p. 182.

16 One was not supposed to eat animal food on the anniversary of somebody's death, and certainly not on the night before, which is when Yuranosuke deliberately flaunted this taboo by ordering raw octopus at the tea-house.

17 Mishima Yukio, *Yukoku (Patriotism)*, translated by Geoffrey Sargent. Mishima later turned this story into a rather gory film, starring himself as the suicidal hero.

18 See John Nathan, *Mishima; A Biography*, London, 1975.

19 Mishima Yukio, op. cit., p. 103.

10 *Yakuza and Nihilist*

1 Taoka Mitsuru, the son of Taoka Kazuo, the most powerful gang boss in Japan before he died in 1981.

2 It is significant that all popular samurai heroes, Miyamoto Musashi, Kondo Isamu, Horibe Yasubei, etc., were raised in very humble homes.

3 See the article by Yamane Sadao in the *Kyobashi Film Senta* programme of January 1982.

4 See Watanabe Takenobu's contribution to *Ninkyo Eiga no Sekai*, Tokyo, 1969, pp. 29–55.

5 *Jingi Naki Tatakai*, directed by Fukasaku Kinji in 1973.

6 The theme song from *Jinsei Gekijo*.

7 Yamamoto Jocho, *Hagakure*, quoted in *Yukio Mishima on Hagakure*, N.Y., 1977, p. 89.

8 Mishima Yukio, op. cit., p. 89.

9 Ibid.

10 *Ninkyo Eiga no Sekai*, p. 76.

11 'Showa Kyokyakuden', directed by Ishii Teruo in 1963.

12 See Donald Richie and Ian Buruma, *The Japanese Tattoo*, Tokyo and New York, 1980.

13 In *Gendaishi Techo* (a journal), September 1966.
14 Donald Richie, *Japanese Cinema*, New York, 1971, p. 75.
15 Quoted in Paul Schrader, *Yakuza-Eiga* in *Film Comment*, February 1974.
16 *Kadensho*.
17 Kurt Singer, *Mirror, Sword and Jewel*, London, 1973, p. 35.
18 Antonin Artaud, *Le théâtre et son double*, Paris, 1938.
19 *Zankoku no Bi*, Tokyo, 1975, p. 21.
20 Sato Tadao, *Nihon Eiga Shisoshi*, Tokyo, 1970, p. 393.
21 Ibid.

11 *Making Fun of Father*

1 R. H. Blyth, *Japanese Life and Character in Senryu*, Tokyo, 1960.
2 George de Vos, *Socialization for Achievement*, London, 1973, p. 480.
3 Harumi Befu, *Japan, An Anthropological Introduction*, paperback edition, Tokyo, 1981.
4 Mikiso Hane, *Peasants, Rebels and Outcasts*, New York, 1982, p. 69.
5 Harumi Befu, op. cit., p. 39.
6 Ibid., p. 41.
7 Sato Tadao, *Nihon Eiga Shisoshi*, Tokyo, 1970, p. 147.
8 Kawai Hayao, quoted in *Sei to Kazoku*, 25 August 1976, p. 131.

12 *Souls on the Road*

1 *Kotei no Furusato* (*Home at the Bottom of the Lake*).
2 Quoted in Sawagi Kotaro's article in a special issue on film of *Jinsei Dokuhon*, Tokyo, 1979, p. 114.
3 Mikiso Hane, *Peasants, Rebels and Outcasts*, New York, 1982, pp. 266–77.
4 In the arts magazine *Bijutsu Techo*, June 1975, p. 237.
5 *Manyoshu*, translated by the Nippon Gakujutsu Shinkokai. Reissued by Columbia University Press in 1965.
6 'Matteimashita!', 'We waited for this!' is a ritual shout from the audience at climactic moments in the Kabuki theatre.

Index